"Joe Koenig provides a compelling case t[...]
if the reader is sitting in a courtroom exp[...]
step by step case, presenting relevant fact[...]
—*David G. Bishop*, Retired Chief of Police, Beav[...]

"Joe Koenig once again demonstrates his passion for acquiring the truth. His diligent search for what's true through thorough investigation has identified the infamous criminal legend D.B. Cooper to be the real life Walt Reca."

—*Jim C. Esposito*, Retired, Special Agent in Charge, FBI.

"Unequivocally, Joe Koenig provides a powerful case that Walt Reca is D.B. Cooper. Koenig's well-reasoned analysis makes a very strong case that any prosecutor would consider. Joe Koenig's objective analysis leaves little doubt that Walt Reca is D.B. Cooper."

—*Michael D. Robinson*, Director, Michigan State Police, retired
and Past President, International Association of Chiefs of Police

"In meticulous detail Joe Koenig traces every step of Reca, a.k.a Cooper's life and career, and pieces together a compelling case that Walt Reca is indeed the infamous hijacker D. B. Cooper. If I were still the Prosecuting Attorney in Oakland County and this hijacking occurred within my jurisdiction, based on the investigative work of Joe Koenig, I would charge Walt Reca with the hijacking of the Northwest Orient Flight 305 on November 24, 1971."

—*L. Brooks Patterson*—Former Prosecuting Attorney for Oakland County
and current Oakland County Executive

"Joe Koenig makes a convincing argument for identifying the late Walt Reca as the elusive hijacker of Northwest Orient Flight 305 in November 1971. Joe's assiduous review of the available documentary evidence and the application of his well-established forensic linguistics skills to the interviews of living witnesses and associates undergirds his investigative findings about this famous cold case."

—*Hon. James G. Huse, Jr.*, Former Inspector General of Social Security
and retired Assistant Director of the United States Secret Service

"Joe Koenig's exceptional ability to gather and analyze information from key witnesses and documents has resulted in a truly compelling case that Walt Reca is the "real" D.B. Cooper."

—*Kathleen McChesney, Ph.D*. Dr. Kathleen McChesney, former Special Agent in Charge and Executive Assistant Director, Federal Bureau of Investigation.

"Joe Koenig has done a masterful job in objectively marshaling the evidence and applying forensic language analysis to the recorded conversations of Walt Reca. I am left with the firm conviction that there is probable cause to believe that Walt Reca is D.B. Cooper. The FBI would be remiss if it did not re-open its case to apply Mr. Koenig's findings to the evidence known to the Bureau."

—*Carl Marlinga*, Former Macomb County (Michigan) Prosecuting Attorney

"Joe Koenig remains one of the most accomplished investigators the Michigan State Police has ever had in its ranks. This is a complicated news story dating back to November 24, 1971. Joe Koenig spent considerable time traveling throughout the country, interviewing those who knew Walt Reca. I believe that Joe, with extensive and meticulous work, has without question identified Walt Reca as D. B. Cooper."

—*Col. R. T. Davis*, Retired Director, Michigan State Police

"Joe Koenig's meticulous assessment of the case against or for Walt Reca as D.B. Cooper is objective, deep and highly persuasive. It should be a model for writers of critical analyses of other cases yet to be offered of other mysteries. Precious few of the tens of thousands of police reports I have reviewed as federal and state prosecutor match this work."

—*John Smietanka*, Former US Attorney and Principal Associate Deputy US Attorney General

GETTING THE TRUTH

"I AM D.B. COOPER"

JOE KOENIG

PRINCIPIA
MEDIA

Principia Media, LLC
678 Front Avenue NW
Suite 256
Grand Rapids MI 49504
www.principiamedia.com

ISBN 978-1-61485-326-8

19 18 17 16 15 14 7 6 5 4 3 2 1

Printed in the United States of America

For Jackson, Ruby, Ava, Joe, Taylor,
and my big sister, Dawn (1941–2018)

CONTENTS

Tribute   1

Foreword by Vern Jones   5

Chapter 1 The Beginning   7

Chapter 2 Perspective and Focus   12

Chapter 3 Could Walt Be D.B. Cooper?   21

Chapter 4 The Tapes, the Transcripts, and Carl's Veracity   37

Chapter 5 The DNA   41

Chapter 6 The Truth-Getting Process   43

The Parking Lot   45

The Forensic Linguist   52

Communication Patterns   67

Chapter 7 Analysis of Walt Reca's Statement   75

Chapter 8 Analysis of Jeff ("Cowboy") Osiadacz's Statements   247

Chapter 9 More Evidence, D.B. Cooper and Walt Reca Comparisons, Abbreviated Timeline   271

Chapter 10 Summary and Conclusions   283

Appendix Complete Walter Peca/Reca Timeline   305

More about the Author   340

TRIBUTE

First of all, to the love of my life and my life companion, my wife, Julie. Without her love, wise counsel, care, and support, there would be nothing.

To my kids, Katie, Jodie, Matt, and Alex; my grandkids Jackson, Ruby, Ava, Joe, and Taylor—this is for you. It's all about you.

To my late parents, Kathryn and Francis; Francis and Mary Louise Vogelsang; my sisters, the late Dawn Badgley, the late Janet Ewing, Francy O'Donnell, and Barb and Kathy Vogelsang; my brothers, Ferm Badgley, Bill Ewing, Mike O'Donnell, and Phil, John, Bill, and Michael Vogelsang. And to my late grandpa Joe Koenig, an inventor and a kind man; my hero and late uncle Albert Muvrin (World War II); and my late cousin Ron Jackson— all wonderful persons who positively impacted my life.

My sister, Dawn Badgley, died on January 21, 2018. She was my big sister, my protector, and I will forever miss her love, insight, and guidance.

To my close friends Jack Minckler, Dick Dykehouse, Roger Bittell, Bruce Williams, the late Steve Courtney, Dr. Stuart Starkweather, my biker buddies John Van Slambrouck, Jeff Steffel, Larry McCart, and my golf partner Mike Murphy. And I cannot forget my great classmates in the 122nd Class of the FBI National Academy.

To the mentoring and friendship of the following important people in my life: Jim Malczewski (my Senior Trooper, to whom

I owe my work ethic—he drove me to work hard and have fun doing it); Pat McTigue (my godfather and example-setter); Pat's wife, Vivian; my high school teacher and coach Lyle McCauley; the late Harvey Heyer; the late Bob Robertson; the late Floyd Garrison; Sam Hutchings; Bob Nyovich; Mike Robinson; the late Dick Meloche; Phil Asiala; Bill Hassinger; Richie Davis; Frank Smith; Avinoam Sapir; John Wojnarowski; Frank Smith; Eldon Beltz; Dan Fitzgerald; Marty Iverson; and John Sadak—all mentors and teachers who helped mold my mind, my focus, and my work ethic.

To Ron, Paulette, Dick, Sue, Terry, Betsy, Paul, Karen, Paul, Linda, the late Pete Panaretos, Nancy, Dean, Jack, Mary, Phil, Fay, Ricky, Marge, Maury, Phyllis, Fred, Joyce, Ade, Marge, Steve, and Kathy—neighbors past and present who are all wonderful friends.

To my good friend Joel Schaaf, who introduced me to the professionals at Principia Media: Vern Jones and Dirk Wierenga. They convert my raw, obtuse scribblings into comprehensive and more meaningful works. And to my gifted editor Patricia Waldygo—a conscientious expert who makes the final edit a delightful educational experience, often forcing me to say, "Gee, I didn't know that!"

I owe special thanks to Avinoam Sapir, whose work developing SCAN (Scientific Content Analysis, *http://www.lsiscan.com/index.htm*) forms the basis for much of what I explain in this book. He is the consummate teacher, as he mixes humor with challenge, subtleties with hammer blows. In short, he makes you think. He is inspirational, and I recommend him to everyone.

Reid Interview and Interrogation (*http://www.reid.com*) also contributed much to my learning and my grasp of the interplay between body language and statement analysis.

I also need to thank the medical doctors Andre Gauri, MD (electro-physiologist, West Michigan Heart); Gilbert Padula, MD

(St. Mary's Hospital, Grand Rapids, Michigan; radiation oncologist, now with Summa Health Cancer Institute); Sherman Sprik, MD (ENT); Jared Knol, MD (St. Mary's oncologist); Jamie Meyer, NP (formerly Lacks Cancer Center, now in private practice); the entire St. Mary's staff for their professionalism and expertise in saving my life—and a special thanks to Dr. William Shimp, MD, of Minneapolis, Minnesota, who provided me with wise counsel and support. None of you have to be as good as you are.

I owe my love and passion for getting the truth to the great organization called the Michigan State Police, recently celebrating its 100th Anniversary. If you have an interest in law enforcement, there is none better.

FOREWORD

by Vern Jones, Publisher, Principia Media

In telling a story that purports to unravel one of the great unsolved crimes in U.S. history, accuracy is critical. Like all the other skeptics, I questioned the validity of many stories and achievements Carl Laurin claimed to be true about his friend Walt R. Reca, as described in Carl's book *D.B. Cooper and Me: A Criminal, a Spy, My Best Friend*.

As our investigative team began to use the technology available today, we discovered more corroborative information to support Carl's findings. For example, we determined the exact dates of events critical to the Reca story, verified the house Walt purchased a couple of months after the hijacking and the name of the seller, confirmed the name of the band Jeff Osiadacz sang with on the night of the hijacking, and located Walt's approximate landing area after the hijacking. Due to the complexity of interrelated events, I found it necessary to create a timeline as the story evolved over two-plus years of our investigation.

The assistance of Joe Koenig in this investigation cannot be underestimated. We needed his investigative instincts, experience, and forensic linguistics expertise. He helped provide us with the evidence we needed to conclude what Carl knew all along: that Walt Reca was D.B. Cooper.

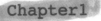
THE BEGINNING

It was November 24, 1971, a Wednesday, the day before Thanksgiving. The weather was rainy, with a temperature of just below 50° F. Northwest Orient Flight 305 departed on schedule at 2:50 p.m. PST from Portland International Airport (KPDX), destined for Seattle, Washington (Sea-Tac). A man who registered as Dan Cooper, later to be known as D.B. Cooper, was one of the thirty-seven passengers on the Boeing 727 and sat in the rearmost seat on the plane. Eyewitnesses described him as in his mid-forties, between 5 feet 10 inches and 6 feet, and wearing a white shirt, a dark suit, a necktie with a mother of pearl tie pin, and a raincoat. He wore penny loafers and carried an attaché case. He told the stewardess he had a bomb and showed her his satchel containing explosives, wires, and a battery. It did indeed look like a bomb to all who saw it. D.B. Cooper announced he was hijacking the plane and demanded four parachutes and $200,000 in $20 bills. When the plane landed in Seattle, he allowed the passengers to depart and ordered the plane to be refueled, while the authorities acceded to his demands and loaded the plane with the parachutes and the cash.

Before he departed, the hijacker offered to give the stewardesses money. "At one point, he offered to pay for his drinks with a $20 bill and insisted the stewardess keep the rest ($18) as change."[1]

---

1   October 21, 2007, http://nymag.com/nymag/features/39593/index1.html.

In an FBI 302 (report form for the FBI) generated by FBI Special Agent H. E. Hinderliter [sic], File LV 164-60 (NORJAK file) on the interview of stewardess Tina Mucklow, he writes,

"Miss Mucklow recalled that she, in an attempt at being humorous, stated to the hijacker while the passengers were unloading that there was obviously a lot of money in the bag and she wondered if she could have some. The hijacker immediately agreed with her suggestion and took one package of the money, denominations unrecalled by Miss Mucklow, and handed it to her. She returned the money, stating to the hijacker that she was not permitted to accept gratuities or words to that effect. In this connection Miss Mucklow recalled that at one time during the flight the hijacker had pulled some single bills from his pocket and had attempted to tip all the girls on the crew. Again they declined in compliance with company policy."

It's important to note the FBI seldom tape-records its interviews with witnesses. So, the FBI's 302 reports reflect what the agents remember the witnesses saying—not necessarily the actual words of the witnesses.

The temperature on the ground in Seattle at the time of departure was at or under 40° F, and at 10,000 feet the temperature was much less.[2] Some say the temperature that night at that altitude was 20° F. At about 2200 (military time), when the plane was flying at the requested 10,000 feet and a slow speed, with little visibility, and rain and cold air outside, D.B. Cooper took the money and jumped from the plane, never

---

2   The Weather Underground, https://www.wunderground.com/history/airport/ KSEA/1971/11/24/DailyHistory.html. See also Gene Johnson, "D.B. Cooper Enigma Still Fascinates," *USA Today*, November 25, 2011, Associated Press. Retrieved August 27, 2012.

to be seen or heard from again—until now. The FBI eventually named this case NORJAK and closed the case in 2016.

I remember this case as a young Michigan State Police (MSP) trooper, newly married and assigned to the New Baltimore Post. Soon thereafter, I was promoted to detective in the Detroit Intelligence Organized Crime unit and began my formal investigative career. I say "formal" because the MSP requires all troopers to conduct investigations, in addition to having patrol duty. During my twenty-six-year career with the MSP, I discovered my passion for getting the truth, learning, conducting research, studying, and applying the tools I'd learned to discover the real message. Now, after more than fifty years of investigative experience in the public and private sectors, I offer my opinion on the D.B. Cooper case.

Before I do, it's important to add some crucial information about the James R. Hoffa case. I was the Michigan State Police's lead investigator on that case. A lot of public resources were spent on this notorious case, and the public needs to know the payoff, the benefits of that huge expenditure of time and resources. During his tenure as president of the Teamsters, James R. Hoffa did much for the membership. Teamsters loved Hoffa, despite the rumblings about his criminal activities and mob connections. There was intense public interest in his disappearance. The "mob" undoubtedly had a hand in the crime. It's a little known important fact that even though we never officially solved the Hoffa case, it provided the catalyst for the decimation of the Detroit La Cosa Nostra ("this thing of ours"). The extreme public interest enabled investigators and authorities to create a federal grand jury and obtain court-ordered wiretaps and search warrants—all necessary and powerful tools we needed to get the evidence to take down organized crime. So, the great investment of time and resources in the Hoffa case paid off handsomely.

I was assigned to the Hoffa investigation on the day of Hoffa's disappearance, July 30, 1975. Our (Julie's and my) wedding anniversary was July 31, and Julie didn't see me for at least three days. I was taking 16 credit hours toward my bachelor's degree at Wayne State University and missed two and a half weeks of classes and three midterms. The phone rang incessantly, at home and in the office. Things were hectic during this active, high-profile case. By contrast, working a cold case, even a high-profile one like D.B. Cooper, is an entirely different setting—you have much more time to think and act. Cold case investigators (like all investigators) need to know one important thing: relying on past investigations and reports almost always creates investigative bias and prejudice. However, the former investigation and case reports are all the investigator has to rely on. As a result, cold case investigators have to tread very carefully, trying to be as objective as possible when evaluating the reports and the evidence, resisting political pressures, and overcoming the inevitable unhealthy personal motives to solve the case. In this case, my publisher and editor Vern Jones and Dirk Wierenga of Principia Media gave me a suspect.

While discussing the critical issue of bias and perspective, I acknowledge that the people at Principia Media have become my friends. I need to suppress (overcome) the influences of that friendship to render an objective opinion. Principia would want no less, even though the publisher invested a great deal of time and money in this project. This is what makes investigations difficult. Whether it's pressure from government officials, the public, friends and associates, or one's ego, the investigator must make sure all the evidence he or she senses is objectively evaluated. Bias and prejudice kill objectivity, leading to the wrong results, the wrong conclusions, and false confessions. So, rest assured, I will do everything I can to provide you, the reader, with an objective and honest opinion.

I was somewhat skeptical when Vern and Dirk first approached me in June of 2016 to assist them in investigating the D.B. Cooper case and helping them determine whether Walt Reca was D.B. Cooper. Soon, however, in looking at Walt Reca's documents, identification papers, transcripts, and diary and listening to the tape recordings, I became much more interested and intrigued. After all, there aren't many investigators involved in two of the three greatest mysteries in American history (Amelia Earhart, Jimmy Hoffa, and D.B. Cooper), so to be a part of this investigation was exciting, to say the least, even to a grizzled senior investigator like me.

Chapter 2

PERSPECTIVE AND FOCUS

My assignment was to apply my experience and expertise to evaluate the evidence and conduct interviews of key persons to help determine truthful information. I had to grasp all that was before me, what we needed, what we could realistically obtain, and what conclusions I could draw from the evidence and my analysis. First, I need to discuss some historical information to help readers put things in perspective and better understand the evidence I had to evaluate.

In June 1965, Walt committed and was arrested for armed robbery of a Big Boy restaurant in the Detroit area. From later conversations with Walt, Carl Laurin knew that Walt had given money to the manager at the restaurant just before he was arrested, thanking her for being nice to him.

When Carl first saw the TV news about the hijacking, he immediately suspected Walt, knowing Walt's capabilities. Carl shouted to his wife, Loretta, "What the hell did Walt just do?" Several years later, his suspicions were confirmed. While watching a TV show about the hijacking, Carl learned that D.B. Cooper had offered money to one of the Northwest Orient stewardesses before he made his leap to infamy. Carl immediately noted the similarity between Cooper's behavior and Walt's gift to the Big Boy manager.

The Complete Walter Peca/Reca Timeline fully explains the close friendship between Walt and Carl. Carl rarely saw or spoke with Walt after the Big Boy robbery in 1965 until the first Billabog reunion in 1998. He lost contact with Walt, having no idea where he was or what he was doing during that time. The only two exceptions were a brief visit from Walt in 1967, when he came to borrow a parachute from Carl when Carl and Loretta lived on Portage Lake, and once in 1975, at a get-together at Joni's house in Westland, Michigan. Joni is Joan Marie Feldhoffer, who became Walt's wife on November 6, 1930.

The Principia film documentary *D.B. Cooper: The Real Story* shows Walt on tape announcing himself at the first Billabog in 1998. Jim McCusker filmed that reunion. It was the first time anyone other than Willard and Art had seen Walt in decades.

After that reunion and prior to the next one in 1999, Carl wrote a chapter in his unpublished book *The Last Barnstormers* about Walt being Cooper. Carl presented copies of the book to everyone during the spring 1999 Billabog reunion.

Not long after that, Carl wrote an expanded version with more details of Walt carrying out the D.B. Cooper hijacking, titling it "Immaculate Deceptions." He mailed it to Walt in late 1999 or early 2000.

Walt didn't acknowledge what Carl had written about him. Carl then called him to ask whether he'd read it. That's when Walt said, "You gave me too much credit for having a plan," adding to Carl's belief that Walt was D.B. Cooper.

Gently, during the next few years, Walt and Carl discussed various aspects of the hijacking, along with many other things, as they rekindled their friendship. In the fall of 2008, Walt gave Carl permission to record their conversations. Carl always went to his daughter's house in Florida to record these phone calls to Walt because he couldn't figure out how to hook up the recorder to his home phone. Carl's recordings were rudimentary, yet even though he used old tape recorders, he effectively captured the conversations.

When Carl phoned Walt in their first recorded call, Walt wouldn't admit he was D.B. Cooper.

> **Carl:** Here *I*– *I*– *I* gotta ask you this, and– and– and *I* need– *I* need the absolute honest– honest answer.
>
> [03:07:49] **Walt:** Yup.
>
> [03:07:51] **Carl:** Are you D.B. Cooper?
>
> [03:07:52] **Walt:** *I* ain't saying nothin'.

Following that first recorded call, Walt phoned Carl on November 27, 2008, and said in an unrecorded call (because Carl was at his home and unable to record it):

> **Walt:** Charlie?
>
> **Carl:** Yes?
>
> **Walt:** I am D.B. Cooper.
>
> **Carl:** I know.

Then later,

> **Carl:** Why now, Walter?
>
> **Walt:** Because it's time.

Walt told Carl (Charlie) he couldn't lie to his old friend anymore.

The taping of these conversations occurred for eight to twelve weeks. This was also when Walt began mailing Carl the cavalcade of evidence and artifacts shown throughout this book. It's important to note that Loretta, Carl's wife, listened in on these conversations and recordings as well. So I evaluated Loretta simultaneously with Carl to determine whether her communication patterns were consistent with Carl's when he provided his accounting of events and information. I concluded that Loretta's communication patterns supported Carl's statements.

Thus, the transcripts of the phone call recordings are merely a slice of all the many phone conversations between Carl and Walt from 1998 until late 2013. However, the recordings and the transcripts are excellent evidence (new evidence to the FBI) and became a major focus of my efforts to find the truth. Carl and Loretta both provided me with written permission to evaluate, analyze, use, and publish the transcripts in this book. I conducted forensic linguistic analyses of the tapes and the transcripts of these tapes and those from other witnesses. Then I compared the very specific information Walt disclosed in the tapes to the known FBI 302 reports of the crew and passenger statements. Cases are solved when we make comparisons between specific information from a suspect and what only the FBI, the hijacker, and the crew on Northwest Orient Flight 305 would know.

For example, here's what Walt Peca told Carl Laurin in the 2008 recordings made with Walt's permission (thirty-seven years following the hijacking), and it is similar to stewardess Tina Mucklow's statement:

[01:51:57] **Carl:** Right. Uh, did— did you make kind of an issue out of that or did you just— just say, "Well, this is where the people get off," or, "This is where we part company," or—?

[01:52:12] **Walt:** No, *I* was asked, "Can *they* get off?"

[01:52:14] **Carl:** Okay. And you said yes?

[01:52:19] **Walt:** "Yeah, Happy Thanksgiving."

[01:52:20] **Carl:** Yeah. Um, and at what point did you offer something?

[01:52:29] **Walt:** What, the four thousand dollars?

[01:52:30] **Carl:** Yeah.

[01:52:32] **Walt:** <u>Right there</u>. *I* don't know how much *it* was <u>right there</u>. *It* was a handful of money, and *I* just offered *it* to a stewardess.

[01:52:38] **Carl:** Yeah. And you said the same thing that you said on the Eight Mile Road job.

[01:52:46] **Walt:** Yeah, the insurance'll cover *it*.

[01:52:50] **Carl:** Uh, didn't you say something like, uh, "You've been nice to me"?

[01:52:57] **Walt:** Yeah, kindness.

[01:52:59] **Carl:** Huh?

[01:53:00] **Walt:** Well, polite and kindness.

[01:53:03] **Carl:** Uh, Okay. An—, and she wouldn't take it and you told her the insurance would cover it?

[01:53:10] **Walt:** Yeah.

Carl, Loretta, and Walt's family knew Walt was a smoker. Lisa Story, Loretta Laurin, and Walt's sister, Sandy, all reported that Walt smoked Sir Walter Raleigh cigarettes. Loretta remembers Walt using coupons to buy that brand. She didn't like smoking Sir Walter Raleigh cigarettes and remembers reluctantly smoking his only when she ran out of her favorite brand. The FBI reports specify that D.B. Cooper smoked Sir Walter Raleigh cigarettes. In the same FBI 302 report on the interview of Tina Mucklow, she stated,

> "... she also recalled that he was a chain smoker. At one time she lit a cigarette for him with the last match in the paper match folder, ... She recalled that he smoked Raleigh Filter tips."

Here's more on this from the FBI's 302 report, SE 164-81: "Unsub is allegedly a smoker of Raleigh filter-tip cigarettes. The search of the plane involved in Norjak conducted at Reno, Nevada, revealed eight Raleigh cigarette butts found near Unsub's seat."

This evidence (Raleigh cigarette butts found near Unsub's seat) is of particular interest to me. Discarded cigarette butts investigators believed were smoked by D.B. Cooper would be a wonderful source for Cooper's DNA. However, investigators back then (the 1970s) had no idea DNA would eventually become the powerful investigative tool it is today. From the University of Leicester (United Kingdom): "DNA was first used to aid a criminal investigation by Professor Jeffreys in 1986."[3] So, the agents probably didn't place the Raleigh cigarette butts into containers that would preserve those butts for future DNA analysis. If those butts were not stored properly, the DNA would degrade and become useless. That's probably why we have no information

---

3   University of Leicester, https://www2.le.ac.uk/departments/emfpu/to-be-deleted/explained/profiling-history.

about DNA from that evidence. However, it's possible the FBI does have it and is keeping that secret. We'll see.

In another December 3, 1971, FBI 302 (164-133) interview of Tina Mucklow, written by FBI SA Joseph Kelly and SA William Culpepper, Ms. Mucklow described the hijacker as irritated. It was taking too long for the parachutes to be delivered, and she explained that the chutes had to come from McChord Air Force Base:

> "The hijacker said, 'McCord is only 20 minutes from Tacoma. It doesn't take that long.' She called the cockpit back over the interphone [sic] and they said that the chutes were enroute [sic] and the cockpit requested permission from the hijacker to start their descent without the parachutes being present at the airport. The hijacker said yes, provided they don't have to wait for the chutes after the fueling was completed. A few minutes later, the pilot called Tina back on the interphone [sic] and advised the chutes were there and he was going down."

Here is Walt talking to Carl about this on the 2008 recording:

```
[01:19:26] Carl: —yeah. Okay, you ordered,
four parachutes, from— from McChord?

[01:19:33] Walt: Yeah, but they didn't
come from McChord.

[01:19:35] Carl: Where'd they come from?

[01:19:37] Walt: Skyhomish [sic: Snohomish].
The jump center, that's right next to the
airport.
```

Remember, these recordings were made in 2008, thirty-seven years after the skyjacking. Memories fade, and you will find confusing details about the parachutes in this transcript. Rarely do statements accurately reflect all the information and facts, even truthful ones. I present this transcript as is, with all the warts and bumps, because I want you to see what investigators often see in statements. In this case, we don't know what evidence or information the FBI held back from the public. Truth-getting is a difficult process, and the investigator has to know that even truthful persons' recollections of events are not always clear and consistent. That's why a good forensic linguist can "see" through the confusion and lack of consistency, the conflicts, to determine whether the speaker is simply not remembering the facts or is deceptively creating the facts. Some inconsistencies are due to Carl's (Charlie's) leading questions. Here, Carl suggests the chutes were ordered from McChord, and Walt agrees (even though he stated later the chutes were ordered from Skyhomish (combining Skyhomish and Snohomish— Snohomish is the correct skydiving center). Poorly structured and leading questions can promote misleading answers, and the forensic linguist knows that.

Walt offers a great deal of detailed information. People who wish to be deceptive are reluctant to provide details that can be used to disprove their statements.

Adding to that is a short videotape of Walt taken in 2009 when he gives a toast:

> "A toast to anybody and everybody that jumped out of a 727. Have I got a story to tell you."
>
> Then he said in Polish, "Wszystko sie zaczelo jak bylem maly dzieciak. Na Zdrowie."
>
> Which, interpreted in English, means: "Everything started when I was a little kid. Cheers."

Following Walt's admission and permission to record their conversations, they agreed the information would be kept secret until after Walt's death. Carl honored that agreement.

One thing struck me as I listened to the recordings to evaluate Carl's and Walt's speech rhythms, pitch, volume, nuances, and idiosyncrasies. The characteristics of both men's voices were consistent throughout the recordings. Walt's demeanor while describing the hijacking and all other past events revealed a matter-of-fact accounting, showing a lack of hubris. One would expect that if Walt were deceptive or creating a story, he would paint himself in a very favorable light. Instead, Walt consistently spoke of his poor judgment, and his tone showed he was embarrassed, almost mocking himself in a self-deprecating way. Those attributes are consistent with truth-telling.

Chapter 3

COULD WALT BE D.B. COOPER?

One of my first tasks was to determine whether the suspect was capable of doing and surviving what D.B. Cooper did. Could Walt Reca have been D.B. Cooper? As Walt Reca confided to his niece Lisa Story, when she asked him why he would do such a thing (the hijacking), he replied, "I was so poor. Better off dead than poor." So, consistent with his contemplation of diving off the dam to secure worker's compensation money for his family, he was willing to die. (see Complete Walter Peca/Reca Timeline).

Walt was a paratrooper (Army 11th or 13th Airborne) and Rescue and Survival Specialist with the Air Force Reserve.[4] He was one of the pioneers in skydiving, along with his lifelong friend Carl Laurin (a.k.a. [*a.k.a.* means "also known as"] "Charlie Brown"). His jumps included night jumps. There wasn't a jump he didn't think he could handle. He attended Escape and Evasion School and was fluent in the Polish and Ukrainian (Russian) languages. From all reports, Walt was a very experienced paratrooper and skydiver.

He possessed legitimate-appearing passports and identification documents. According to Lisa Story, as told to Dirk Wierenga of Principia Media, Walt forged a driver's license for her so she could go into bars while underage, and it worked.

---

4   *D.B. Cooper and Me*, by Carl Laurin (Grand Rapids, MI: Principia Media, 2018), p. 33. On May 16, 2018, Mr. Laurin advised me it might have been the 13th Airborne.

Then, there is the 1948 Certificate of Competency of an Osage Indian under the name Walter Recca with two c's. In 1948, Walt would have been fifteen years old. Based on the evidence, Walt first used the name Recca in 1972. No other records show him using the name Recca before 1972, which makes the Osage record questionable. He reportedly used that certificate later in life to get work from the union. Furthermore, as told to Dirk, in 2014 Lisa and her mom, Sandy, were cleaning Walt's house following his death and threw away a box of various official-looking government seal embossers. It is not a stretch to believe several of his identification documents were forged. And, I might add, they were pretty good ones.

During the 1970s, he was still a fugitive (for a 1965 armed robbery of the Big Boy restaurant in Detroit, Michigan), and Walt was able to alter even official documents, including his birth certificate. He could easily change his identification records from his given name Peca to Reca, by changing the "P" in Peca to an "R" to make it Reca. (See the attached photo showing under black light the extension of the P to an R on his Department of Defense Immunization Certificate.) Note that he also changed the original from AF (Air Force) to ARMY. To see the original black light photos, which accentuate the different-colored inks, go to *www.kmiinvestigations.com*. Evidence suggests he had been using the name Reca since 1967. In January 1971, he began working for the Vinnell Corporation and used the name Reca then. Walt used the last name Reca in his marriage to ███ in 1974. However, he used the last name of Racca when buying his house in Spokane, Washington, in 1972. He got away with this because the owner didn't conduct background checks on land contracts in those days.

Under black light—showing alterations

Under black light   **Plain light[5]**

When Walt was alleged to be smuggling diamonds and precious stones out of Sierra Leone (see the audiotape transcript at time stamp 02:52:49) in the late 1970s, he posed as a priest calling himself Father Wally. He also used the name Walter

---

5   For black light full-effect photos, go to *www.kmiinvestigations.com*

Drinkell in the mid-1970s on his Great Britain passport (photo below).

One pictured document shows Walter Reca to be a KGB agent. Another shows Walter Reca to be a minister. Yet another document shows his vaccine history, which might correlate with foreign service. On October 1, 1976, Walt officially changed his name from Walter Peca to Walter Reca. Old passports show several trips to the Middle East and Eastern Europe. He gave Carl ("Charlie Brown") his spy camera, a Minox EC miniature camera, alleged to be the camera of choice for spies. Finally, Walt's résumé shows a great deal of interesting activity. Be sure to read the Complete Walter Peca/Reca Timeline.

These identities and identification documents provide evidence Walt worked for U.S. or foreign intelligence services. He worked for at least one company, the Vinnell Corporation, an "international private military company."[6] He provided Carl (Charlie) with stories of clandestine activities, supported by all of his identification papers, his contacts book (which, by all appearances, was written contemporaneously), and details that were never disproved. To the contrary, you will find all the evidence to be corroborative. For example, Walt gave Lisa an envelope during one of her visits to his home in Oscoda, Michigan, saying only this to her: "I did that." When Lisa opened the envelope, it contained an article about the assassination attempt on Abu Daoud, known as the mastermind of the Munich Massacre during the1972 Olympics. (See the photo, below, of that article.) Eleven Israeli athletes and one German police officer were killed on that tragic day. On August 1, 1981, the gunman shot Daoud five times from a close distance while Daoud was

---

6   See *https://en.wikipedia.org/wiki/Vinnell*.

Munich chief shot

supporter in Ferm... Tyrone a fo...

By DAVID ADAMSON Diplomatic Correspondent

ABU DAOUD, the Palestinian terrorist who masterminded the 1972 Munich Olympics massacre was seriously wounded when he was hit by five bullets as he sat in the coffee shop of a Warsaw hotel on Saturday, it was disclosed yesterday.

Mr Mahmoud Yaseen, the Palestine Liberation Organisation representative in Warsaw, said Daoud was in hospital with wounds in the mouth, stomach and chest.

"There was... and he escaped," Yaseen said. "He apparently had people waiting for him outside the hotel."

Mr Yaseen was unable to explain why Daoud was in Wasaw, but said he thought he was "in transit." Where from and where to he did not know.

The most likely connection was with events in Vienna, were two Arabs were arrested at the airport last week after police found four rifles, a sub machine gun, six hand grenades and 525 rounds of ammunition in their luggage.

At the airport to meet them was Mr Ghasi Hussain, the PLO envoy to Austria. He has so far rejected the Austrian Interior Ministry's request to him to leave the country.

The target of this activity may have been President Sadat, of Egypt, whose visit to Austria

Abu Daoud.

next Monday and Tuesday was cancelled yesterday without explanation.

There is considerable traffic between Poland and Austria, largely by Poles seeking to escape the turmoil at home. Daoud might have been attempting to slip into Austria by this route, or he may have been connected with a plot in some sort of back-up role.

Daoud was a member of Black September, the group responsible for the murder of 11 Israeli athletes in Munich in 1972, the murder of the Jordanian Prime Minister, Wasfi Tal in Cairo in 1971, the

in a coffee shop in Warsaw.[7] Walt's passport (see photo below) shows he was in Poland shortly before the shooting (arriving in Warsaw June 28, 1981, and departing July 1, 1981).

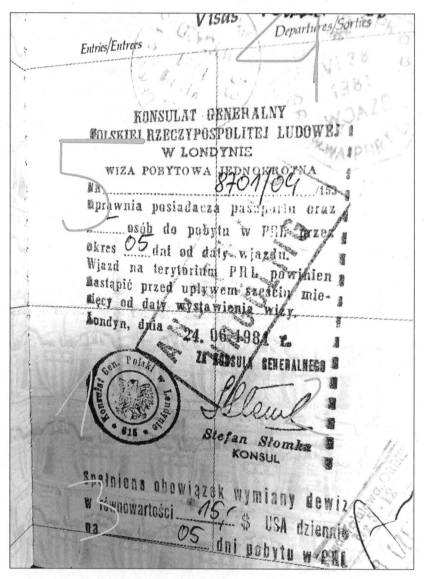

---

7   See *https://en.wikipedia.org/wiki/Abu_Daoud*.

1. **Polish Consulate-General in London;**
2. **Consul-General Stefan Slomka Consul;**
3. **Obligation to exchange foreign currency in the equivalent of $15 U.S./day for 5 days in the PRL met;**
4. **Entry Warsaw airport 28 June 1981—departure appears to be 7/1/1981.**
5. **Consulate-General of PRL London.[8]**

After reading the Complete Walter Peca/Reca Timeline, viewing evidence (identification papers, Walt's contacts book, and other documents), and conducting research, I concluded that there is no question Walt Reca was a capable candidate. He was wild, impulsive, daring, and desperate. Yes, Walt Reca could have been D.B. Cooper.

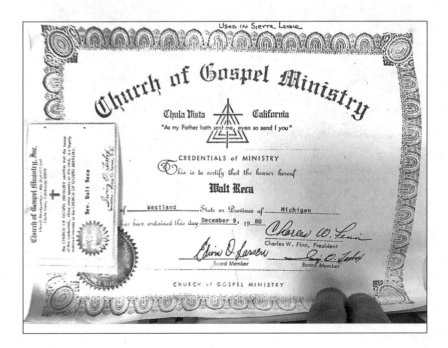

---

8   Polish interpretation from a source who wished to remain confidential.

AMERICAN FOREIGN SERVICE
June 10, 1980
Walter RECA
Steven Coffman
Consul
Oran, Algeria
June 11, 1979
PHOTOGRAPH, DESCRIPTION, AND SIGNATURE OF BEARER
PERSONAL DESCRIPTION
Michigan, U.S.
Sep. 20, 1933
Supervisor
N/A N/A
N/A N/A
None
ARAMCO CONSTRUCTION CAMP
DHAHRAN NORTH
Name
WALTER RICHARD RECCA
Nationality
AMERICAN
Sponsor
ARABIAN BUNDY
Valid Unit
ID NUMBER
Pullman
Kellogg
HOUSTON, TEXAS
WALTER RECA
SOCIAL INSURANCE NUMBER
CANADA
NUMÉRO D'ASSURANCE SOCIALE
SIGNATURE
08 № 00755
S.I.M.
1692/A/IX/77.
Nomor
22 September 1977.
Berlaku dari tgl.
22 September 1982.
Sampai dengan tgl.
Cap jempol

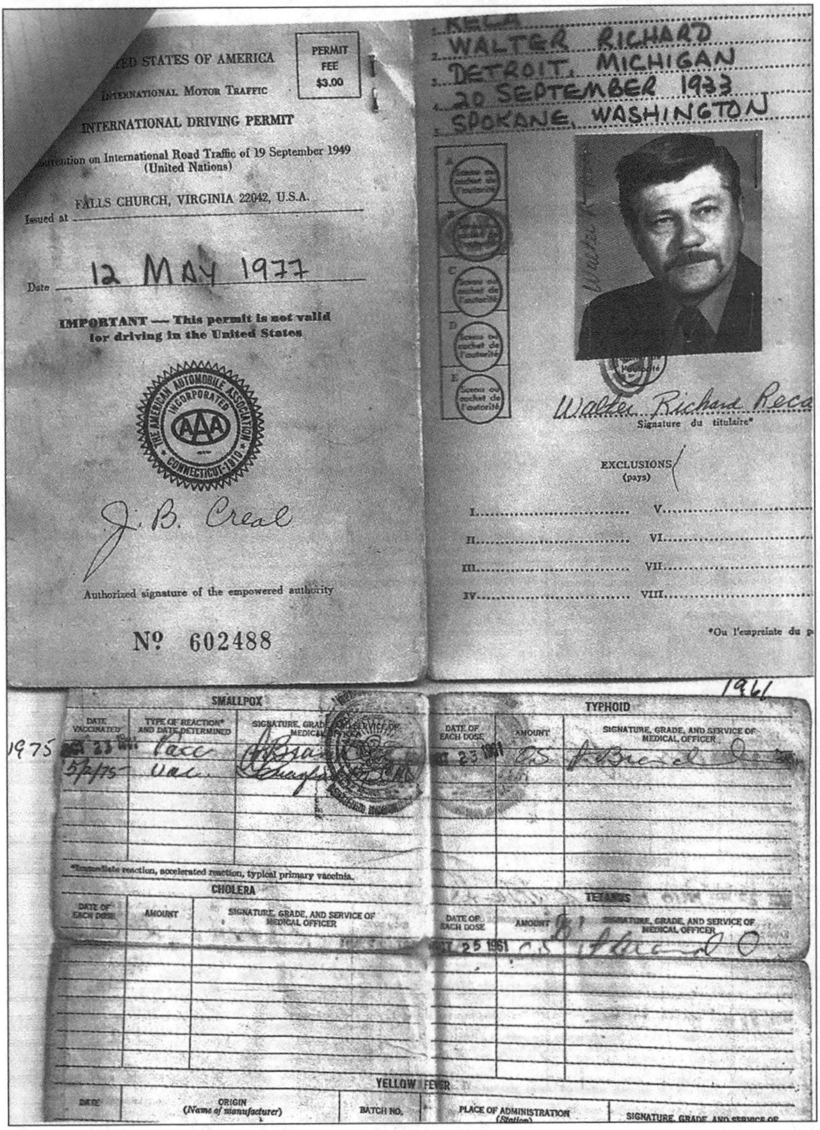

...ED STATES OF AMERICA

PERMIT FEE $3.00

International Motor Traffic

INTERNATIONAL DRIVING PERMIT

...vention on International Road Traffic of 19 September 1949 (United Nations)

Issued at FALLS CHURCH, VIRGINIA 22042, U.S.A.

Date 12 MAY 1977

IMPORTANT — This permit is not valid for driving in the United States

THE AMERICAN AUTOMOBILE ASSOCIATION INCORPORATED AAA CONNECTICUT-1910

J. B. Creal

Authorized signature of the empowered authority

Nº 602488

1. RECA
2. WALTER RICHARD
3. DETROIT, MICHIGAN
4. 20 SEPTEMBER 1933
5. SPOKANE, WASHINGTON

Walter Richard Reca

Signature du titulaire*

EXCLUSIONS (pays)

I. ... V. ...
II. ... VI. ...
III. ... VII. ...
IV. ... VIII. ...

*Ou l'empreinte du p...

1961

SMALLPOX

DATE VACCINATED	TYPE OF REACTION* AND DATE DETERMINED	SIGNATURE, GRADE, AND SERVICE OF MEDICAL OFFICER
1975 ... 23 ...	Vacc	
5/2/75	Vac.	

*Immediate reaction, accelerated reaction, typical primary vaccinia.

TYPHOID

DATE OF EACH DOSE	AMOUNT	SIGNATURE, GRADE, AND SERVICE OF MEDICAL OFFICER
... 23 1961		

CHOLERA

DATE OF EACH DOSE	AMOUNT	SIGNATURE, GRADE, AND SERVICE OF MEDICAL OFFICER

TETANUS

DATE OF EACH DOSE	AMOUNT	SIGNATURE, GRADE, AND SERVICE OF MEDICAL OFFICER
... 25 1961		

YELLOW FEVER

DATE	ORIGIN (Name of manufacturer)	BATCH NO.	PLACE OF ADMINISTRATION (Station)	SIGNATURE, GRADE, AND SERVICE OF

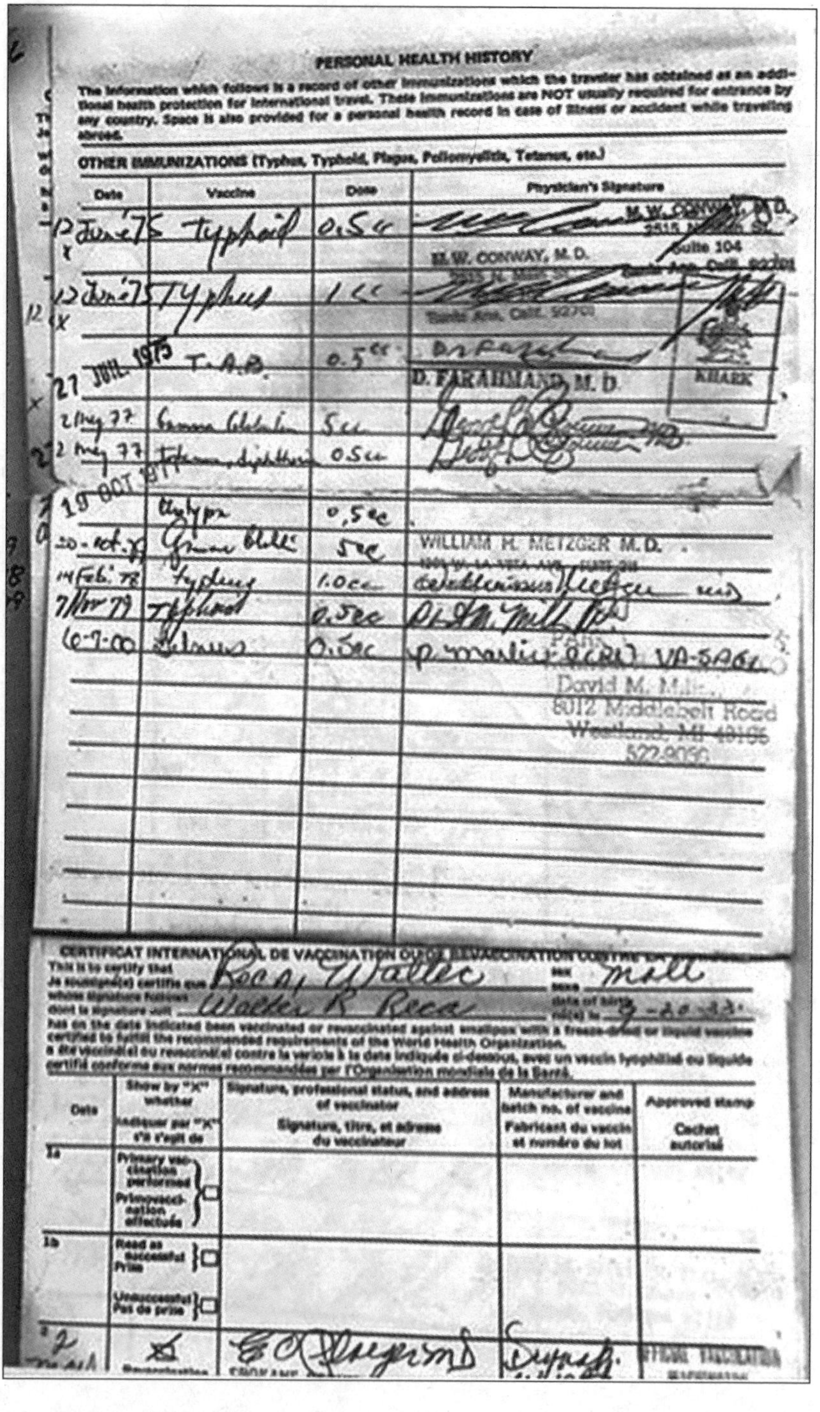

PERSONAL HEALTH HISTORY

The information which follows is a record of other immunizations which the traveler has obtained as an additional health protection for international travel. These immunizations are NOT usually required for entrance by any country. Space is also provided for a personal health record in case of illness or accident while traveling abroad.

OTHER IMMUNIZATIONS (Typhus, Typhoid, Plague, Poliomyelitis, Tetanus, etc.)

Date	Vaccine	Dose	Physician's Signature
12 June 75	Typhoid	0.5 cc	M.W. CONWAY, M.D. 2515 N. Main St. Suite 104
12 June 75	Typhus	1 cc	M.W. CONWAY, M.D. 2515 N. Main St. Santa Ana, Calif. 92701
27 JUIL. 1975	T.A.B.	0.5 cc	D. FARAHMAND, M.D. KHARK
2 May 77	Gamma Globulin	5 cc	
2 May 77	tetanus, diphtheria	0.5 cc	
19 OCT 1977	typhus	0,5 cc	
20 Oct 77	Gamma Globulin	5 cc	WILLIAM H. METZGER M.D.
14 Feb. 78	typhus	1.0 cc	
7 Mar 79	Typhoid	0.5 cc	
6-7-00	tetanus	0.5 cc	David M. Miller 8012 Middlebelt Road Westland, MI 48185 522-9090

CERTIFICAT INTERNATIONAL DE VACCINATION OU DE REVACCINATION CONTRE LA VARIOLE

This is to certify that / Je soussigné(e) certifie que: Reca, Walter — sex / sexe: male

whose signature follows / dont la signature suit: Walter R Reca — date of birth / né(e) le: 9-20-33

has on the date indicated been vaccinated or revaccinated against smallpox with a freeze-dried or liquid vaccine certified to fulfil the recommended requirements of the World Health Organization.

a été vacciné(e) ou revacciné(e) contre la variole à la date indiquée ci-dessus, avec un vaccin lyophilisé ou liquide certifié conforme aux normes recommandées par l'Organisation mondiale de la Santé.

Date	Show by "X" whether / Indiquer par "X" s'il s'agit de	Signature, professional status, and address of vaccinator / Signature, titre, et adresse du vaccinateur	Manufacturer and batch no. of vaccine / Fabricant du vaccin et numéro du lot	Approved stamp / Cachet autorisé
1a	Primary vaccination performed / Primovaccination effectuée ☐			
1b	Read as successful / Prise ☐ Unsuccessful / Pas de prise ☐			
2	X Revaccination			OFFICIAL VACCINATION

INTERNATIONAL CERTIFICATE OF VACCINATION OR REVACCINATION AGAINST CHOLERA
CERTIFICAT INTERNATIONAL DE VACCINATION OU DE REVACCINATION CONTRE LE CHOLÉRA

This is to certify that — RECA WALTER R — sex / sexe — MALE
Je soussigné(e) certifie que

whose signature follows — Walter R Reca — date of birth / né(e) le — 9-20-33
dont la signature suit

has on the date indicated been vaccinated or revaccinated against cholera.
a été vacciné(e) ou revacciné(e) contre le choléra à date indiquée.

Date	Signature, professional status, and address of vaccinator / Signature, titre, et adresse du vaccinateur	Approved stamp / Cachet autorisé
1. 12 June 75	0.5cc — M.W. CONWAY, M.D. 2515 N. Main St. Suite 104 Santa Ana, Calif. 92701	OFFICIAL VACCINATION CALIFORNIA A-09745 U.S.A.
2. 27 JUIL. 1975	D. FARAHMAND. M.D.	KHARK ISland IRAN KHARK 100 No 17
3. 23 April 1976	SPOKANE COUNTY HEALTH DISTRICT North 819 Jefferson Street Spokane, Washington 99201	OFFICIAL VACCINATION WASHINGTON 46-063-0720 U.S.A.
4. 1 November 1976	Dr. M. Meresh M.D. SPOKANE COUNTY HEALTH DISTRICT North 819 Jefferson Street Spokane, Washington 99201 S.	OFFICIAL VACCINATION WASHINGTON 46-063-0720 U.S.A.
5. 2 May 1977	GEO. B. PFOERTNER, M.D., F.C.C.P., INTERNAL MEDICINE & PULMONARY DISEASE 99 N. Curtis SUITE 404 BOISE, IDAHO 83705	OFFICIAL VACCINATION IDAHO
6. 19 OCT 1977	Cholera Vaccine Lot .774M	MORRISON-KNUDSEN INTERNATIONAL CO. INC. GWESH THIRD EXPANSION MEDICAL DEPT.
7. 14 Feb. 1978	0.5c WILLIAM H. METZGER M.D. 1201 W. LA VETA AVE. SUITE 211 ORANGE, CA. 92668	OFFICIAL VACCINATION CALIFORNIA G-21079 U.S.A.
8. 31 Dec 1979	0.5 cc — Kenneth R. Steinoff	PARK VALLEY CLINIC Kenneth R. Steinoff, D.O. David M. Miller, D.O. 8012 Middlebelt Road Westland, MI 48185
9. 25 Nov 1981	0.5CC #646-496	DAVID M. MILLER, D.O., P.C. 9460 Middlebelt Livonia, Michigan 48150
10. 3 July 1982	0.5CC #106605 A	DAVID M. MILLER, D.O., P.C. 9460 Middlebelt Livonia, Michigan 48150
11.		

Form 5-132

UNITED STATES
DEPARTMENT OF THE INTERIOR
BUREAU OF INDIAN AFFAIRS
OSAGE AGENCY

Certificate Of Competency Of An Osage Indian

Whereas, ... Mr. Walter E. Recca ....
an adult unallotted member of the Osage Tribe of Indians, is of less than one-half Indian blood.

Now, therefore, pursuant to Section 242.5, Title 25, Code of Federal Regulations, and in compliance with the Act of February 5, 1948 (Public Law 408, 80th Congress, 2nd Session) the Superintendent of the Osage Agency does hereby issue to the said ..... Walter E. Recca ....
this Certificate of Competency.

Done at Pawhuska, Oklahoma this ....1.....day of...June, 1948................................

Superintendent of the Osage Agency

STATE OF OKLAHOMA }
OSAGE COUNTY } ss.

This instrument was filed for record on the ....1....day of ...June....... A.D.
19 y..... at ..... o'clock ..... M., and duly Recorded in Book..... 2 ....of C. C. on Page.... 271.....

W. H. LUNDAY, County Clerk

When work was slow I got my dispatches from the Union Hall as a minority, a Osage Indian

WALTER R. RECA
2207 Otter Street
Warren, Michigan 48092
(313) 268-0467

PERSONAL:

Social Security Number
U.S.A.
Canadian
Saudi Arabia

Passport Number — 24520543

Place of Issue — Dhahran Saudi
Arabia by Consulate General of the
United States of America

Description — 5' 10" — 170 lbs.

Date of Birth — September 20, 1933

Place of Birth — Detroit, Michigan

Health — Excellent

POSITION OBJECTIVE:

Direct field management . . . quality control, construction management team, inspector heavy horizontal/vertical/underground structural steel rigging, erection & welding, offshore barge or vessel superintendent, supervisor.

GENERAL BACKGROUND:

Over 21 years diversified experience in structural steel erection, heavy rigging and welding (12 years at supervisory levels). Over 10 years experience in Direct Field Management, Inspector and Quality Control, with 8 satisfactorily completed overseas contracts, 5 in Saudi Arabia, Iran, Indonesia, Scotland. Experience encompasses responsibilities as Superintendent performing structural erection and rigging steel beams, piping and miscellaneous iron, offshore oil platform, fabrication of buildings being barged to Alaskan pipeline project. Grand Coulee Dam, suspension bridges, industrial aluminum plants, steel mills, towers, high-rise commercial buildings, including fabricating, burning, layout, welding, rebar, etc. Experienced in heavy duty rigging and utilization of 200/400 ton cranes and various models and truck cranes in 35/100 ton class. Capable in all phases of rigging, i.e. tri- and quad-block reaving and rigging for outhaul and horizontal movements inclusive of marine barge mounted crane operations in setting, connecting, welding heavy bridge sections, etc. Capable of loading/installing heavy (150 + tons) equipment. Successful in supervision of subordinate personnel, cogent when required to meet Company Policy, or to be in correlation with customers specifications. Largest complement supervised 25 Americans, 40 nationals, 350 TCN's. Get around very well on high steel structures.

FOREIGN LANGUAGES:

Speak and comprehend Polish and Ukrainian. Working knowledge of Indonesian.

MILITARY:

2/50 to 1/54 U.S. Army Honorable Discharge.

PAST AFFILIATIONS:

American Welding Society Ref. #535583
American Concrete Institution Ref. #113-612567
Canadian Institute of Steel Construction
Iron Workers Local #14 Spokane, Washington
Amalgamated Society of Boilermakers
Shipwrights, Blacksmiths, and Structural Workers of Great Britain and Ireland
Lodge #19, Branch of Nair, Scotland
Letters of recommendation on request

COUNTRIES EXPERIENCED

Algeria, Austria, Bahrain, Belgium, Canada, Chile, Denmark, Ecuador, Egypt, France, West Germany, Greece, Greenland, Guatemala, Indonesia, Iran, Japan, South Korea, Netherlands, Nigeria, Panama, Peru, Poland, Saudi Arabia, Sierra Leone, Singapore, Switzerland, Thailand, and United Kingdom.

The parachutist who landed in the Michigan underpass wasn't the only one to goof in the course of Funarama sky leap. . . . Another chutist waved so enthusiastically to the pilot as he jumped from the plane that he slammed his arm against the machine, and broke it in five places. . . . Despite his injury, he came down safely and parachuted again a few hours later, with his arm in a cast.

Walt Peca (a.k.a. Reca) in the late 1950s or early '60s (photo provided by Carl Laurin).

Loretta and Carl ("Charlie Brown") Laurin (l. to r.), with the author, during a lunch break following my first interview of Carl.

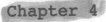

Chapter 4

THE TAPES,
THE TRANSCRIPTS,
AND CARL'S VERACITY

Carl gave Dirk and Vern ten mini-cassette audiotapes that comprise all the recordings of his telephone discussions with Walt from approximately late October 2008 to late December 2008 or early January 2009. There are about 3.5 hours of recordings.

It is safe to say that Carl is not savvy in modern-day electronics or computers. He has no email. He handwrites all correspondence. He handwrote his first manuscript about the parachute team, called *The Last Barnstormers*. It could be said that Carl is brilliant and a little behind the times. His wife, Loretta, handles their email correspondence and anything Internet-related.

The recordings were done at his daughter's house because she had a tape recorder. So, Carl went to his daughter's house to initiate all the recorded calls to Walt. The recordings were undated, scattered in a box, and of poor quality. None of the recordings were date stamped or numbered, and there was no reference to dates or times on or inside the cassettes/recordings. We pieced together the cassettes as best we could to put them in chronological order. I don't know whether the transcripts accurately reflect the chronological order of the conversations.

Carl and Walt began talking about and continued to talk about Walt being D.B. Cooper long before and after these recordings. They began talking in 1998 and continued through 2014, ending with Walt's death.

In 2008, Walt was seventy-five years old, and Carl was seventy-four. These recordings cover a series of incidents that occurred thirty-seven years earlier. I expect there to be discrepancies, inaccuracies, and contradictions, as I point out in Walt and Carl's discussions about Snohomish versus McChord as the source of the parachutes. I know, from experience, that truth-tellers, years younger than Carl and Walt, often make errors in their accounting even of recent events. Again, we need to keep this in mind as we evaluate the transcripts and the evidence. Luckily, we have actual recordings, FBI 302 reports, and evidence with which we can make comparisons to help us determine our final conclusions.

I obtained an initial transcription that didn't meet the standards I needed to effectively conduct my analysis. My wife, Julie, stepped up and did a fabulous job of fine-tuning them, making them accurate reflections of the actual discussions. Both Julie and I repeatedly listened to the tapes with the completed transcripts many times to make sure the transcripts precisely captured the conversations. In doing so, I was able to get a fix on Walt's communication patterns, his voice, his articulation, the volume, his reactions to the questions, how long he took to respond to each question, the nuances in his voice, his voice inflections, and the pace of his speech. Listening to his voice and responses, I found his communication patterns to be consistent throughout the discussions, regardless of topic. This was an important first step in my analysis.

Walter R. Peca Jr. (Recca, Racca, Reca), in his Last Testament, told Carl Laurin (a.k.a. "Charlie Brown"), "I was never a liar; I was a robber, a thief, and a hijacker, but never a liar." And in that testament, he again told Charlie, "I am D.B. Cooper." Later, Carl asked, "Why now, Walter?" Walt replied, "Because it's time." After many months of discussions, Walt dictated his Last Testament to Carl Laurin ("Charlie Brown") over the phone, and Carl handwrote it. Carl had a neighbor type his handwritten document into a word processor and print out the finished document. Walt reviewed and confirmed that the written document was accurate. Walt's niece Lisa Story and his sister, Sandy, reviewed the Last Testament with him, and they also attested to the document's accuracy after discussing it at length with him. Walt decided not to sign the Last Testament after Lisa and Sandy advised against it because they didn't want him to incriminate himself before his death.

The sentence "I am D.B. Cooper" is a powerful one. Start with the pronoun *I*, which is a powerful pronoun, unique in that it compels the possession of what follows—"am D.B. Cooper." It is present tense, meaning the teller believes he is D.B. Cooper. It's a simple, precise, and direct statement—all trademarks of truthful statements. There's no wiggle, no hesitancy, no misdirection. Walt's statement powerfully compelled me to take on this project.

I need to talk about Carl's veracity, the stories he told us, the evidence he accumulated, and the actions he took to help procure the evidence I (we) used to verify and help corroborate his account. We studied all the documents Carl said he had. I interviewed the various persons he said he'd contacted, and I verified Carl's account. The evidence Carl provided is corroborative. My analysis of the communication patterns of his wife, Loretta, also corroborated his statements and assertions. The documents/evidence provided appeared to be written contemporaneously, meaning the writings apparently were made when the incidents occurred. That makes the records more likely to be authentic. With much expense, we could have submitted these records to a lab to determine when the various entries were made, but the cost was prohibitive. As a seasoned investigator, I felt the documents were probably authentic.

Carl Laurin is not a trained investigator. The transcripts show his questions and interview style to be leading, contaminating, and suggestive. Carl had to "pull" the information out of Walt, and he did. Analyzing transcripts of this sort is difficult for a forensic linguist. I commend Carl for his spectacular work in obtaining and retaining this information. While his questions were leading, he allowed Walt enough latitude and freedom to reveal communication patterns that are the heart of linguistic analysis. And Carl was repetitive in his questions, going over and over ground already tilled, again providing a good record for me to review and enabling me to compare previous responses for consistency. I often repeat questions in my interrogations, primarily to determine the subject's consistency, accuracy, and fluency. Although Carl is not a trained investigator or interrogator, he more than got the job done. I salute him and his passion for telling this story. He's a remarkable man.

Chapter 5

THE DNA

In 2009, Carl said he acquired a bodily sample that would identify Walt's DNA and gave it to his attorney David Damore, instructing Damore to submit it to the FBI for comparison with D.B. Cooper's alleged DNA. Carl didn't reveal Walt's name to either Damore or the FBI. Mr. Damore's records show he sent that DNA sample to FBI Special Agent Larry Carr on July 27, 2009 (copy of submission below). Mr. Damore verified each and every detail Carl told us. Seventy-four days later, Agent Carr informed Mr. Damore that the submitted DNA did not match the FBI's sample. According to Damore, Agent Carr asked him who had picked up Cooper from the landing site. This statement was of particular interest to Carl. He wondered why Agent Carr would focus on the identity of the person who picked up the hijacker, rather than on the identity of the hijacker. We have no idea why Agent Carr posed this question.

DNA, especially in those days, was a nascent science. Carr told Mr. Damore the FBI's DNA sample could be used only to eliminate a suspect's DNA. The Bureau's DNA sample was obtained from the black tie D.B. Cooper abandoned before jumping.[9] The FBI had no idea who had handled or touched the black tie and whether the DNA was, in fact, D.B. Cooper's. How did FBI agents secure and store the tie to protect it from contamination, if they

---

9   See *https://www.fbi.gov/history/famous-cases/db-cooper-hijacking*.

were unable to use a science unknown to them at the time? Knowing what we know now, that Walt Reca said he bought the tie and the other items of clothing in a second-hand store, it's just as likely the DNA belonged to the previous owner of the tie. And, as discussed earlier, the best DNA source for D.B. Cooper would have been the Raleigh cigarette butts—which apparently were lost by the FBI and never made available for DNA analysis.

227 Seabreeze Boulevard
Daytona Beach, Florida 32118

David R. Damore, P.A.
Aaron D. Delgado, P.A.
Matthew E. Romanik, P.A.++
Robert W. Rawlins, III, P.A.

DAMORE DELGADO ROMANIK &RAWLINS
Your Community Law Firm

Telephone: 386.255.1400
Facsimile: 386.255.8100
www.communitylawfirm.com

Donald W. "Trace" Pendry, P.A.
Of counsel – David D. Ege, P.A. *+
*Admitted Wisconsin Bar
+Board Certified Criminal Trial Law
+ + Board Certified Workers' Compensation

FACSIMILE COVER SHEET

THE INFORMATION CONTAINED IN THIS FACSIMILE MESSAGE IS LEGALLY PRIVILEGED AND CONFIDENTIAL INFORMATION INTENDED ONLY FOR THE USE OF THE INDIVIDUAL OR ENTITY NAMED BELOW. IF THE READER OF THIS FACSIMILE MESSAGE IS NOT THE INTENDED RECIPIENT, YOU ARE HEREBY NOTIFIED THAT ANY DISSEMINATION, DISTRIBUTION OR COPY OF THE FACSIMILE TRANSMISSION IS STRICTLY PROHIBITED. IF YOU HAVE RECEIVED THIS FACSIMILE TRANSMISSION IN ERROR, PLEASE IMMEDIATELY NOTIFY US BY TELEPHONE AND RETURN THE ORIGINAL FACSIMILE MESSAGE TO US AT THE ADDRESS ABOVE VIA THE UNITED STATES POSTAL SERVICE. THANK YOU.

TO: Special Agent Larry Carr
          Federal Bureau of Investigation

FAX: 1-206-262-2525

FROM: David Damore, Esq.

DATE: July 27, 2009

RE: DNA sample

Number of pages: 4

COMMENTS: As per our discussions, please find attached the profile for comparison. I look forward to hearing from you with the results.

SENDER: **Anna**

Chapter 6

THE TRUTH–GETTING PROCESS

I spent many years in the Detroit area. One of my favorite radio shows was WJR's Joseph Priestly McCarthy, also known as J.P. McCarthy. J.P. frequently used the penetratingly accurate saying "It's not the money—it's the amount." We want to know whether Walt Reca *is/was* D.B. Cooper—not whether Walt Reca *could have been* D.B. Cooper. So, let's get to the truth of the matter.

This is a book to get the truth and to promote the processes that will get us there. Was Walt Peca, a.k.a. Recca, Racca, Reca, the real D.B. Cooper? We will answer that question. My passion is to help you understand how we get there.

In *Getting the Truth* (Principia Media, 2014), I detail the essential truth-detecting tools that allow us to understand the real message, to be able to distinguish truth from deception— to evaluate statements and transcripts for truthfulness and deception. For a much greater understanding of my analysis in this book, I recommend reading that one. Here is the one principle you need to master:

People don't tell complete lies; they tell partial truths.

That's what makes truth-detection so difficult. People can lie (mislead) by telling partial truths, leading the listener to believe the whole statement is true when only part of it is. We all too often assume that since a portion of a statement is true, the entire statement is true. A polished deceiver will attach some "wiggle" words that will allow him or her later, if necessary, to say, "Oh, I meant . . ." For example, when Los Angeles Police Department Detective Phillip Vannatter asked OJ a question, OJ used Vannatter's language in his answer (see "The Parking Lot" and contaminating questions). By answering the question in this way, OJ gives few details, and, if asked later why he answered it this way, he can say, "I was just repeating what was asked."

Vannatter: Uh huh. I understand she had made a couple of crime . . . crime reports or something?

Simpson: Ah, we have [sic] a big fight about six years ago on New Year's, you know, she made a report. I didn't make a report. And then we had an altercation about a year ago maybe. It wasn't a physical argument. I kicked her door or something.

Furthermore, bias and prejudice occur in everything we say and hear. So the message one person delivers to another is rarely understood completely. As a result, both the teller and the receiver don't fully understand all the intricacies and inferences of the communication process.

We approach perfect communication when we know:

What is communicated and why;
and,
what isn't communicated and why.

I say we "approach" perfect communication because we rarely achieve it. The orchestra approaches it, with the conductor and the musicians all working off the same sheet music. And they approach perfect communication with the audience only when they've rehearsed, practiced, and executed in a way that provides the audience with the intended message. Once one person in the audience falls asleep, perfection is again denied. We may approach perfection when an old, dear friend gives us a known facial expression that is clearly and perfectly understood because we've sensed that same expression many times before.

Once you master the principles in *Getting the Truth* and *Getting the Truth: "I Am D.B. Cooper,"* you will be able to see the tracks partial truth–tellers leave behind as they try to deceive you. You'll also be able to tell when someone is truthful, which may be even more valuable to you.

Communication is very complex. It's a series of events, actions, and inactions. We can communicate with a glance, a motion, a reaction, a slight nuance in our voice or pronunciation, or even no response. We control some communication, how we interpret, how we project. Most communication, though, is not under our control—inadvertent reactions, innate motions, and erroneous interpretations. Our footprints, our fingerprints, our breath, our ancestors' DNA and appearance, our posture, our appearance, the volume of our voice, our confidence or lack of— all convey information about us, telling others something about us. All of these are communication mechanisms, even if invisible and/or unintended. As we communicate (send and receive), we're constantly selecting, evaluating, analyzing, and sensing each and every communication mechanism.

THE PARKING LOT

The communication process is like a huge parking lot. The "parking lot attendant" is our mind. This model serves to help explain the intricacies of the communication process: the timing, our individual and unique nuances of speech, our body language, and the infinite combinations of the thousands of variables involved. The communication elements (vehicles) constitute most of the ways we uniquely communicate: our vocabulary, our communication habits, our experiences, our unique physical traits, and the library of all our communication tools and components. Think of each element in this parking lot as a word, a physical reaction, a grunt, a raised voice, a voice inflection, eye movement, hand movement, silence, or a phrase. Each element is a communication component. Our mind (the "attendant") selects a combination or a string of these elements to create a message and to interpret and understand received messages. Each element has its own uniqueness. And when an element is selected, not selected, moved, or changed, a track is laid like a wolf's footprints in the snow—to be detected by the trained observer to help interpret the real meaning of the message.

We also use other methods to communicate in both intended and unintended ways: our scents, fingerprints, tattoos, footprints, blood pressure, skin color, and many other evidence-leaving characteristics that communicate something to someone. No wonder we misinterpret or don't understand one another.

When we express ourselves, our communication mechanism (our mind, the "attendant") deliberately selects a communication element or a series of elements, and each appears and disappears as needed. This is a very fast but deliberate process. Mistakes are important and discernible, measureable, and meaningful. Everything matters. Our response contains all the elements we selected (as well as those we pondered but chose not to select), which move very quickly to deliver the message. We see the response like we see a waterfall—an apparent uninterruptable stream of water that, when examined closely, is the fast flow of the basic elements of communication.

Like a computer, our communication process's operating system is based on a series of *Yes* and *No* decisions. As we compose our thoughts and select our unique communication mechanisms (vehicles), our parking lot attendant (our mind) evaluates each and every vehicle in our parking lot to form our response. In a flash, we ask the *Yes* or *No* questions: "Use this vehicle?" If the answer is "Yes," the vehicle (component) surfaces. If "No," our attendant moves on to the next. "Use this vehicle with others?" If yes, then another vehicle is selected to surface. It happens in milliseconds, like computer calculations, computer code, and it's very precise. When the answer is *"Yes,"* all the "yes" vehicles surface to form our response. The *"No's"* leave tracks. The evidence is there for everyone to sense. The die is cast. The track is laid.

Some vehicles and combinations of vehicles are favorite selections and surface frequently. These are the "communication patterns" I refer to later. These favorites (phrases, words, physical movements) represent habitual, persistent, and recurrent patterns. They surface during non-stressful conditions, when the responder is comfortable, at ease. In the transcripts that follow, I identify Walt's favorite phrase as "right there," which I characterize as an idiosyncrasy, an informal response. I then see where that phrase appears and draw conclusions on how often he uses it ("right there" is used 214 times), where he uses it, and when he uses it (see the beginning of my analysis of Walt's transcript).

The responder's "attendant" has several bosses, all divisions within our minds. Some are our Memories, Instincts, Genetics, Visions, Mental Creations, Defense Mechanisms, Habits, Biology, and Truth-Teller. All impact our responses. Some are autonomic (Habits, Instincts, Biology, and Genetics), which create responses without our knowledge or input. Others are very thoughtful and calculating (Memories, Visions, Mental Creations, and Defense Mechanisms), which create responses to protect us, to indemnify us, to deceive others. Each has its own unique communication patterns. And there are gradients of each, depending on the circumstance. So, suffice to say, our communication process is a very, very complex one.

The Habitual "attendant" responses are less discriminating, almost autonomic. This "attendant" frequently uses certain vehicles repetitively, almost without reason, almost without caution. Walt's "right there" is a good example, which he uses throughout the transcript in both low-stress and important stressful portions of the transcript. The fact that he uses that phrase throughout his transcript in both stress and no-stress areas connotes comfort, confidence, and a careless quality—all consistent with truth-telling.

The Defense Mechanism "attendant" tries to suppress telltale communication patterns when there is stress, when extra care is needed before the response, and when the response is new or unique. For example, when you write to the president of your company, you will avoid using contractions. You won't say, "I'm determined to find . . ." You'll say, "I am determined to find . . ." We talk differently in formal and informal settings.

Consider the reluctant, deceptive witness who consistently answers questions with the wiggle phrase ". . . as far as I can recall." The witness's Defense Mechanism "attendant" is adding that phrase (vehicle) because it wants to create deniability if evidence later shows the witness is not recalling correctly or knows or should have known the specific answer. Or, the "attendant" reacts to questions with a question to steal more time to safely process all the possibilities for answers.

The Truth-Teller "attendant" is programmed from our early days when our parents, teachers, and thought leaders taught us to tell the truth. Later, as we matured, we evolved to tell partial truths to avoid telling complete lies. The Truth-Teller "attendant" works very hard to create responses that obfuscate the real meaning of our partially truthful and deceptive responses.

The Biological "attendant" is, to a large extent, autonomic and beyond our control. If we experience sudden severe pain, our faces distort to communicate our distress even before we know what's going on.

Each of these "attendants" affects our responses. Communication patterns emerge and changes surface, revealing evidence of communication decisions, both willing and unwilling. Forensic linguists recognize these changes as opportunities to help them understand the real message, to detect truth and deception.

Recent events, actions, and exchanges (our Memories "attendant") also affect the selection of communication components. How often do you see the words in the question show up in the response? For example, the following exchange appeared in the interview of OJ Simpson by Los Angeles Police Department detectives Phillip Vannatter and Thomas Lange:

O.J.S.: Eleven o'clock. yeah. somewhere in that area.

P.V.: And you went by limo?

O.J.S.: Yeah.

P.V.: Who's the limo service?

O.J.S.: Ah, you have to ask my office.

another example of response containing interviewer verbiage.

T.L.: Did you converse with the driver at all? Did you talk to him?

O.J.S.: No. he was a new driver. Normally, I have a regular driver I drive with and converse. No, just about rushing to the airport, and about how I live my live on airplanes, and hotels, that type of thing.

T.L.: What time did your plane leave?

O.J.S.: Ah, eleven forty-five the flight took off.

P.V.: What airline was it?

O.J.S.: American

P.V.: American? And it was eleven forty-five to Chicago?

O.J.S.: Chicago.

T.L.: So yesterday you did drive the white Bronco?

O.J.S.: Mmm hmm.

T.L.: And where did you park it when you brought it home? *where's the 2nd ti...*

O.J.S.: Ah, the first time probably by the mailbox. I'm trying to think. or did I bring it in the driveway? Normally, I will park it by the mailbox. sometimes.

T.L.: On Ashford, or Ashland?

O.J.S.: On Ashford, yeah.

T.L.: Where did you park yesterday for the last time, do you remember? *or he lie no he knew to say he can rem...*

O.J.S.: Right where it is. *∴ no one else drove it.*

9

The word *converse* in Detective Lange's question led to OJ using that word in his response. I call this "Question Contamination." The wording in the question contaminates the response. OJ's "attendant" uses the same word the questioner uses to OJ's advantage. OJ never used that word before but uses it now. Untruthful people will hide behind undefined words.

Over time, the "attendant" alters almost every vehicle. Some receive tune-ups, reupholstering, or bodywork, and others get removed and replaced. We constantly work on our communication mechanisms and components, changing and fine-tuning them.

The receiver then interprets the sender's communication using his or her own parking lot full of his or her own unique vehicles. This is where the receiver's "attendant" interprets messages. If the interpretation matches the intended message, the message is communicated accurately, and we deem the words used to be mutually understood. If something is different, there's a misunderstanding; the communication was not mutually understood. Now, the parties (the sender and the receiver) might not yet know the receiver misunderstood the sender. In that case, the mistake was inadvertent. So, when I say, "I like the way you expressed yourself at our meeting," and you think I'm referring to the first meeting when, in fact, I'm referring to the second, that is inadvertent and not intended.

If, however, the sender misleads the receiver intentionally, we have deception. In my previous example, I would be deceptive if I intentionally phrased my statement to mislead the receiver into thinking I meant it when, in fact, I didn't.

See how Abbott and Costello reveal the feigned unintentional miscommunication beautifully in the classic "Who's on first?" (Costello is learning about baseball.)

Abbott: Strange as it may seem, they give ball players nowadays very peculiar names.

Costello: Funny names?

Abbott: Nicknames, nicknames. Now, on the St. Louis team we have Who's on first, What's on second, I Don't Know is on third—

Costello: That's what I want to find out. I want you to tell me the names of the fellows on the St. Louis team.

Abbott: I'm telling you. Who's on first, What's on second, I Don't Know is on third—

Costello: You know the fellows' names?

Abbott: Yes.

Costello: Well, then who's playing first?

Abbott: Yes.[10]

Costello didn't catch Abbot's initial definition. Instead, he fell back on his own definitions, his own vehicles in his own parking lot, his Memories "attendant."

THE FORENSIC LINGUIST

The beauty of forensic linguistics hits you when you find the rhythm and patterns of communication. It's like enjoying a symphony. You need to experience it.

We're looking for changes in those patterns, but you first have to discover the patterns. The forensic linguist calibrates to the individual, identifying his or her communication patterns, then determining when those patterns change. The next step is determining what caused the change. The change could be the result of many variables, such as noise, distraction, deception, and so on. Only skill, patience, practice, and perseverance will uncover it. Absorb, absorb, absorb the evidence and information. The trained observer senses all that is there and all that isn't there that should be. You solve the puzzle when you discover the actual cause.

---

10   See *http://www.psu.edu/dept/inart10_110/inart10/whos.html*.

Like water seeking its own level, the body relieves itself of stress, seeking calmness. The greatest stress reliever known to man is truth-telling. It's a relief valve, a bloodletting, a purging. Nature demands it in order to begin the rebuilding process. Forensic linguists, interrogators, and investigators use that force to their advantage. We know the default is truth-telling.

As we communicate, our "attendant" examines each vehicle to compose the thought we wish to communicate. Retrieving the vehicle is very fast—it's a millisecond, a decision. Sometimes when that vehicle appears, we want it to disappear—but it's too late, it has already appeared. We try to send it back into the parking lot, even though it was already detected, seen, and heard and has left evidence. These are Freudian slips, parapraxes, "slips of the tongue." **Everything** matters in communication. The "slip of the tongue" gives us a window into the thought process of the communicator. The intended or unintended thought(s) that caused that "slip," illuminating that vehicle, is there for us to evaluate, to interpret.

In short, forensic linguistics requires the methodical study of each and every word, each and every communication mechanism. We seek to identify communication patterns and changes in those patterns. For example, take a look at the following statement:

"I saw him come up from the basement with **a** gun. He went outside and shot **the** gun in the air."

That sentence makes sense and has truthful traits—the change from the article "*a*" in "**a** gun" to article "*the*" in "**the** gun" is expected. Logically, it appears as if the speaker is referring to the same gun and the same shooter. The speaker uses the active voice (I saw; He went), and the past tense (saw, went, shot). We probably know what happened. The "active voice" tells you who did what: "I threw the ball." You have no doubt who threw the ball. In contrast, we often see, "The ball was thrown," which is the "passive voice." The passive voice doesn't tell you who the actor was. Truthful people want you to know the truth. Untruthful people want you to think you are being told the truth. So, we often see deceptive people use the "passive voice."

Accordingly, what if the speaker said this?

"I saw him come up from the basement with **a** gun. He went outside, and **a** gun was shot in the air."

This is different. Now we don't know which gun was shot or, for that matter, who shot the gun. In the first example, we assume (assumptions are never safe) the guy who went from the basement to the outside is the one who shot the gun. In the second example, we're left wondering who shot the gun or what gun because the speaker changed the communication pattern. Something happened to cause the change. We know the speaker *can* use the active voice, as shown in the first 1.5 sentences, but he or she chooses to change to the passive voice (". . . and **a** gun was shot in the air"), effectively concealing the gun used and the person who shot the gun. Something caused that change. Notice that the use of passive language forces sentences to be longer, wordier, cloudier. The active voice, conversely, provides clarity and precision. The passive voice is imprecise and causes confusion, often intentionally. Deceptive people often use the passive voice to subtly conceal knowledge, the identity of the actor, or their intent. Applying forensic linguistics will allow us to better understand what really happened. It enables us to identify changes in communication patterns and help determine why those changes occurred, ultimately leading us to understand what really happened.

"Truth is Peace, the resting place, the beginning."

Telling the complete truth relieves stress, allowing the rebuilding process to begin.

- Be an active listener—a trained observer.
- Always use mutually understood words in your questions.
- Be on the lookout for what is there and, more important, what isn't.
- We are all different, unique. Each of us communicates uniquely.
- Analysis, therefore, must be calibrated each and every time, uniquely.
- It is harder to lie than to tell the truth.
- We experience more stress when telling a lie.
- The truth hides in obscurity and confusion.
- You can lose the truth in how you ask a question, how you structure and sculpt a question, and how you time and position a question.

Absorb, absorb, absorb information. Be a sponge. Delay judgment until after absorbing all the information.

Again, truth-getting is more about discovering partial truths than uncovering lies. A partial truth that is misleading is a lie—let's make no mistake. However, it's much easier and more productive to get the whole truth from someone by calling a lie a **partial truth**. The key to truth-getting is to look through the eyes of the prevaricator, not the investigator. Feeling and showing empathy, knowing the feelings of others, are essential aspects of truth-getting.

Each of us communicates uniquely. **Each and every** word we use, **how** we use those words, and **how** we say/write those words result from our own unique communication style. Everything is important—everything. Words used, the cadence and rhythm of the discourse, the emphasis on parts of words, breathing, blinking—all go into getting a fix on a person's communication pattern. Remember, each person's pattern is unique, and our job as forensic linguists is to detect changes in that pattern, then eliminate all possible causes, before concluding a person was deceptive. In a way, our communication is coded. My previous book, *Getting the Truth,* and this book will help you decode what others are saying, writing, and communicating so you can understand the real message, the real communication. When people tell partial truths, they leave tracks. Those tracks allow us to decode their communications. In doing so, we become better and better at getting the truth.

I'm not sure what caused me to become a forensic linguist. Maybe it was my formal education. When I earned my bachelor's degree in accounting, Wayne State University required me to pass a writing test. I flunked it (see "More About the Author"). Surprised, because I and others had always thought I was a good writer, the test revealed that I consistently wrote in the passive voice. Many military and police organizations teach their young agents to write in the passive voice, thinking it "sounds" more professional. As an officer, I would write, "The scene was secured by the undersigned, and evidence was seized."

Instead, I finally learned I should write this in the active voice: "I secured the scene, and Tpr. Jones seized the evidence."

See how different these two sentences are. The first contains 11 words, and the second 10 words—yet the second sentence is much clearer and contains much more information. The second sentence is written much more professionally. All police and military organizations need to change their report writing policies.

Following that revelation, I assiduously tried to improve my writing every chance I got. I attended and graduated from the FBI National Academy in Quantico, Virginia (1980, 122nd Class,

University of Virginia) and Northwestern University's Staff and Command School (1989). From all over the world, departments and organizations select their top performers to attend these much sought-after academies. The attendees gain worldly perspectives and exceptional training. While attending these schools, I learned that many top police professionals wrote just like I did, in the "passive voice." Ironically, the passive voice is the preferred style for the deceptive person. The "active voice" shows the actor; the passive voice obscures the actor. Take a look at this statement of a subject who submitted a fraudulent claim to an insurance company, claiming his car was stolen:

> I came home around 10:00pm in the evening. I parked the car in our driveway. The doors were locked and the alarm was activated.
>
> I went to bed about 11:00pm. When I came out at 7:00am in the morning I discovered that the car was gone and a part of the driver side window was still on the ground, broken out. A police report was filed immediately at the local precinct.

Look at the first paragraph. He uses the active voice in the first two sentences, then shifts to the passive voice when saying, "The doors were locked [by whom?] and the alarm was activated [by whom?]." Again, forensic linguists look for changes in communication patterns. This is a communication pattern change when he goes from using the active voice to the passive voice. If he had stayed in the active voice and written, "I locked the doors and activated the alarm," I would have told the company, "Pay the claim." Instead, I called the man in for an interview, and he confessed that he couldn't continue to pay his loan on his car, and he'd filed a false report. Over the years, I have accumulated many more examples of these kinds of changes in communication patterns that led to confessions.

Eastern Michigan University required a great deal of writing for my master's degree, which added to my desire to improve my writing abilities. My formal training in statement analysis through SCAN (Avinoam Sapir's Scientific Content Analysis academies) interview and interrogation schools and academies, including the Reid School of Interview and Interrogation, and more than forty-five years of investigative experience honed my passion for forensic linguistics.[11] I saw the power of knowing the real messages people were communicating.

All this led to my first book, *Getting the Truth*, which in turn brought about my career as a speaker to many professional organizations, such as the IIA (Internal Auditors' Association), MAHA (Michigan Association of Healthcare Auditors), the ACUA (Association of College and University Auditors), the Michigan Certified Fraud Examiners Association, the Michigan CPA Association, and some that, for privacy reasons, won't allow me to mention them. I have also been a guest on numerous radio and television shows.

---

11   LSIS SCAN, *https://www.google.com/search?client=safari&rls=en&q=scientific +content+analysis&ie=UTF-8&oe=UTF-8*. Also see John E. Reid & Associates; *https://www.reid.com*.

Furthermore, several associations often requested that I write articles for their members on these powerful concepts:

- "Getting the Real Message," *College and University Auditor*, vol. 60, no. 2 (Summer 2018).
- "Getting the Truth," webinar for the Association of Certified Fraud Examiners, March 29, 2018.
- "Anatomy of Denials," *Association of Certified Fraud Examiners' Fraud Magazine* vol. 33, no. 1 (January–February 2018).
- "The Right Questions, the Right Way, the Right Time," *Compliance and Ethics Professional Magazine* (April 4, 2017).
- "Taming the Perfect Storm, Security Gaps in the Banking Industry" (December 2006).

Objectivity is the key to truth-getting. If you have bias or prejudice (and we all do!), you have to be aware of those very effective barriers to understanding. You won't sense the truth if you are predisposed to believe something else. You can only look at politics to see how seemingly fair-minded and intelligent people differ in how they see and react to apparently obvious "facts." We all "see" and "sense" things differently. If we all suppressed our biases and prejudices, we might have a chance to agree. Our biases and prejudices contaminate how we interpret facts. Eyewitness accounts of an event often conflict. DNA evidence, particularly in Innocence Projects, all too often shows the unreliability of eyewitness testimony in criminal cases.[12]

Contamination also plays a large part in how the forensic linguist asks questions. Questions must be properly structured to minimize contamination, to promote truth-telling.

---

12 "Why Science Tells Us Not to Rely on Eyewitness Accounts," by Hal Arkowitz and Scott O. Lilienfeld, Scientific American, January 1, 2010; *https://www.scientificamerican.com/article/do-the-eyes-have-it/*.

Minimizing contamination will help you to get the truth. Contamination is defined as anything that affects the subject's responses. Unintentional contamination can occur as you walk into the interview room, as you begin the questioning process, and in the type of interview room itself (such as noises inside and outside the room).

Factors to consider when you attempt to minimize contamination are the way you present yourself, your choice of interview rooms, your questioning strategy or question structure, and how and when you ask your questions, as well as your question presentation. Consider how each of these variables may affect the subject's responses.

Poorly-structured questions can keep you from getting the truth. For example, let's look at the following questions:

"What can you tell me about . . ."
"What do you know . . ."
"Would you say . . ."
"To the best of your knowledge . . ."

Questions such as these, with introductions, will contaminate the response by allowing the deceiver to wiggle out of telling the truth. "What can you tell me about" creates the opportunity for a person who wishes to be deceptive to answer truthfully by answering what he or she "can tell you." The person can't tell the complete truth because that may incriminate him or her. So, the question "What can you tell me" allows people to tell only that which they "can tell" without incriminating themselves. The deceptive person seizes subtle opportunities to tell partial truths. The compliance officer who asks, "Did you follow procedures?" or the auditor who asks, "What are the risks in your operation?" is just asking for a misleading answer. The truthful subject will answer truthfully; the deceptive person might seize the opportunity. The words *procedures* and *risks* first need to be defined and mutually understood before you use them in questions. If cornered on an answer, the deceptive person can always use the excuse, "I took the question to mean..." Even truthful people may unintentionally provide misleading answers. The old adage "Garbage in, garbage out," applies. So, what is a well-constructed question?

Well-constructed questions (or commands) contain mutually understood words constructed simply and precisely. Consider these examples:

"Were you ever at 765 Moross?"
Better: Show a picture of 765 Moross and ask, "Were you ever inside that building?" ("At" is not precise; "inside" is better. Also, the subject might not know the address.)

"Did you kill your wife?"
Better: "What happened to your wife?"
"She was killed."
"What do you mean?"
"Someone shot her."
"Did you shoot her?" ("Kill" needs to be defined.)

"What do you think happened?"
Better: "What happened?"

Telling lies is stressful, and a body under stress seeks peace. Use that force to your advantage. The forensic linguist will structure questions to allow truthful people to tell the complete truth and make it very difficult for deceptive people to tell partial truths.

Objectivity was one of the biggest concerns I had when presented with this challenge. Carl was convinced Walt was D.B.

Cooper from the day of the hijacking. Carl's questions, laced with information, insinuation, and accusation, contaminated all the discussions and the transcripts. I was left with transcripts of those contaminated discussions to determine whether Walt was telling the truth—a very difficult assignment. However, we can look for consistency of communication patterns, details that only the hijacker would know, and compare these details to FBI evidence and expert interpretations to help lead us to logical conclusions. Logic, however, doesn't necessarily equate with what really happened. Once this analysis and information are released, the FBI will determine whether it believes Walt was D.B. Cooper.

In linguistic analyses, we're looking to answer why the speaker uses specific words, particular tenses, and other grammatical elements and where there are unexpected or expected changes in those words, tenses, voices, communications, and grammatical patterns. For example, if someone frequently uses the word *like*, then suddenly quits using that word, there is a reason for that change, and we need to find out why. Change alone is not necessarily important; the reason for it is. We need to know why the change occurred—because only one of the many options is deception. Change in communication patterns can be caused by sounds, movement, flashbacks, activities within the room or outside the room, the way the question was asked—almost anything. We do our best to eliminate all but the greatest stress creator, deception. So, step one will be to get a lock on Walt's communication patterns and whether he expresses himself using consistent communication patterns. When he doesn't, we need to analyze everything to carefully identify the reason. Does he offer information, or does he simply respond to the questions? Does he respond directly, simply, and precisely, or is he unnecessarily circuitous in his answer, lack of an answer, or the way in which he answers? We also need to keep in mind what he doesn't say—whether he leaves out something you would expect him to say. That, too, is a change. What is said is very important. What isn't said may be doubly important.

If the speaker's patterns are consistent, we then examine content. Is the content relevant? Does the speaker use mutually understood words? Does he or she define words that can be misunderstood? Does the questioner use mutually understood words? If the answer to any of these preceding questions is "no," the truth-getting process is in jeopardy. And it goes on and on. Forensic linguistics requires patience, study, passion, focus, and perseverance.

I'm including the entire transcript made from the tape recordings of the Carl Laurin and Walt Peca discussions because what is there is important, and what isn't there may be doubly important. Remember, Walt first admitted to Carl in November 2008 that he was D.B. Cooper. Carl began recording the conversations with Walt about the D.B. Cooper case, with Walt's permission, which resulted in the tapes and the transcription reviews that follow. I will highlight the consistencies and changes in Walt's communication patterns to help us determine his veracity. It was clear to me that Walt engaged in these conversations and recordings freely and voluntarily, not under duress.

The keen eye of the reader might detect that the transcript begins with the time stamp 03:07:49, not 0. That is because I received one audio recording that was a compilation of many undated and unnumbered recordings. When I received the first raw transcript, the events didn't flow chronologically. The tape showing 03:07:49, the last tape in the original raw transcript, included events that had occurred before all the others. So I cut and pasted the last tape transcript, beginning at 03:07:49, and put it at the beginning. The time stamps are important to get a feel for how long it took Walt to respond, to identify pauses, and to measure the pace of the conversation. The transcript used in this book now reflects a more accurate chronology of the events.

I also include my analysis of Jeff ("Cowboy") Osiadacz's statement, transcript, and recording. Although Carl Laurin was the first to contact and talk to Jeff in late June or early July 2012, the information I relied on for Jeff was obtained in 2016 and 2017.

The Complete Walter Peca/Reca Timeline is essential reading to help us get the truth. My linguistic analysis will focus on the recordings and the transcripts of Carl Laurin ("Charlie Brown") and Walt and on Jeff Osiadacz's recording, transcript, and written statement. Getting the truth in a linguistic sense is only part of the story. As indicated in the following passages, a person can be truthful without being factual. Look at the complete timeline of the events to get a good feel for not only what happened, but how all the characters fit into this famous crime. How does all the evidence fit? I'll help determine whether Walt is truthful about being D.B. Cooper, but what does all the evidence say? Do the truth and the facts all lead to our making the factual case (cold case) that Walt was D.B. Cooper?

Please keep in mind that the recordings between Carl Laurin (a.k.a. Charlie Brown) and Walt occurred in 2008 and 2009, more than thirty-seven years after the hijacking took place on November 24, 1971. The transcripts, which I analyzed along with the recordings, were produced in 2017. Walt Reca (a.k.a. Peca, Recca, Racca) confirmed his confession in his Last Testament, dictated to Carl Laurin in June 2013, which Carl wrote down and subsequently had typed. They agreed that Carl wouldn't release Walt's confession to being D.B. Cooper until after Walt's death. Carl Laurin kept his promise. Walt Reca, a.k.a. Peca, died on February 17, 2014.

My analysis will help us determine Walt's and Jeff Osiadacz's truthfulness. I'll calibrate Walt's communication patterns to determine whether these patterns change, and I'll apply the same methods to Jeff Osiadacz. *Calibrate* means I will determine Walt's communication patterns when he is talking casually, in nonthreatening portions of the transcript—not responding to questions about D.B. Cooper. Once we establish that calibration or foundation, we can then move on to analyze Walt's communication patterns to see whether they change and under what circumstances. When, and if, his pattern changes, we need to analyze those changes to carefully identify the reason(s). Consistent patterns indicate truth-telling. If Walt's communication patterns remain consistent even when he's talking about his role as D.B. Cooper, that is powerful evidence he's telling the truth.

A person can be truthful without being factual.[13]

---

13   Courtesy of Brian Solis, *http://www.briansolis.com/2017/05/innovation-begins-shift-perspective/*.

A person can be truthful without being factual. For example, if I'm color-blind, and I say a sign is blue, I'm being truthful even if the sign is green. The fact that the sign color is green doesn't make my statement untruthful. If I say something happened, and I truthfully believe it did, my statement is still truthful, albeit wrong. "Truth is an instance of quoting one or many of the facts while describing or discussing the subject. The difference between truth and fact is that fact is something that cannot be combated with reasoning, for it is logic itself. But truth is something which depends on a person's perspective and experience."[14] So, we need to be aware of the difference between truth and fact—and the relevance of each.

Some details provided by Walt don't comport with the D.B. Cooper (NORJAK) case information released by the FBI. For example, the FBI contends Northwest Orient Flight 305 flew along Victor 23, on an approximate flight line from Seattle through Longview, Washington (the pilot Scott says Ariel, Washington, which would put the flight path about 60 miles west of where Walt stated he landed.[15] As I discuss further on, I as an investigator wouldn't want hundreds of people walking through and contaminating the drop site. Was that a factor in promulgating the suspected flight path? Knowledgeable sources advise that the real path of Northwest Orient Flight 305 could not be determined with the equipment available in 1971 because of the altitude (10,000 feet), the plane's slow speed (inhibiting the much faster tailing jets' surveillance), and the weather conditions. So, we shouldn't be quick to eliminate Walt as a suspect just because of the FBI's promulgated flight path.

---

14   See *https://philosophy.stackexchange.com/questions/8053/what-is-the-difference-between-fact-and-truth.*

15   See *Questersite.com; https://questersite.wordpress.com/2015/10/11/finding-d-b-cooper-part-2-the-first-clues/.*

Jeff Wierenga, a commercial pilot since 1987, certified in flying the Boeing 737 and a pilot for the 727 for more than 1,500 hours, told me: "I wouldn't fly the FBI's [given] flight path because at some point you would have to cross the spine of the Sierra Mountain range, which is over 12,000 feet on average. The Cascade Mountain range near Cle Elum, Washington, has an average elevation below 10,000 feet."[16]

Another discrepancy concerns the money found on the beach along the Columbia River (lat. 45.717888, long. −122.759500) at Tena Bar, Washington, near Longview, Washington, a location that would put the flight path even farther west of Walt's landing site.[17] The prevailing 18-knot wind was from the southwest, which could—at 10,000 feet altitude—account for some of the discrepancy but not all. How did that money, which showed serial numbers from the stolen $200,000 in $20 bills, get there? We simply don't know. And the FBI reportedly doesn't know either.

So, do we dismiss Walt's admission just because of this conflicting information? No. We don't because we really don't know what the FBI knows. As an investigator, I would withhold sufficient information to help eliminate non-truthful confessors and to identity the only one who could be D.B. Cooper.

COMMUNICATION PATTERNS

As part of the linguistics analysis process, I conducted searches of the transcript for clues to measure the frequency and consistency of the use of words and phrases. The following spreadsheet shows some of the work I did:

---

16 Jeff Wierenga provided this statement to me on June 11, 2018.

17 See Citizens *Sleuths.com; https://citizensleuths.com/tenabar.html.*

Walt Variable	No. of Times Appeared	Avg. per Page of Walt's Statements (46 pgs.)	
just figured	1	0.02173913	
selling	1	0.02173913	
shouldn't of	1	0.02173913	
walkin	1	0.02173913	
walking	1	0.02173913	
wanta	1	0.02173913	
would have been	1	0.02173913	
woulda	1	0.02173913	
didn't even know	2	0.043478261	
I seen	2	0.043478261	
makin	2	0.043478261	
sellin	2	0.043478261	
want no	2	0.043478261	
would've	2	0.043478261	
I gotta	3	0.065217391	
gun	4	0.086956522	
have been	4	0.086956522	Not significant—all non-critical.
could have	4	0.086956522	Not significant—all non-critical.
would have	4	0.086956522	Not significant—all non-critical.
wanna	4	0.086956522	
fucking	5	0.108695652	
guns	5	0.108695652	
nothin'	5	0.108695652	
and I got	6	0.130434783	
gotta	8	0.173913043	
had to	9	0.195652174	

going to	12	0.260869565	
all that	14	0.304347826	
don't remember	16	0.347826087	
I've	17	0.369565217	
gonna	21	0.456521739	
fuckin'	23	0.5	
and then	24	0.52173913	
missing I/pronoun	24	0.52173913	No meaningful pattern.
come	30	0.652173913	
so	38	0.826086957	
have	39	0.847826087	Not significant—all non-critical.
would	43	0.934782609	No passive voice —4 "would have"s.
like	50	1.086956522	
I'm	69	1.5	
but	79	1.717391304	All used to add, not to disagree/ contradict.
don't	135	2.934782609	
you know	170	3.695652174	
right there	214	4.65217	One pg. = 0, non-hijack. 3 pgs. 1, 2 hijack. 1 non-hijack.
uh	257	5.586956522	
was	270	5.869565217	
yeah	305	6.630434783	
I	748	16.26086957	No pages w/o an "I."

Author: Joe Koenig ©2018

You can see Walt uses the words highlighted in gray most often. "Right there" is the most unique, and is used an inordinately large 214 times. "Right there" is a colloquialism and offers a forensic linguist a wonderful opportunity to see when and where Walt uses it. What's the origin of the colloquialism "right there"? The *Dictionary of American Slang* defines it as, "in there pitching, there."[18] Carl Laurin said Walt learned that phrase while living in the Polish neighborhoods in Detroit, where he grew up. It is a unique phrase and, for me, a diamond in the rough.

One would expect a "colloquialism" to be used in informal, non-stressful, nonthreatening, social-like situations—in a setting where the speaker is very comfortable. We wouldn't expect to see a colloquialism in a formal conversation or situation. Certainly, Walt's conversations with Carl (Charlie) are informal, even though they are talking about a very serious incident: the hijacking that took place on November 24, 1971. So, within that conversation, is there a pattern when Walt uses his colloquialism and when he doesn't? That is a question I aim to resolve because it may provide insightful information to help determine Walt's credibility. Note, the "right there" appears an average of 4.65 times per page of the transcript—a powerful sign of casual use. If, for example, Walt uses that colloquialism in questions relating to non-hijacking questions and never when talking about the hijacking, that would be a change in his communication pattern. Changes in communication patterns are meaningful and require us to try to explain the change. No communication pattern change is a good indication Walt is comfortable, whether talking about the weather or the hijacking—lending credibility to his story.

Pronouns are very important to getting the truth. The first person singular pronoun "I" identifies the actor. "I" is the one

---

18   *The Dictionary of American Slang*, 4th edition, by Barbara Ann Kipfer, PhD, and Robert L. Chapman, PhD (New York: HarperCollins, 2007).

who threw the ball in this active voice sentence, "I threw the ball." No one else threw it. "I" is unique, specific, and revealing. Walt frequently uses "I" throughout his statement, an average of 16.26 times per page of his statements, showing a high degree of responsibility, accountability. There were no pages without his "I," and I found no significant number of missing "I"s. When someone uses "I," especially in the active voice, the listener knows only one person is accountable and responsible for what follows. In addition to looking for the "I"s in a statement, we must look for when the "I"s are missing. For example:

"I went to the store. Went in and bought a candy bar, then went to the bar." The "I" pronoun is missing when she (or someone) "went in and bought a candy bar, then" she (or someone) "went to the bar." Now, these missing pronouns may be insignificant—but forensic linguists can't make that assumption. To the forensic linguist, she "might" have gone into the store and bought a candy bar, and she "might" have gone to the bar. Why did she change her pronoun use? Was it because she didn't go into the store and didn't go to the bar? Or is it because she felt the "I" was unnecessary? That's where our calibration kicks in, and we compare her known communication pattern to this sentence. Did she do that before, and were we able to explain why to our satisfaction?

When I conduct an analysis, I usually circle all the pronouns, the articles "the" and "a," and important (unique) words and phrases. In the following transcripts, the legend reveals how to identify the pronouns; Walt's responses; Carl's (Charlie Brown's) questions; important words/phrases, such as "right there"; threatening vs. nonthreatening questions; and Walt's admissions. Often, I'll also highlight objects (door, ball, gun), verbs that indicate voice change, and sentences that seem to reflect a different cadence, rhythm, or emotion. If you're looking at a written statement, that job is a little more difficult because you don't have the sound and visual hints that tell you there is a change. In this case, I listened to the audiotapes that led to these transcriptions. So, I did have the luxury of listening to the audio but not the visual, and I took advantage of that. Walt is very consistent in the audio, straightforward, with no discernible changes in his rhythm, cadence, or emotion. That is a good indicator of veracity, but only one.

Finally, to identify discrepancies and similarities, I went through much of the voluminous information/evidence the FBI released to the public and compared it with the information offered by Walt. I also compared factual information to disprove or corroborate information Walt provided to Carl in these transcripts of conversations tape-recorded at least thirty-seven years after the hijacking (For example, Walt states in the transcripts that he put "crazy glue" (known as Super Glue—cyanoacrylates) on his fingers while in the airport just before he boarded Northwest Orient Flight 305 to avoid leaving fingerprint evidence. He discovered this process earlier and experimented with "Super Glue" to make him fingerprint-less. Was "Super Glue" even available in 1971? Yes, Super Glue was invented in 1941 by Dr. Harry Coover (while working for Eastman Kodak) and has been available since 1958.[19] The FBI reported there were no useable suspect fingerprints obtained from the scene. Ironically, in the 1980s, police crime labs around the world discovered the value of cyanoacrylates' vapors in detecting and developing latent print evidence for use in identifying suspects.

The Last Testament was written by Carl almost five years after the tape recordings between Walt and Carl. Walt's Last Testament is undated and unsigned, but Walt's niece Lisa Story provided the envelope Carl used to mail this typed statement

---

19   See *https://gunthertoodys.com/1950s-inventions-superglue/*.

to Walt, and the postal date is June 20, 2013. When Lisa and her mother asked Walt about the contents of this document in August 2013, he confirmed to them that it was true and accurate and he was D.B. Cooper. Then she and her mother (Walt's sister, Sandy) talked him out of signing it, fearing he would go to prison.

From an investigator's and best-evidence standpoint, Walt's Last Testament is less important than the audiotapes and related transcripts because Carl wrote it, not Walt. Thus, I didn't analyze it. Walt confirmed the details in his Last Testament verbally to his sister, Sandy, and his niece Lisa but chose not to sign it on their advice. With that in mind, and the fact that I didn't analyze it, I use only excerpts from Walt's Last Testament and don't provide the entire document.

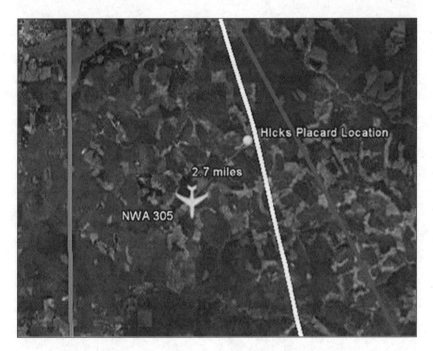

Suspected flight path from Citizen Sleuths.com[20]

---

20   See *https://citizensleuths.com/flightpath.html.*

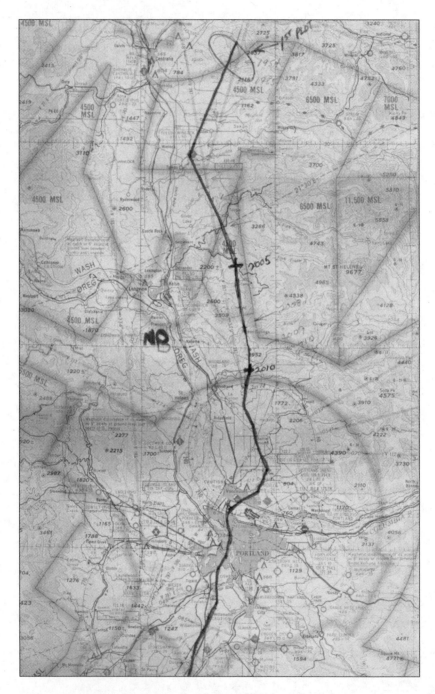

Suspected flight path from the FBI archives.

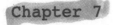

Chapter 7

ANALYSIS OF WALT RECA'S STATEMENT

LEGEND:

Pronouns (and pronoun-like articles)

Walt's statements

Carl ("Charlie Brown") Laurin's statements

Analysis

Important words/phrases

Walt's admissions

Hijacking-related discussions

(nonthreatening = Walt is just talking, not responding to questions about D.B. Cooper)

*Note: Please read the entire transcript to get a feel for Walt's speech patterns and a full appreciation of my analysis.

Carl: Here *I— I— I* gotta ask you this, and— and— and *I* need— *I* need the absolute honest— honest answer.

[03:07:49] **Walt:** Yup.

[03:07:51] **Carl:** Are you D.B. Cooper?

[03:07:52] **Walt:** *I* ain't saying nothin'. ***One usually denies something that isn't true. This is not a denial. It's avoidance. If the person doesn't deny it, the allegation may well be true.***

[03:07:55] **Carl:** Okay. Here's the problem. There's another guy writing a book. *I* just found this out yesterday. If— If you're not, we gotta find out because it's gonna destroy us. It's gonna destroy us.

[03:08:18] **Walt:** No, *I*'m not admitting to anything. ***Another opportunity missed. Even more evidence the allegation might be true.***

[03:08:22] **Carl:** Okay. So we really don't know then.

[03:08:28] **Walt:** If *they* wanta claim anything, let them claim everything *they* want to. *I* don't care.

[03:08:34] **Carl:** *I* know but that's— The problem is— the— the problem is— is— is— Put yourself in the agent's place or the publisher's. We're just another couple of guys or guy, whatever there's been in the past, coming up and— and saying this stuff. We really don't have any proof. <u>You know</u>, we're— we're just—

[03:09:02] **Walt:** *I* understand that, but *I*'m not gonna go to prison <u>right there</u> just to prove, <u>you know</u>, a point to a publisher and to an agent. ***Use of the phrase "right there" in a threatening discussion.***

Also note that throughout this transcript, Walt uses "right there" 214 times and "you know" 170 times. The "right there"s constitute an unusual and unique communication pattern for Walt. According to Carl ("Charlie Brown"), Walt's "right there" phrase was general parlance in the Polish neighborhoods in Detroit, where Walt grew up. I would expect a colloquialism, general parlance phrases like "right there," to be used during relaxed conversations, during times of little stress. Let's see where Walt uses his phrase "right there." I highlight every "right there" with double underlines. If Walt is talking about planning or executing the hijacking, I characterize that as a "threatening" situation. If he's not talking about the planning or execution of the hijacking, I characterize that "right there" as a nonthreatening discussion.

His first use of "right there" happens at 03:09:02, *during his response to Carl's accusation that Walt is D.B. Cooper. So, if I'm correct, Walt doesn't perceive this conversation as stressful since, by this time, Carl and he had discussed this topic many times in the past. And, later, Walt admits to Carl that he is D.B. Cooper. During this taped conversation, Walt uses "right there" seven times (the conversation is about whether he is D.B. Cooper), further evidence he views this as not stressful. Furthermore, he uses "right there" at least once on almost every page of this entire transcript. I look for patterns and changes in patterns. Walt's use of "right there" is a pattern that just doesn't change. This suggests Walt is under little stress when responding to any of Carl's questions about D.B. Cooper.*

Wouldn't it be nice if the suspect, D.B. Cooper, used that phrase during the hijacking and the stewardesses made note of it? There is nothing in the FBI reports about the suspect using unusual phrases or language. But Walt states in this transcript that he was very stressed during the hijacking. One would expect he wouldn't use a colloquialism ("right there") during stressful periods, that his speech would be very guarded. So, what's this all mean?

It means we have more work to do. We need to figure out whether Walt is making up the whole story and enjoying his deception; he is making up the whole story and now believes it; or he is telling the truth about a significant event that occurred in 1971, more than thirty-seven years earlier.

Walt uses the phrase "you know" 170 times. Many of those follow Carl's use of "you know." So, unlike the "right there"s, Walt's "you know"s could be due to contamination by Carl's use of "you know." Carl is the first to use "you know" at 03:08:34 and uses the phrase 216 times—so much contamination that it greatly diminishes the value of Walt's use of "you know." Therefore, I'm not emphasizing its use in this analysis. The "right there"s are an even more unique communication pattern and more frequently used. Again, consistent patterns indicate truth-telling. If Walt's communication patterns remain consistent, even when he's talking about his role as D.B. Cooper, that is powerful evidence he's telling the truth.

We'll also look at other key words and phrases to try to fully understand Walt's real message. This analysis will tell us with some degree of certainty whether Walt was, in fact, D.B. Cooper. Let's begin our analysis.

[03:09:10] **Carl:** Well, okay, *I— I— I* understand that, uh—

[03:09:14] **Walt:** If anybody come up to *me*— That's how come *I* said, "Okay, go ahead and print *it* <u>right there</u>," because if anybody come up to *me* afterwards, *I*'d deny everything. *I*'d say that's the imagination <u>right there</u>, of the author, the publisher, or whoever. *Use of the phrase "right there" in a threatening discussion. By threatening discussion I mean this question and answer pertain to the hijacking.*

[03:09:28] **Carl:** Okay. But knowing that it's going to destroy us if we're wrong, should I— Should I keep going on with— with it? With the book?

[03:09:43] **Walt:** That's your choice, Charlie.

[03:09:47] **Carl:** I know.

[03:09:50] **Walt:** My choice is I wanna be free of everything, you know.

[03:09:56] **Carl:** I understand.

[03:09:57] **Walt:** I don't want nothin' hanging over my head.

[03:09:59] **Carl:** I understand. *[Seems to be a break here.]* Are we the only guys that— that know pretty much your story? You've never told this to anybody else in the past?

[03:10:09] **Walt:** Never told anybody anything.

[03:10:11] **Carl:** Okay. *[Seems to be another break here.]* Can you think of any more reason, um, why you're telling this— this now?

[03:10:23] **Walt:** Uh, probably because we got into it gradually. [Charlie interjects: Okay, but— but—] It wasn't, uh, like, "Hey, Walt— what about this?" You know?

[03:10:34] **Carl:** Yeah, yeah.

[03:10:35] **Walt:** I think this has been going on for a couple of years now.

[03:10:37] **Carl:** A couple of years, yeah.

[03:10:38] **Walt:** Yeah.

[03:10:39] **Carl:** And nobody's believed it at all, <u>you know</u>—

[03:10:42] **Walt:** *I* never told nobody. [Carl interjects: Right.] *You're*— yeah, *you*'re the only one and that's because, uh, *I*— *I*— *I*'ve got— *I* trust *you*, <u>you know</u>. **This shows additional weakening of his denial.**

[03:10:50] **Carl:** Okay, so what do you want us to do, um, with this book? Do you want us to hold it until a certain time because for example— Let me just give you an example. Right now, if they said, "Well, we're gonna put that book out tomorrow," even if *I* didn't talk to you, *I*'d say, "Don't do it. *I* want that book held. *I* don't want that book put out right now."

[03:11:15] **Walt:** Well, that's up to *you* and Michael <u>right there</u>, 'cause Michael can get a hold of the attorneys and find out what to do with *it*. **Use of the phrase "right there" in a threatening discussion.**

[03:11:23] **Carl:** Well, now, uh— Now, *I*'ve talked to different people, not— not, uh— uh, whatever *I*— *I* didn't tell 'em what we're doing or nuttin'— but he— *I*— *I* just— he said, "Well, hijacking is a federal crime," and he said, "And *I*'m sure that there's no statute of limitations on it."

[03:11:54] **Walt:** For a while let *me* think this over.

[03:11:56] **Carl:** Yeah well— Yeah, well, we are. _I_ mean, nothing's gonna happen within a month or nothin' anyway, but— but, um, uh, <u>you know</u>, _I_ mean, it's— This is, uh— This is a big deal. This is a big thing and, uh— But it isn't so big to me. It isn't so big to me that— that _I_ would, uh, <u>you know</u>, want— want you to go to jail over this thing. <u>You know</u>, nothing— _[crosstalk]_ —nothing that big.

[03:12:29] **Walt:** Yeah. Well, Michael's got publishers, and _they_'ve got attorneys, <u>right there</u>. _They_ can decide what to do about that situation. _**Use of the phrase "right there" in a threatening discussion. The Michael here is Michael Abrams, a writer of the book cited below who Carl was considering to write Carl and Walt's story.**_ [21]

[03:12:41] **Carl:** Okay, but— but _I_ don't want, <u>you know</u>, _I_ don't— _I_ wanna make sure that— that we're covered on this thing. [Walt interjects: Yeah.] This thing doesn't get out of hand— out of— out of our hands and— and, uh— uh— Okay, and, uh, but— _I_ mean, it's went on a long time, but you kept the secret for thirty-seven years, uh, give— give or take a week or two, and, uh— uh, <u>you know</u>, _I_— _I_— _I_ still— wh— when _I_ still find it hard to believe that we are talking about it, <u>you know</u>, for me.

[03:13:18] **Walt:** Yeah. _Me_, too. _[laughs]_

---

21 Michael Abrams — writer and author of "Birdmen, Batmen, and Skyflyers: Wingsuits and the Pioneers Who Flew in Them, Fell in Them, and Perfected Them" published 2006 Crown Publishing.

[03:13:22] **Carl:** Um, yu-<u>you know</u>, *I* thought there had to be maybe some health reason or something like that, that you're— that you're talking about it.

[03:13:33] **Walt:** Well, *I* gotta go Monday <u>right there</u> for nuclear medicine. *They* gotta check *my* heart, all sorts of shit. *Use of the phrase "right there" in a nonthreatening discussion.*

[03:13:42] **Carl:** Oh, that's this coming Monday?

[03:13:43] **Walt:** Yeah.

[03:13:44] **Carl:** Oh, wow.

[03:13:45] **Walt:** 'Cause *my* valve's not working right, in *my* heart.

[03:13:48] **Carl:** Yeah.

[03:13:48] **Walt:** And so *they* got, uh— *They* got all sorts of stuff to, uh, tests going on.

[03:13:54] **Carl:** Yeah. Um, but did— did that have anything to do— that or something like it have anything to do with you finally fessing up?

[03:14:05] **Walt:** No. *I* don't think so. *A tacit admission that he is about to "fess up."*

[03:14:09] **Carl:** Wow.

[03:14:11] **Walt:** In other words, talking to *you* is different than talking to somebody else, you know? Uh, *I* mean *I* don't feel that *I*'m exposed talking to *you*, where *I* do with somebody else.

[03:14:25] **Carl:** Well, you're not to me personally, but don't forget, uh, this thing, uh— And *I*— <u>You know</u>, *I* know the editors just don't come right out, but sooner or later— sooner or later, uh, if we write this in a book, it gets out there, <u>you know</u> what *I*'m saying? Sooner or later if— if a book goes out and this is there, it's just like you reading the *Detroit News*, it's there. And people see it. And— And, uh— *I* mean, <u>you know</u>, the FBI'll see it, everybody will see it.

[03:15:00] **Walt:** Well, *I* figure <u>right there</u>, *you*'ll know what to do about that, Charlie. ***Use of the phrase "right there" in a threatening discussion.***

[03:15:04] **Carl:** *[laughs]* It— Th— The only thing that we can do is— is sit on it. Is tell 'em, uh— wh— <u>you know</u>, we just can't— can't publish this— this thing at this time.

[03:15:19] *[END OF AUDIO]*

[00:00:11] **Carl:** Yeah, Just like making your first jump. *I* mean, you can say to me, "Well, describe something on your first jump." Your, your first jump or your second jump, or your third per— <u>You know</u>, when you were Fort Bragg. And the only thing *I* can tell ya is *I*— is *I* got onto a C-119, along with a-about forty other saps that were scared out of their mind. And uh, we sat there in the thing, and then the guy said, "Stand up and hook up." <u>You know</u>.

But *I* can't remember anybody's face or any um, or any um, <u>you know</u>, um, describe anything other than just it was an airplane, and we were all— all on it, <u>you know</u>.

[00:00:52] **Walt:** *I* don't— *I* don't remember even getting to the door. 'Cause *my* face was in the other man's backpack, right in front of *me*. And all *I* knew that happened was daylight then, and somebody said, "Go." You know, at *me*. ***Now Walt is beginning to confide in Carl once he believes that Carl will not publish anything until after Walt's death.***

[00:01:04] **Carl:** Yeah. Yeah. Yeah. Now— *[audio aborts]*

[background noise]

[00:01:18] **Carl:** Well, where were you working then, and what were ya supposedly, you know, in other words, if you lived in Detroit, what were you doing for a living, like— ?

[00:01:28] **Walt:** *I* was, like, more or less, in the gun business.

[00:01:33] **Carl:** Well, okay, you mean, for the Hamsters? ***Carl and Walt frequently speak of the Hamsters, which is their code word for Teamsters.***

[00:01:36] **Walt:** Yeah, well, if *you* put *it* that way.

[00:01:38] **Carl:** Okay. Um—

[00:01:41] **Walt:** *I* would get guns over from uh, machine guns and all that, from Earl's gun shop, and then *I* would sell *it* to different locals. And uh, uh, to Whitney Elliott.

[00:01:53] **Carl:** Oh, okay.

[00:01:55] **Walt:** *We* had Marcus right there and offload guns into the car and that, um. ***Use of the phrase "right there" in a nonthreatening discussion.***

[00:02:03] **Carl:** Um, at Marcus? You mean, the Red Fox?

[00:02:08] **Walt:** No, Marcus. The uh, there's a Marcus Hamburgers and *they* used to have *it*. *They* use to be loose fried hamburger. And *they* would put chili over *it* <u>right there</u>. *They* were famous all over uh, Detroit, uh, if *you* ever were in the Detroit area. The only time *we* ever seen another Marcus was at Pattaya Beach in Bangkok, Thailand. *Use of the phrase "right there" in a nonthreatening discussion.*

[00:02:30] **Carl:** <u>You know</u> that— that— not being funny, the place that *I*'m used to seeing Marcus *[sic]*, 'cause *I* never went to that place you're talking about, and *I* used to go right by it if we were going to a baseball game or, or whatever.

[00:02:43] **Walt:** Yeah, yeah, that's right round that area there.

[00:02:46] **Carl:** But that was— the thing that they called Marcus, er, was on the— the sign was the Marcus *[sic]* Red Fox, that— that big eating place. *The Machus Red Fox Restaurant, then on Telegraph Rd. Bloomfield Township, MI, was the alleged place James R. Hoffa was to meet Detroit mob boss Anthony "Tony Jack" Giacalone and New Jersey mob boss Anthony "Tony Pro" Provenzano on July 30, 1975, the day of Hoffa's disappearance.*

[00:02:59] **Walt:** Well, this was no Red Fox. This was just a hamburger and chili joint.

[00:03:02] **Carl:** Well, okay.

[00:03:04] **Walt:** *They* were— *They* were famous for their hamburger though.

[00:03:06] **Carl:** Yeah. Yeah. Uh, okay, so, uh, so anyway, you were wearing a suit. Um, and— and were you— you're still getting money from the cookie company then?

[00:03:22] **Walt:** Yeah.

[00:03:24] **Carl:** Um, okay. Um—

[00:03:28] **Walt:** *It*'s all on that paper, Charlie, *you* gotta find that paper. *I* got all the information on *it*. *Once Walt admitted to Carl he was D.B. Cooper, he began sending Carl some equipment (one item was the small Minox camera (shown above in "Could Walt be D.B. Cooper?") allegedly used by spies to photograph documents) and a great deal of paperwork, including documents, letters, articles, and photographs. Walt would then discuss those items with Carl in subsequent phone calls.*

[00:03:34] **Carl:** Okay.

[00:03:35] **Walt:** *I* don't—

[00:03:36] **Carl:** <u>You know</u> what, are you positive you give that to me, or did you give that to Michael?

[00:03:41] **Walt:** Yeah. *I*'m positive *I* sent *it* to *you*.

[00:03:43] **Carl:** Man, *I* can't— *I* don't remember— *I* don't remember that part of it on— here um, shit. *I* gotta dig all that stuff out. Okay, uh—

[00:03:56] **Walt:** *It*'s from the Birmingham Police Department, has letterhead on top of *it*.

[00:04:03] **Carl:** You didn't send me that.

[00:04:05] **Walt:** Yup. [Carl interjects: *I*— *I*] Walt continues: *I* know *I* did.

[00:04:14] **Carl:** *I* tell you the truth, *I* don't ever remember getting anything with the Birmingham Police Department on it. And *I* remember most of the— almost all of those letters, at least, something about them. <u>You know</u>, that one there— that one there um, *I*'ll tell you—

[00:04:30] **Walt:** *You* got the one with— with *me* from South America bringing back the machine gun— didn't ya?

[00:04:35] **Carl:** Yeah. Yep. Yeah, and of course *I* got the one, um, that the guy sent from the *Detroit Free Press*, <u>you know</u>, telling you to go back to uh, um, Vienna or somethin' like that, <u>you know</u>, that one—

[00:04:48] **Walt:** Yeah.

[00:04:49] **Carl:** —um, but *I*— but *I* sure as hell don't remember anything with the Birmingham Police Department on it. *I*'ll— *I*'ll go back and *I*'ll search through that relentlessly. But *I* honestly do not remember. That one seem like it would've caught my attention just— just because it was from a police department, <u>you know</u>.

[00:05:09] **Walt:** Okay, *I*'m gonna have to look right here and see if *I* got a copy. ***Use of the phrase "right there" in a nonthreatening discussion.***

[00:05:13] **Carl:** Yeah.

[00:05:14] **Walt:** <u>Right there</u> 'cause *I* sent *you* the original. ***Use of the phrase "right there" in a nonthreatening discussion.***

[00:05:16] **Carl:** Okay.

[background noise]

[00:05:19] Carl: Where did you say you were living, in what fancy place?

[00:05:24] **Walt:** Uh, in those apartments by Palmer Park.

[00:05:27] **Carl:** And that's— that's in— in Detroit?

[00:05:29] **Walt:** Detroit, yeah.

[00:05:32] **Carl:** And, and at this time, um, you had not got back with Joni yet. Is that right? *Joni is Joan Marie Feldhoffer, who became Walt's wife on November 6, 1930.*

[00:05:44] **Walt:** Well, *I* never got back with Joni 'til thirteen years later.

[00:05:47] **Carl:** So you were actually living there in Detroit, and she didn't know nothing about it?

[00:05:53] **Walt:** No, *[inaudible 00:05:53]*

[00:05:55] **Carl:** *[laughs]* God. What if— what if she'd a bumped into you somewhere? Just by sheer luck or—

[00:06:07] **Walt:** Oh, nothing like that. Joni— Joni was just a very nice girl, she wouldn't have said anything, you know.

[00:06:15] **Carl:** You're kidding?

[00:06:16] **Walt:** Yeah.

[00:06:17] **Carl:** *[chuckles]* Yeah. She'd a seen you in a, in a store or something, she wouldn't have even said, "What the—

[00:06:23] **Walt:** Oh, yeah, yeah. *We* would've talked and all that.

[00:06:27] **Carl:** Yeah. Yeah. But um, oh God, that would've been awkward to me, <u>you know</u>. *[laughs]* *I* can't— *I* can't imagine if *I*'d did anything like that other than a whole bunch of screaming. All— All *I* can imagine, <u>you know</u>.

[00:06:44] **Walt:** Yeah.

[00:06:45] **Carl:** *[laughs]* God damn, you're lucky that way. *[laughs]* Okay, so—

[background noise]

[00:06:54] **Carl:** You were getting paid by the cookie company a little bit and you were— you were making some— *I* guess, you call it side money or somethin', working for the Hamsters and doing this other um, <u>you know</u>, gun stuff or whatever.

[00:07:10] **Walt:** Um, here's what happened. *It*'s also in the letter, *I* was on the books to get paid, <u>you know</u>, from the cookie company—

[00:07:18] **Carl:** Yeah.

[00:07:19] **Walt:** Not a lot of money.

[00:07:20] **Carl:** Yeah.

[00:07:21] **Walt:** But this is in the letter from the Birmingham. *They* said, "Where were *you* this night?" This is years later. And *I* said, "Well, *I* was at work at the cookie company." *I* give them the name of the cookie company, *I* don't even know what *it* is, *it*'s in the letter. ***The Birmingham, Michigan Police Department investigated Walter*** *two years after his 1967 attempted robbery of a jewel show at the Birmingham House Motel.*

[00:07:35] **Carl:** Yeah.

[00:07:36] **Walt:** Right there. Then, uh, *they* denied that *I* was working that night. *Use of the phrase "right there" in a nonthreatening discussion.*

[00:07:40] **Carl:** The cookie company did?

[00:07:42] **Walt:** Yeah. *They* didn't wanna get involved in that shit.

[00:07:45] **Carl:** Yeah. Huh. So, well, so then what did you do?

[00:07:53] **Walt:** *I* didn't take the lie detector test.

[00:07:56] **Carl:** Oh, okay. Yeah, *I* remember— *I* remember you telling me about the lie detector. *I* don't remember— *I* don't remember reading about it, though. *I* really really don't. *I*'m gonna go through my stuff. But *I*'ll tell you what, if *I* find that letter, *I*'ll, *I*'ll really be amazed, because *I*— *I* generally at least, remember 'em. If, if *I* can't 'member everything, uh, er, *I* generally always remember, <u>you know</u>, the letter it— itself. <u>You know</u>, *I* mean *I* would *I*— if there was one that— that said Birmingham Police Department on it.

[00:08:38] **Walt:** Yeah, *I* talked to *you*— after. *You* said *you* got the letter.

[00:08:42] **Carl:** Well, if *I* got it, it's somewhere out there in all my stuff b-but *I*'ve been thinking—

[00:08:49] **Walt:** *It*'s one *sheet* of paper.

[00:08:51] **Carl:** Just one page?

[00:08:53] **Walt:** Yeah.

[00:08:54] **Carl:** Okay, well, *I*'ll go look again. <u>You know</u>, *I* will go look again, *I* promise ya. Um, so anyway, you had on a suit when you went in and did that thing. And uh, um, did you drive there in a car er—? Or is this the time when the Hamsters were chauffeuring you around?

[00:09:16] **Walt:** No. *I* drove there in a car.

[00:09:17] **Carl:** Okay. Was this—

[00:09:19] **Walt:** *I* didn't want them to know too much about what I was doin' neither, <u>you know</u>. *They* don't go for this outside *[unintelligible— quirky?]* one.

[00:09:25] **Carl:** Now, in what years you think that you were— what was it that they were chauffeuring you around in that black Cadillac?

[00:09:35] **Walt:** Oh—

[00:09:39] **Carl:** That had to be about the same time, approximately.

[00:09:43] **Walt:** Yeah.

[00:09:46] **Carl:** Maybe later than— than *[crosstalk]*

[00:09:50] **Walt:** *I*— *I* can't remember the year right. <u>You know</u>, this is a long time ago. *I* even forget how to spell now and read, too.

[00:09:57] **Carl:** *[laughs]* Yeah, yeah. Uh. Okay, yeah, but anyway, yeah, son of a gun and, uh— Well now, wait a minute. When, uh, when, when they were chauffeuring you around in the Cadillac, they were also chauffeuring ▇▇▇ around in it. Is she in a separate Cadillac?

[00:10:21] **Walt:** Oh, yeah, yeah, <u>right there</u>. That's when *I* had trouble with the uh, with the union, union workers. ***Use of the phrase "right there" in a nonthreatening discussion.***

[00:10:26] **Carl:** Right. And that was, that had to be, that was about the same time, too. That couldn't have been very . . .

[00:10:34] **Walt:** No. That was after *I* got extradited to Michigan.

[00:10:39] **Carl:** What year would that be?

[00:10:42] **Walt:** Let's see, uh, about '66, '67.

[00:10:49] **Carl:** Yeah, so that, that would be just after this— this jewel thing.

[00:10:53] **Walt:** No, that was about '64.

[00:10:56] **Carl:** The jewel thing was about '64?

[00:10:58] **Walt:** '64 or '63.

[00:11:00] **Carl:** Okay now, in '64 you lived, you told me you lived in California out there, because *I* said, "Well, *I* lived in California in San Bernardino in '64."

[00:11:15] **Walt:** Yeah.

[00:11:17] **Carl:** Oh you and *I* talked about that. *I* didn't know you lived there 'til then. And *I* said *I* lived in San Bern—

[00:11:21] **Walt:** *I* lived in Tehachapi.

[00:11:24] **Carl:** Yeah.

[00:11:25] **Walt:** That's one of the, uh, when the FBI came out to the job in Washington State. *The FBI interviewed Walt on or about November 1965 (details at [00:44:07] thinking Walt was Indian Kelly, a murder suspect.*

[00:11:31] **Carl:** Right.

[00:11:32] **Walt:** And *they* were looking for that killer Indian.

[00:11:34] **Carl:** Yeah.

[00:11:35] **Walt:** <u>Right there</u> and then, uh, uh, that's when *they* got *me* in there, uh, *they* wanted to see if *I* had a tattoo. That's when *I* dyed *my* hair to look like, <u>you know</u>— *Use of the phrase "right there" in a nonthreatening discussion.*

[00:11:43] **Carl:** Yeah.

[00:11:44] **Walt:** —somebody else and *I* did. *I* looked like a fuckin' murderer.

[00:11:46] **Carl:** *[laughs]*

[00:11:54] **Walt:** So, *I* was already wanted, <u>you know</u>. And when *they* called *me* in there and *I*— uh, *I* didn't fit the description exactly. *They* were looking at the picture, and the guy had a tattoo on his arm.

[00:12:05] **Carl:** Yeah, yeah.

[00:12:07] **Walt:** *I* had the— a burn from welding on *my* arm.

[00:12:09] **Carl:** Yeah.

[00:12:09] **Walt:** And *they* took the bandage off, and *they* saw *it* wasn't a tattoo.

[00:12:13] **Carl:** Yeah.

[00:12:14] **Walt:** <u>You know</u>. And that's when *I* left there and *I* went down to California. And *I* went, uh, seeing Bob Sinclair. *I* stayed over at his place a little bit. And *I* was parachuting there. Then *I* went and got a dispatch for the Union Hall. Bob showed *me* where the Union Hall was at, the Iron Workers.

[00:12:33] **Carl:** Uh huh.

[00:12:34] **Walt:** And *I* got a dispatch from the Union Hall, and *I* was going to the job 'cause *I* was— Bob Sinclair had an apartment *he* was going to sublease *me* that belonged to his girlfriend.

[00:12:43] Carl: Uh huh.

[00:12:44] **Walt:** And uh, uh, *I* was going ah to the job <u>right there</u> in the fuckin' traffic, eight lanes going in one direction, and *I* couldn't make the turnoff so *I* said, "Fuck *it*." And *it*'s the only place *I* kept on going and then *I* read in *my*, looked through the Union Hall in Fresno. *I* went to Fresno, and *I* got a dispatch with <u>Tehachapi</u>. *Use of the phrase "right there" in a nonthreatening discussion.*

[00:13:06] **Carl:** Okay. Yeah.

[00:13:09] **Carl:** That— that was something. And, and *I* was out there and you were there and we didn't even know each other were there, <u>you know.</u>

[00:13:15] **Walt:** Yeah. *[laughs]*

[00:13:16] **Carl:** Yeah.

[00:13:17] **Carl:** But *I*, for some reason or other *I* wasn't aware that you lived in Detroit at this— at this time either at— at Palmer Park and all that, where *I* don't know where that's at, but, um.

[00:13:30] **Walt:** Oh, that's on uh, Seven Mile and Woodward, that big, big park across from the Fairgrounds.

[00:13:36] **Carl:** Oh, okay.

[00:13:37] **Walt:** In the apartments, uh, south of there.

[00:13:40] **Carl:** Across from Fairgrounds. *I*'m writing that down. During this time then, going back to that— that jewel robbery, you must have— you must have been doing fairly well, *I* mean money-wise.

[00:13:54] **Walt:** Yeah. Ah sure. *I* mean, uh, *I* was getting uh, monetary resources <u>right there</u>. Uh, *I* didn't have to show up at work. That's the way, uh, the Hamsters paid us, <u>*you know*</u>. ***Use of the phrase "right there" in a nonthreatening discussion.***

[00:14:04] **Carl:** Yeah.

[00:14:05] **Walt:** Not only *me*, but other people. *I* don't know who the other people were, *you* know what *I* mean. All *I* know is where *I*'ve worked, and *I* didn't ask any questions. And one thing *I* was told *they* had a phone booth in the hallway. A telephone booth.

[00:14:19] **Carl:** Yeah.

[00:14:20] **Walt:** *He* told *me*, "Don't use that phone booth if there's any important, <u>*you know*</u>—

[00:14:23] **Carl:** Yeah.

[00:14:24] **Walt:** —calls 'cause *it*'s bugged."

[00:14:25] **Carl:** Yeah. Yeah. *[laughs]* So— so they knew it was bugged, and they just, just let 'em keep it there, <u>you know</u>.

[00:14:36] **Walt:** Yeah. Tell everybody don't use *it*.

[00:14:39] **Carl:** Yeah. Yeah, except for—

[00:14:40] **Walt:** <u>*You* know</u>, *I* mean, if *you* want to call your wife or something.

[00:14:42] **Carl:** Yeah.

[00:14:43] **Walt:** That'd be good. Yeah.

[00:14:44] **Carl:** Yeah.

[00:14:45] **Walt:** *They* had the places checked out about, uh, every two weeks. So *[unintelligible 00:14:51]* with all kinds of fuckin' electrical equipment to see what office could be bugged and all that. *They* paid for that.

[00:14:56] **Carl:** Yeah. Did, did they ever find any?

[00:15:01] **Walt:** *I* don't know.

[00:15:03] **Carl:** Yeah.

[00:15:04] **Walt:** *It*'s— *it*'s not something *you* ask questions about, <u>you know</u>.

[00:15:07] **Carl:** Yeah. Yeah. Okay, so you're doing okay money-wise, and this is about '64 and that. So then what was— and— and— and y-you pull this stick up and you didn't get any, any mo, anything to amount to anything.

[00:15:26] **Walt:** Okay, so did *you* find that letter?

[00:15:28] **Carl:** No. *I* didn't look for it. *I—* *I* haven't had a chance to look for it. *I*'m going to tear tear that apart and—

[00:15:31] **Walt:** Okay. *I* made a cop, *I* made a, *I* found *it*.

[00:15:35] **Carl:** Good.

[00:15:37] **Walt:** *I* sent *you* the original, but *I* kept myself a copy, and *I* just made a copy here. Want *me* to read *it* off to *you*?

[00:15:45] **Carl:** Yeah. Yeah.

[00:15:47] **Walt:** Okay. Hold on, *I* have to get some glasses.

[00:15:50] **Carl:** Okay.

[00:15:51] **Walt:** Let's see here.

[00:15:54] **Carl:** What was the date on it?

[00:15:55] **Walt:** What?

[00:15:57] **Carl:** What's the date on it?

[00:15:59] **Walt:** *It* was written in 1968.

[00:16:04] **Carl:** '58 or '68?

[00:16:07] **Walt:** '68.

[00:16:09] **Carl:** Wait a minute.

[00:16:11] **Walt:** This is when this letter was written.

[00:16:14] **Carl:** Yeah.

[00:16:14] **Walt:** So *you know*.

[00:16:16] **Carl:** Okay.

[00:16:16] **Walt:** *It*'s uh, City of Birmingham, 151 Brighton Street Birmingham, Michigan. To: William E. Matz. 33314 Grand River Avenue Farmington, Michigan.

[00:16:30] **Carl:** Okay.

[00:16:31] **Walt:** Re: Walter Peca.
Dear Sir, *I* interviewed Mr. Walter Peca in the Probation Officer *[sic]* on December 14th, 1967. At this time, Peca, Mr. Peca was advised of his rights and denied any involvement with our robbery, armed, of Birmingham House Motel. June 7th, 1965 at 12:11 a.m. Mr. Peca called December the 15th, 1967 and stated *he* was employed at the Sunshine Biscuit Company, 1217 Coyle, Detroit at the time of this offense occurred.

Mr. Ken Hunter, Personnel Manager at Sunshine Biscuit, Incorporated reports Mr. Walter Peca was not employed at this time. Hours were 3:30 PM thru 12:00 o'clock a.m. on the 8th of June, his first day of employment.

We would like to clear our files and if Mr. Walter Peca is involved, uh, would close our case with his five years probation by Judge Beer. Thank *you* for your co-cooperation. If *we* can be any further service, please contact us. Yours truly, Richard Chambers, Detective. *[phone beeps]*

[00:17:56] **Carl:** *I* don't ever remember reading that letter.

[00:18:02] **Walt:** *[unintelligible 00:18:03]* *I* sent *you* the original.

[00:18:05] **Carl:** *I*— *I*— *I* can't help it. *I* just—
I— *[phone beeps]* *I* can't remember. *I*— *I* would
have remembered that, *I* think. Maybe, may not.
Maybe *I*'m slipping. *I* don't know, but *I*— *I*, —
[phone beeps] *I* don't remember. Is your phone
going dead? Walt?

[00:18:24] **Walt:** No. *I* got an online phone now.

[00:18:25] **Carl:** Oh, oh, okay, um.

[00:18:26] **Walt:** And all the other phones *I*
bought batteries for.

[00:18:30] **Carl:** Okay, hey, anyway, that thing
happened in— it didn't happen in '63. It happened
in June of '65 right?

[00:18:37] **Walt:** Yeah.

[00:18:40] **Carl:** The actual robbery; so actually,
I was right in my first notes. *I*— *I* had up there
'65 and then crossed it out and went back to '63,
but it actually happened in— in '65. So, uh—

[00:18:54] **Walt:** If *it* wasn't for these papers,
I couldn't even tell *you.*

[00:18:57] **Carl:** *I* know. *I* know. That's what *I*'m
sayin' that if this stuff— y-you did so much stuff.
You went back and forth, out to California and
Washington and got extradited back and all this
here kind of stuff. And if— if, <u>you know</u>, it 'd
be— it's almost like writing a dictionary. Uh—

[00:19:15] **Walt:** Like books like *War and Peace.*

[00:19:17] **Carl:** Yeah. Yeah.

[00:19:18] **Walt:** *You* ever try to read that?

[00:19:20] **Carl:** No. No.

[00:19:21] **Walt:** That was terrible, <u>right there</u>. *You* had to look in the back to find out who *they*'re talking about, what their nicknames are, there are so many characters. *You* have to go to the index to find out. *I* couldn't read *it*. *I* got half way through *it*, and *I* still didn't know what the fuck *I* was doin'. Believe *me*. **Use of the phrase "right there" in a nonthreatening discussion.**

[00:19:37] **Carl:** Hey, *I* think *I*'ll let it go then. *I* was intending someday to read that, but *I* might— *I* might just— might— might just sit on that one. Uh, so okay. So you did that in '65. Did you ever work your way up to at least a halfway decent job with them where you made decent money?

[00:19:59] **Walt:** Well, *I*— *I* was making decent money then. Well, *I* mean— *I*, <u>you know</u>, *you* couldn't get rich off of *it*.

[00:20:06] **Carl:** Yeah. Yeah. Huh. Okay. Well, let's see.

[00:20:13] **Walt:** *I*— *I* was, *my* wages were the same thing *they* would pay somebody working on the dock or loading truck.

[00:20:20] **Carl:** Yeah. Yeah, but you were taking a lot more risks.

[00:20:25] **Walt:** A lot of times *I* did nothing.

[00:20:28] **Carl:** Well, true.

[00:20:29] **Walt:** Yeah. *I* went home and slept.

[00:20:30] **Carl:** Yeah. A lot of times. Probably for two or three months at a time. You probably had very very little to do. That's true.

[00:20:37] **Walt:** Yeah.

[00:20:37] **Carl:** Yeah, uh, but other times, <u>you know</u>, uh, it would seem like, <u>you know</u>, ah, seem like that some of the stuff that these people do— let's take this Tom guy, seems like they should have made pretty good money, <u>you know</u>, for what they do. <u>You know</u>, because uh—

[00:20:57] **Walt:** Yeah. *He* had *it*. *He* was gettin' a good wage. *He* owned the horse farm.

[00:21:02] **Carl:** Yeah. Yeah.

[00:21:04] **Walt:** *He* had a barn with horses and everything, and all of a sudden, *they* didn't need *him* no more.

[00:21:08] **Carl:** Yeah.

[00:21:10] **Walt:** In other words, *we* can get *you* a job at a bakery or *we* can get *you* a job with the warehouse or *we* can, but, <u>*you know*</u>, "*We* don't need *you* no more," and that was *it*, "Get the fuck out."

[00:21:19] **Carl:** Wow. Wow. Well, he must have done something to piss somebody off, too, though.

[00:21:27] **Walt:** Oh, but that's the way *they* work. *I*—

[00:21:29] **Carl:** Going back, y-y-you must have been working, doing some work, before this all started for the Hamsters because they— they had you on this Sunshine Biscuit payroll.

[00:21:42] **Walt:** Yeah.

[00:21:47] **Carl:** So at that time you were just working your way up with them?

[00:21:51] **Walt:** Yeah. Working *my* way up, under charge of picket lines. *We* picketed here. Picketed there for, *you know*, different problems, like different locals *we* had. *You know*, but *I* mean the Teamsters were paying *me* right there, Sunshine Biscuit or whatever the name of that biscuit company was. *Use of the phrase "right there" in a nonthreatening discussion.*

[00:22:12] **Carl:** Yeah. That was it.

[00:22:14] **Walt:** Yeah.

[00:22:15] **Carl:** Yeah.

[00:22:15] **Walt:** And, uh, and *I* got paid, too, right there from Tastee Bread. So, *I*'m getting two checks right there, *you know*, to be working for these different locals, on picket lines. Going on in and talkin' to people, uh, who our girls would tell, um, *you*'re not doing right by your employees or whatever, *you know*. *Use of the phrase "right there" in a nonthreatening discussion.*

[00:22:36] **Carl:** Yeah.

[00:22:37] **Walt:** Right there then and *they* agree [unintelligible] which other people would come in to take care, but *I* had a different way of talkin', *you know*, for— *Use of the phrase "right there" in a nonthreatening discussion.*

[00:22:45] **Carl:** Yeah. Yeah. *[laughs]* Um, okay. You seem like you were— should have been making enough money but, <u>you know</u>, so—

[00:23:05] **Walt:** *I* was <u>right there</u> but, <u>you know</u>, *I* thought *I* could make more at— other things, <u>you know</u>, and um, oh, and <u>you know</u> *I* think *I* fought for that *[unintelligible]*. Oh, that that had a whole bunch of dope come down on *me*, <u>you know</u>. *Use of the phrase "right there" in a nonthreatening discussion.*

[00:23:23] **Carl:** For— for the Teamsters.

[00:23:25] **Walt:** Yeah.

[00:23:27] **Carl:** Yeah.

[00:23:29] **Walt:** *My* pension with them was gone! *[laughs]*

[00:23:33] **Carl:** Huh. Let's see, so— yeah. Okay. That kind of clears up right where *I*— *I* always— *I* had my times wrong on when you did all this stuff and one thing. Uh. That kind of clears that up, but but you did go back to work for the Teamsters later, didn't ya? Well, it—

[00:23:59] **Walt:** Uh, yeah.

[00:24:00] **Carl:** Well, for example, them times that because when ███████ was back there with you—

[00:24:08] **Walt:** Well, there was nothing like that, nothing like that. *I*'d just take us out for dinner. █████ and *I* and all our, <u>you know</u>, and uh, like when guys got sick. *He* out— come back out— *I* was working iron then, and *he* took *me* out someplace <u>right there</u>, uh, to put in an application for a job with somebody <u>right there</u>. Took the names of the people, put down the license plates on the public parking lot, <u>you</u> know. *Use of the phrase "right there" in a nonthreatening discussion.*

[00:24:37] **Carl:** Oh. Okay.

[00:24:40] **Walt:** Nothing wrong, nothing wrong, wasn't gonna go anywhere.

[00:24:45] **Carl:** Oh. Okay. *[pause]* Wh-when you finally left Detroit, you left to go to see Art down in Lauderdale.

[00:25:05] **Walt:** No, that was another time when *I* went down to see Art. See, *I* was already brought back and *I* was on probation then. *I* was extradited back to Michigan 'cause of Big Boy.

[00:25:17] **Carl:** Yeah. Uh huh.

[00:25:19] **Walt:** And then, when everybody was getting on *my* ass. The Teamsters, not the Teamsters, but the Iron Workers, and *I*, uh, <u>you know</u>, *I* went and filed charges against them and then, uh, and then *they* were threatening *me*, and *I* called up the FBI. *I* was protected under the Hobbs Act. *I* was a federal witness.

[00:25:36] **Carl:** Uh huh.

[00:25:36] **Walt:** And *they* went down to the union hall. Right there, "But that don't mean *they* still couldn't kill *me*," <u>you know</u>. *Use of the phrase "right there" in a nonthreatening discussion.*

[00:25:42] **Carl:** Right.

[00:25:43] **Walt:** And then after a while *I* said, "Fuck *it*, though." *I* just might as well, <u>you know</u>— head up and head out <u>right there</u>, <u>you know</u>, and that's when *I* left. And went down to see Art in Lauderdale. ***Use of the phrase "right there" in a nonthreatening discussion.***

[00:25:56] **Carl:** Right but this that would— that would be about '65—

[00:26:00] **Walt:** '68 or '69.

[00:26:03] **Carl:** Now somewhere, somewhere between '65 and '68 to '69 then, you— you fell on hard times, more or less.

[00:26:19] **Walt:** Yeah. Real hard times.

[00:26:21] **Carl:** Well what— Okay. Wh-what do you think— what was the reason for that or why do you think?

[00:26:30] **Walt:** *I* was workin' iron, but, uh, uh— *I* wasn't a union member. *I* was working on core bit. Yeah, *you*'re the last one out of the hall and the first one to be laid off.

[00:26:40] **Carl:** Okay but, you were collecting money from the biscuits company, right? Or did that stop for some reason?

[00:26:51] **Walt:** Oh. That stopped, that there, uh, after Big Boy.

[00:26:58] **Carl:** Okay. *[pause]* So basically, well— well, hadn't you been working with the Hamsters during this time and collecting somethin'?

[00:27:11] **Walt:** Yeah. *I* was working with them, but *I* was paid by the Biscuit Company.

[00:27:15] **Carl:** Okay.

[00:27:16] **Walt:** *My* pay wasn't coming from the Teamsters—

[00:27:18] **Carl:** Yeah.

[00:27:20] **Walt:** —that's the way *they* pay people off. *They* call up, uh, biscuit companies, uh, and whoever *it* is and order, "You put this man on your payroll." *I* worked for, um, Tastee Bread, <u>right there</u>, for one payroll for about six months, uh, <u>you know</u>, and, but *I* was, then *I* was in charge of picket lines. **Use of the phrase "right there" in a nonthreatening discussion.**

[00:27:39] **Carl:** Uh huh. Okay. Uh. Well for the work that you did for those guys, they, they are really um, y-you didn't really make a whole lot of money.

[00:27:58] **Walt:** No.

[00:28:00] **Carl:** Well how— how come um, *I*'m not, <u>you know</u>, how come you worked for them and did stuff if you weren't making hardly any money?

[00:28:09] **Walt:** *I*— *I* was hoping for a better position.

[00:28:13] **Carl:** Oh. Okay. *[pause]* *I*'m just writing it down. *[pause]*

[00:28:24] **Walt:** Yeah. *I* always tried to work *my* way up. *I* mean, *you* just don't get in there,

<u>right there</u>, for doing nothing. *Use of the phrase "right there" in a nonthreatening discussion.*

[00:28:30] **Carl:** Yeah. Um—

[00:28:32] **Walt:** No business agent and that. *You* gotta do something. *[pause].* Yeah. In other words, *I* was proving myself.

[00:28:40] **Carl:** Yeah. Well, okay. Did-did-did you ever kinda— did you ever prove yourself? In other words, did you ever get up to where you were making at least a decent uh, a decent wage, <u>you know</u>, 'cause *I* know, like Loretta knew— knew, this one guy. *I* think you knew him, too, um, ████ ██, and he always made good money with 'em.

[00:29:08] **Walt:** *I* don't know what— what's considered good money, <u>you know</u>.

[00:29:11] **Carl:** Well, *I* mean, he um, he was—

[00:29:14] **Walt:** What was *he* doing? What was his job?

[00:29:16] **Carl:** Well *I-I—* He was a— He was pretty much a goon and, uh, ██████ was, you've heard this name, uh. Joni used to run around with, uh, Loretta and this girl named ██ ██, who was a-actually, uh, Montgomery Cliff's cousin, <u>you know</u>, ████████. But not that that had anything to do with it, but— so this ██████, he was uh, and ███, the daughter, he, she never— she never knew what her dad did, and Loretta didn't know either, but one time she was over at her *[Uncle Eddie's]*, he was a

Hamster and, uh, *[Eddie]* and, uh and uh, Loretta brought up. Well, my— my girlfriend, ███████, her dad works— works with Jimmy Hoffa but none of us know what he did and *[Eddie]* laughed. He was a funny guy, big beer drinker, and he said, "███████]?" He says, "He's a goon. He breaks people's legs," <u>you know</u> *[laughs]* and that's kind of what he said, <u>you know</u> and he laughed when he said it and all that. And, uh, that's the first time that Loretta actually knew what— what he did. Now she never did tell Mary, but Joni knew her real well. They were— they all ran around together. They— they were— about four of 'em— they were—

[00:30:39] **Walt:** Okay, here's what happened. Uh, uh, uh. *I* told *you* about Tom here in that; right there, *he* was a shooter, <u>you know</u>, for the Hamsters. *Use of the phrase "right there" in a nonthreatening discussion.*

[00:30:49] **Carl:** Whi-which one? Tom who?

[00:30:51] **Walt:** Oh, *I* don't— *I* don't wanna say no names.

[00:30:53] **Carl:** No. Okay.

[00:30:54] **Walt:** *He* was a shooter for the Hamsters.

[00:30:56] **Carl:** Yeah.

[00:30:57] **Walt:** And uh, uh, worked for Hoffa.

[00:30:59] **Carl:** Yeah.

[00:31:01] **Walt:** And then uh, like *you*'re talking about this ███ guy. One day, *they* call, Hoffa called *him* in the office and told, uh, uh, Tom that, uh, "*We* don't need *you* no more or any type of work that *you* do." And that was *it*. [Carl interjects: Gol!] He was living— having a horse farm, <u>you know</u>. He lost everything.

[00:31:23] **Carl:** *I* wonder what— *I* wonder what happened to him.

[00:31:29] **Walt:** *He* was an errand boy. *He* was around too long. *They* don't keep people around too long that know too much.

[00:31:33] **Carl:** Yeah.

[00:31:34] **Walt:** Charlie, *I* gotta use the bathroom. *I*'ll be right back. *I* gotta take a piss. These water pills.

[00:31:38] **Carl:** Okay—

[00:31:39] **Walt:** Hold on a second.

[00:31:43] **Carl:** Let's see, so '65 when you did the great jewel—

[00:31:47] **Walt:** The Hiccup.

[00:31:48] **Carl:** *[laughs]*

[00:31:49] **Walt:** *[laughs]* The Maxwell Smart guy *[sarcastically]*.

[00:31:53] **Carl:** Yeah. Ye-yeah. That was just— that was just— you were just doing a little side job to— to uh—

[00:31:59] **Walt:** Yeah. Which *I* shouldn't of been doing because *they* drop *you* then.

[00:32:04] **Carl:** If they catch you doing that—

[00:32:06] **Walt:** Yeah.

[00:32:06] **Carl:** Did they ever? Did they ever know it was you or never— never— did they ever associate you with that? *I* mean the Hamsters?

[00:32:17] **Walt:** No, not till afterwards when *it* was all over. But, *I* mean, *it* was all over for *me* with them with— with the Big Boy. *They* stopped everything <u>right there</u>. ***Use of the phrase "right there" in a nonthreatening discussion.***

[00:32:27] **Carl:** Oh, wow. *[silence]* *I*'m just writing it down.

[00:32:35] **Walt:** *You* can't trust anybody with a felony conviction.

[00:32:41] **Carl:** Okay. Yeah, because— because somebody with a felony, the cops can pull 'em in and— and make 'em talk. <u>You know</u>. Easy— easier than— than somebody without.

[00:32:52] **Walt:** *[crosstalk]* *They* don't make them talk. *They* run down and make a deal with the prosecuting attorney.

[00:32:55] **Carl:** Yeah.

[00:32:56] **Walt:** 'Cause *they* don't get so much time. Nobody has to make *you* talk. Good people with a felony conviction do *it* themselves.

[00:33:02] **Carl:** Well, yeah. That's what *I* meant. <u>You know</u>, they— they're, they're wa-watchin' their own back. <u>You know</u>, and— and uh.

[00:33:09] **Walt**: Right, yeah.

[00:33:10] **Carl**: Yeah.

[00:33:10] **Walt**: *I* want a great deal <u>right there</u>, <u>you know</u>. *I* don't want twenty years <u>right there</u> uh— <u>you know</u>. Give *me* five to— to ten and let *me* out in three, <u>you know</u>. ***Use of the phrase "right there" in a nonthreatening discussion.***

[00:33:17] **Carl**: Yeah.

[00:33:18] **Walt**: And, here's what was goin' on.

[00:33:20] **Carl**: Yeah. Yeah.

[00:33:22] **Walt**: 'Cause when *you* got a felony conviction, *you*'re not even in charge of a picket line.

[00:33:27] **Carl**: Yeah. What year did you rob Big Boy?

[00:33:31] **Walt**: *It* must have been '65.

[00:33:35] **Carl**: Uh. Okay. *I* think it was— *I* think— *I* think it was— and uh, uh, wh-what day did you do that? *I-I-I* have two different dates. One *I* have somethin' like Father's Day.

[00:33:56] **Walt**: *It* was Father's Day in '65.

[00:34:04] **Carl**: Okay, so basically, um. Basically then, what you're saying is that— that after Father's Day of '65 whatever month that is, that you were pretty well out of the Hamsters?

[00:34:22] **Walt**: Oh, yeah.

[00:34:24] **Carl**: And they— they— you were just cut loose.

[00:34:27] **Walt:** Yeah.

[00:34:27] **Carl:** Okay. Um, well, then— then— then this is— this is when basically you fell on hard times.

[00:34:38] **Walt:** Yeah.

[00:34:40] **Carl:** So that's— that's pretty much when everything stopped and but— but the Iron Workers were still after you.

[00:34:48] **Walt:** Not then. *I* wasn't even in Iron Workers then.

[00:34:52] **Carl:** In '65?

[00:34:54] **Walt:** No. That's when *I* went to look for Don Brennan. *I* went to Art's house in Flint <u>right there</u>, and from there Art drove *me* to the airport the next day. *I* wanted to leave out of Flint, not Detroit. ***Use of the phrase "right there" in a nonthreatening discussion.***

[00:35:09] **Carl:** Yeah.

[00:35:10] **Walt:** 'Coz *I* jumped bond.

[00:35:11] **Carl:** Yeah.

[00:35:12] **Walt:** <u>Right there</u>, and *I* left out of there and went to California and went to Huntington Beach, <u>right there</u>. And, *I* knocked on the door where *I* had the address. Was looking for Don. There was nobody home. *I'm* real short on money then. ***Use of the phrase "right there" in a nonthreatening discussion.***

[00:35:28] **Carl:** Yeah.

[00:35:29] **Walt:** <u>Right there</u>, but *I*'m at the restaurant and, uh, *I*'m havin' a cup of coffee and these two ladies are talking and Don Brennan's name was brought up and one was Don Brennan's mother. So *I* told her that *I*'m looking for Don; *I* want to find *him*, and *she* said, "*He*'s up in Washington." So *I* caught a Greyhound Bus for Washington State for uh Wenatchee *[00:35:49]*. ***Use of the phrase "right there" in a nonthreatening discussion.***

[00:35:52] **Carl:** Yeah. Yeah. That's when you stayed with Sadie Thompson and all that stuff.

[00:35:56] **Walt:** Yes.

[00:35:56] **Carl:** That was interesting. Um, and um—

[00:36:01] **Walt:** *She* didn't want *me* to leave there.

[00:36:03] **Carl:** Really?

[00:36:05] **Walt:** Yeah, *she* had uh, an old DeSoto.

[00:36:07] **Carl:** Yeah.

[00:36:08] **Walt:** <u>Right there</u> and about a '46 DeSoto— brand new. *She* told *me*, "*You* could drive this, <u>*you* know</u> and look for this job over here." *She* was going through the paper with *me*. Stay down there. Fix *me* big breakfast and lunches and suppers. Oh, *she* was uh— near ninety. *She* was a nice lady. ***Use of the phrase "right there" in a nonthreatening discussion.***

[00:36:27] **Carl:** Yeah. Now you're back workin'— workin' on your— iron— there, and ▆▆▆ was with you.

[00:36:35] **Walt:** Yeah.

[00:36:36] **Carl:** Okay, *I* gotta— *I*'m just putting a line here where— where ▮▮▮ comes into it, uh.

[00:36:49] **Walt:** *I* mean *we*— ▮▮▮ and *I* right there, *we* went down to the hall, Teamsters' Hall. And *they* took *me* out for dinner with ▮▮▮ and all that at Carl's Chop House and that. *Use of the phrase "right there" in a nonthreatening discussion.*

[00:36:58] **Carl:** Yeah.

[00:36:59] **Walt:** You know, but *I* mean there was no uh—

[00:37:01] **Carl:** Wa— how come, how come and you told me this one. How come they called you Bonnie and Clyde then?

[00:37:10] **Walt:** By being extradited back to Michigan.

[00:37:13] **Carl:** Oh, okay. Alright.

[00:37:14] **Walt:** Stay with *me*.

[00:37:16] **Carl:** Yeah, because you were— okay— because you were in trouble with the hoods, *I* mean the— the— the cops and stuff like that. So this— this is now the time where you're living in the trailer out there off not far from Eight Mile *I* forget where but *I*— *I* had to—

[00:37:35] **Walt:** In Farmington. The trailer park. *It* was right off of Eight Mile but it was Farmington. *It* was a Grand River, Middle Belt uh, right together in that area.

[00:37:47] **Carl:** Oh. Okay.

[00:37:48] **Walt:** At Eight Mile, where *it* crosses <u>right there</u>, confusing place. ***Use of the phrase "right there" in a nonthreatening discussion.***

[00:37:52] **Carl:** Yeah. And so this is where— this is where you found um, um, Walt Junior in the trailer, and the cop had to break the— the window out—

[00:38:08] **Walt:** Well, yeah.

[00:38:10] **Carl:** —to get him out and then after that—

[00:38:12] **Walt:** All the gas was turned on, on the trailer.

[00:38:14] **Carl:** All the gas was on— so then after that, that's when you lit out and went down to Art's.

[00:38:23] **Walt:** Uh, yeah. Uh.

[00:38:25] **Carl:** Down in Lauderdale.

[00:38:27] **Walt:** *I* went to Louisiana first.

[00:38:27] **Carl:** Oh, yeah. That's right. And right, you worked on that bridge thing there.

[00:38:32] **Walt:** Yeah, between uh, Port Allen and uh what's the name of that capital? Baton Rouge.

[00:38:36] Carl: Baton Rouge. Yeah. *I*, *I* had the dates all mixed up when *I* was doing this before. This thing was in, you did this— this— Birmingham House thing in '65. Nineteen sixty—

[00:38:53] **Walt:** Prior to, uh, Big Boy.

[00:38:56] **Carl:** It was what?

[00:38:59] **Walt:** Prior to Big Boy.

[00:39:01] **Carl:** It was prior to Big Boy?

[00:39:02] **Walt:** Yeah.

[00:39:03] **Carl:** Okay. *I*'m gonna write— hold on. This was prior— Big Boy was when?

[00:39:12] **Walt:** On Father's Day, whenever that was.

[00:39:15] **Carl:** Of the same year?

[00:39:16] **Walt:** Yeah.

[00:39:18] **Carl:** Okay. Um.

[00:39:22] **Walt:** Was a Sunday. Father's Day Sunday in uh, whatever— whatever month that comes in.

[00:39:31] **Carl:** *I*— *I* got that written down somewhere in— in that book. *I* got it written down but it was the same year so this— this was shortly after Big Boy, which you'd already been caught from.

[00:39:45] **Walt:** *It* was BEFORE Big Boy.

[00:39:47] **Carl:** Oh, well, this— okay. This was before Big Boy.

[00:39:52] **Walt:** Yeah.

[00:39:53] **Carl:** And you got caught for it, then you done Big Boy anyway.

[00:40:00] **Walt:** *I* didn't get caught for that one.

[00:40:02] **Carl:** Well, yeah. Okay, yeah. They— they thought— they were— they were— they thought maybe you did it. Uh, but they didn't prosecute and they— and they said— and they said that, um, uh, that we would like to clear our files that, uh, he's involved but would close our case, with his five-year probation by Judge Beer. Now that was *[inaudible 00:40:34]*

[00:40:31] **Walt:** The— The five-year probation was for Big Boy's.

[00:40:34] **Carl:** That was for Big Boy?

[00:40:37] **Carl:** Yeah. Okay. Me, *I*'m just writing it down here. Okay. So now during this time, um, this is— is the time where you said that you were making some money, um, selling guns?

[00:41:09] **Walt:** Yeah *I*— *I*— Yeah.

[00:41:14] **Carl:** Okay. Now you can't make a whole lot of money selling guns.

[00:41:21] **Walt:** The kind *I* was sellin', *you* could.

[00:41:25] **Carl:** Okay. Uh.

[00:41:30] **Walt:** *I* was sellin' Sten guns.

[00:41:33] **Carl:** Sten guns?

[00:41:36] **Walt:** Yeah.

[00:41:38] **Carl:** What the hell was that?

[00:41:41] **Walt:** The British— that was the British submachine gun in World War Two.

[00:41:46] **Carl:** Oh, okay. *[pause]* Wow. Hmm. And this is when you were living uh, in that fairly nice neighborhood of Detroit?

[00:42:12] **Walt:** Yeah. *It* used to be a nice neighborhood.

[00:42:16] **Carl:** Yeah, well, back then, yeah. Uh. And you. Okay. Were— were you— were you— you were married then to Joni?

[00:42:34] **Walt:** *We* were separated.

[00:42:36] **Carl:** You were separated.

[00:42:37] **Walt:** *We* were divorced. No, *we* were divorced then.

[00:42:40] **Carl:** Oh okay. You were already divorced at that time?

[00:42:44] **Walt:** Yeah.

[00:42:46] **Carl:** And did— did she know you were living in Detroit?

[00:42:52] **Walt:** Uh, *I* don't know if *she* knew or not, but *I* don't think *she* give a fuck.

[laughter]

[00:43:04] **Carl:** Oh, okay. You took off from the Big Boy thing, and *I* think you went to California, right?

[00:43:10] **Walt:** Yeah, about uh, a year. And here's what happened there is *I* got out on bond for Big Boy.

[00:43:16] **Carl:** Yeah.

[00:43:18] **Walt:** Waiting for a trial, so, uh— uh, *I* just took off <u>right there</u> for California for, uh, Don Brennan's place. *Use of the phrase "right there" in a nonthreatening discussion.*

[00:43:27] **Carl:** Yeah. And so that's when— that's when this whole odyssey started, and *I* got the rest of it right where you— you ended up in, uh, Wenatchee, at Sadie Thompson's and then you—

[00:43:41] **Walt:** Yeah.

[00:43:42] **Carl:** He sent you the— the money and you went up to uh, um—

[00:43:46] **Walt:** *[Unintelligible]*, there.

[00:43:47] **Carl:** Bill— Bellingham, was it?

[00:43:50] **Walt:** Yeah.

[00:43:51] **Carl:** That's almost in Canada. Bellingham is just a couple of miles from Canada, isn't it?

[00:43:50] **Walt:** No, that's Blaine *[sic]*. Bellingham's about fifty miles from Canada.

[00:44:02] **Carl:** Oh, well, fifty miles. But then what year was it that you married █████?

[00:44:07] **Walt:** Uh, █████ and *I* started living together— oooh uh, about November of '65. *I* went down to— That's when the— the FBI thought *I* was that Kelly, that Indian Kelly, and they surrounded the work around *[unintelligible 00:44:35]*.

[00:44:36] **Carl:** Yeah.

[00:44:37] **Walt:** <u>Right there</u> and then *they* found out *I* wasn't this Indian Kelly <u>right there</u>, and *I* went from there. *I* went down to California. Uh. Got a hold of Bob Sinclair, and *we* were jumping together at California City. And then *I* got into *[unintelligible]* from the Union Hall. So *I* started getting some jobs in California, yeah. And uh, <u>you know</u> how, what the fuck is *it*? Eight lanes? ***Use of the phrase "right there" in a nonthreatening discussion.***

[00:45:03] **Carl:** Yeah. Yeah.

[00:45:04] **Walt:** *I* crossed over too many cars.

[00:45:06] **Carl:** *[laughs]* Yeah.

[00:45:08] **Walt:** So *I* just kept on going.

[00:45:10] **Carl:** *[laughs]* You were so screwed up, then if you missed your turn, you didn't even care. <u>You know</u> it?

[00:45:18] **Walt:** <u>You know</u> that. Didn't care less. The closest place *I* could get off was Victorville *[??]*, <u>right there</u>. How many miles is that? Seventy-five? Eighty? ***Use of the phrase "right there" in a nonthreatening discussion.***

[00:45:28] **Carl:** Straight through from LA? No. Yeah. It's— it's at least that long. It's out in the desert there. Um.

[00:45:36] **Walt:** Yeah.

[00:45:37] **Carl:** It's even further than that. <u>You know,</u> it's probably a hundred and— from LA, probably a hundred and fifty. Mm.

[00:45:44] **Walt:** *[unintelligible 00:45:48]* and *I* looked up in *my* book *they* had a suboffice from, uh, *I* worked for a local office there. Anyhow *I* looked *it* up in *my* book and *I* went over there and *I* got a dispatch for *it* to Tehachapi.

[00:45:58] **Carl:** Yeah. That was a woman's prison.

[00:46:05] **Walt:** *It* was when *I* was there. Yeah.

[00:46:07] **Carl:** Yeah. Yeah.

[00:46:08] **Walt:** *We* were putting an addition on to *it*.

[00:46:11] **Carl:** Yeah.

[00:46:12] **Walt:** What *it* was, *I* was running out of money to where *I* figured *I*'d work long enough and get the fuck out of there.

[00:46:18] **Carl:** Yeah. You didn't like— you didn't like that job.

[00:46:23] **Walt:** *I*— *I* had to get— *I* didn't have no money. *I* had to get a hotel. *I* told them *I*'m working here. Can *you* hold *me* over 'til payday? Then *I* went down to a convenience store, there *I* told them the sad part so *I* got canned goods there to eat. Then *I* went to work. When *I* got enough money <u>right there</u>, *I* paid off the motel, paid off the uh, uh, grocery store <u>right there</u>. Then took right off for fuckin' Washington. Got the fuck out of California and them eight-lane fuckin' freeways. ***Use of the phrase "right there" in nonthreatening discussion.***

[silence] This is the beginning of a new tape and new topic.

[background noise]

[00:47:29] **Carl:** Why— why Spokane? That seems like a-a-an out of the way. *I* mean, just— just this isn't that important, but it seemed like so far, a hundred and fifty miles to Spokane.

[00:47:43] **Walt:** Well, *I* wouldn't drive *it* to Portland. *Spokane is 85 miles west of Walt's home in Hartline, WA. Walt then took a bus to Portland.*

[00:47:46] **Carl:** No. No. *I* know.

[00:47:48] **Walt:** No. <u>Right there</u>. In Spokane, <u>right there</u>, *you* leave *it* in the lot, and nobody pays no attention. Hartline's a ghost town. *Use of the phrase "right there" in a threatening discussion.*

[00:47:54] **Carl:** Yeah. Yeah. Well you couldn't catch a Grey— couldn't catch a Greyhound from Hartline anyway, could you?

[00:48:00] **Walt:** No. <u>Right there</u>. But that way, *it*'s— there's no connection. *Use of the phrase "right there" in a threatening discussion.*

[00:48:05] **Carl:** Yeah.

[00:48:07] **Walt:** When *I* left ah, uh, Michigan, okay, *I* went to Art's <u>right there</u> with Art at the airport in Michigan. But *I* don't remember whether the plane landed in Detroit or not, but Art was with *me*, *he* gave *me* $50 extra in case *I* needed *it*. And that's when *I* was James J-Johnson. And *I* become James Johnson by looking at the name tag. *Use of the phrase "right there" in a threatening discussion.*

[00:48:28] **Carl:** Okay. Yeah.

[00:48:30] **Walt:** When *I* got to the counter, that's when *I* became, you know. There was no planning before that.

[00:48:36] **Carl:** Well—

[00:48:37] **Walt:** "What's your name, sir?" And *I* looked at her name tag and said, "James Johnson."

[00:48:41] **Carl:** Yeah. Well, you know there— there— there— there— there might have been— y-you think there was no planning but— but there is some planning because like you say, you rented a typewriter, took it back, and uh, uh, drove to Spokane because um, the— the car would sit in the lot and not be, you know, nobody'd uh—

[00:49:03] **Walt:** Yeah.

[00:49:03] **Carl:** —think a thing of it. So there— had. There was planning, you know, in other words, or when— when you did something, there was a reason you— that you did that and you and— and— and— and as— as— as opposed to uh, going some other place, you know. Uh, to a smaller town, maybe where you know, uh, not that many people— take—

[00:49:24] **Walt:** Yeah— *you*'re too conspicuous there— small town.

[00:49:26] **Carl:** Too conspicuous, yeah. Okay. So, there was— there was planning, more— more than you think of. Yeah. When did you put the— the wraparound sunglasses on? At what point?

But, uh, in other words, as you were sitting. *I* would— If *I*— *I*'m making a guess, *I*—

[00:49:44] **Walt:** *I* had them on all the time. *I* still even wear some wraparound sunglasses. Even today. Here's— here's— here's what the planning was right there. *I* loved them two kids, you know. The babies? *Use of the phrase "right there" in a threatening discussion.*

[00:49:56] **Carl:** Yeah.

[00:49:57] **Walt:** Right there. *I* didn't have much money right there. *They* were ready to start school. There was no future. So prior to that, *I* was thinking if *I* fell off the iron and got killed, at least workman's compensation would give 'em enough money right there so *they* could buy a home. And that's what was going through *my* mind at the time. *Use of the phrase "right there" in a threatening discussion.*

[00:50:19] **Carl:** You were kind of like in in a way then you were kind of down and out.

[00:50:23] **Walt:** Yeah. *[inaudible]*

[00:50:24] **Carl:** In other words, yeah.

[00:50:27] **Carl:** But *I* mean, usually you don't act like you're down and out, you know, usually, uh, um, even when you didn't have any money when *I* knew you, you were never, um, bummed out, shall we say?

[00:50:39] **Walt:** Yeah, but *I* didn't have the responsibility that *I* had then. And plus, uh, uh, at this time right there, *I* jumped probation also. So *I* was still wanted. [Carl interjects: Yeah.] You know, in other words at the time *I* thought *I* had no future. **Use of the phrase "right there" in a threatening discussion.**

[00:50:52] **Carl:** Okay. So, yeah, you've told me that before. [Walt interjects: Yeah]. Yeah. Do you remember what you wrote on the first note? You know, the— the one that you borrowed the typewriter?

[00:51:14] **Walt:** No.

[00:51:16] **Carl:** Just that it was gonna be a hijacking.

[00:51:19] **Walt:** Yup and, uh, uh, and then *I* made a mistake with the typewriter. *I* was supposed to turn *it* back on a certain date. *I* didn't turn *it* back on that date. So then *they* made reference right there, and *they* wrote letters to Hartline. Hartline, *you* couldn't get no, uh, no mail unless *you* went to the post office. [Carl interjects: Uh huh.] You know, so *I* mean, uh, *I* was worried about that, the exposure, you know, from this stationary company writing the letter. **Use of the phrase "right there" in a threatening discussion.**

[00:51:46] **Carl:** Yeah, yeah. Huh.

[00:51:52] **Walt:** And *it* all blows up in your mind, you know, *it* over-exaggerates right there, your fears. **Use of the phrase "right there" in a threatening discussion.**

[00:51:57] **Carl:** What would have happened, okay, um, here's another thing that *I* thought of. Okay, you were sitting in seat 18 E or F or E, one of them. You had, actually you had that whole thing *I* think there's three seats or wider, something like that, at least two. Anyway, you had that seat all to yourself. There were only thirty-five people on the airplane. What if— what if they would of assigned you a seat and there would have been a guy sitting right next to you? What would you have done?

[00:52:32] **Walt:** *I* never thought that far ahead.

[00:52:36] **Carl:** You never thought of that?

[00:52:37] **Walt:** No.

[00:52:38] **Carl:** So just— just getting the empty row of seats was just the luck of the draw?

[00:52:44] **Walt:** Yeah.

[00:52:46] **Carl:** Okay. Um, you're— you're— you're on the airplane now. You took off out of Portland, and you ordered a drink. Er, you lit a cigarette.

[00:53:02] **Walt:** *I* always liked cigarettes.

[00:53:02] **Carl:** Yeah. But you lit one too soon, and the gal come back and told you, "Sir, the seat belt sign is on. Would you mind putting it out?" Um, and you *I* guess you put the cigarette out for a while. And that's when you handed her the note.

[00:53:23] **Walt:** This is vague, Charlie.

[00:53:24] **Carl:** The airplane was— wasn't even off the ground yet when you handed her the note. Did you know that?

[00:53:30] **Walt:** Mm-uh. This is all vague.

[00:53:34] **Carl:** And, uh, anyway it wasn't—

[00:53:37] **Walt:** Anxiety, probably.

[00:53:38] **Carl:** Yeah. So in fact the airplane was just taxiing, it was taxiing, come to think of it. And, uh, you handed her the note and, uh, uh, she— she put the note in her pocket like, you know, or some place and, uh, and you even [Walt interjects: smoked] Now you must have planned something because you said you put you put—

[00:54:01] **Walt:** Yeah. Super Glue.

[00:54:03] **Carl:** On your on your fingers?

[00:54:04] **Walt:** Yeah.

[00:54:05] **Carl:** Where did you do that? In a hotel room in Portland or what?

[00:54:10] **Walt:** I did it once in Spokane before I left and I had the Super Glue with me and, uh, I did it at the airport, waiting. But to put another coat on.

[00:54:22] **Carl:** Okay. Um, was there anything else that that you did that was precautionary like that?

[00:54:33] **Walt:** Not that I know of right there. I can't think of it now. Let me give— give me some time right there to think about things

<u>right there</u>, <u>*you know*</u>, these kind of questions. *I* can add to *it* later. **Use of the phrase "right there" in a threatening discussion.**

[00:54:42] **Carl:** Oh, yeah.

[00:54:43] **Walt:** Right now *it*'s a little, uh, *it*'s difficult to talk about at the present time.

[00:54:50] **Carl:** Did you come up with the number 200,000 because you— you, uh, figured it out how much, uh, a pack of $20 bills weigh and you added it up and it come to 20, 21 pounds and you figured that that's all you could carry? In other words, was— how do you arrive at the at the figure, uh, 200,000? Just— just a nice round number sounded right?

[00:55:16] **Walt:** Yeah, right. Sure giving *me* a lot of credit that *I* figured *it* out what *I* could carry. <u>Right there</u> was the number come out of the top of *my* head, and if *it* was so much that *I* couldn't carry, *I*'d throw *it* out the door anyhow. **Use of the phrase "right there" in a threatening discussion.**

[00:55:33] **Carl:** Right. *[laughing]* Okay.

[00:55:35] **Walt:** Just to have everybody guess, "How did *he* carry all that?" <u>*you know*</u>.

[00:55:39] **Carl:** Yeah. Well, you were in in, um, Portland waiting for the airplane. *I* went over this before, but, anything at all that you could remember in there while— while you were waiting for the airplane? Anything at all?

[00:55:57] **Walt:** Yeah, right there *it* was going through *my* mind *I* should forget all this shit and go home. *Use of the phrase "right there" in a threatening discussion.*

[00:56:04] **Carl:** Even then?

[00:56:05] **Walt:** Yeah. Yeah.

[00:56:08] **Carl:** And once you got on the airplane *[crosstalk]*, once you actually walked up there and they shut the door, you were pretty much committed then? (Walter interjects: Yeah.) *I* mean, you could have backed out, you could have just said, "Well, screw it. *I*'ll rent a car at the airport at Seattle," or some darn thing, you know, but it would have been a lot more hassle basically, basically when you went up and got on that airplane you were 99.9 percent committed then.

[00:56:36] **Walt:** Yes. [Carl interjects: *I* would say yeah.] That was beyond changing, you know, changing my mind then.

[00:56:42] **Carl:** Yeah. Yeah. When you were on the bus, when you were on the bus going from, uh, Spokane to Portland, um, where did you— where did you keep the, uh, the dynamite thing? You know the— you know the—?

[00:57:04] **Walt:** Between *my* legs, you know, between *my* feet and ankles.

[00:57:07] **Carl:** Oh, okay, you kept it on the floor?

[00:57:09] **Walt:** Yeah.

[00:57:10] **Carl:** Yeah. Did anybody sit next to you?

[00:57:15] **Walt:** Yeah. Right there but *they* got off in a little bit, you know. *Use of the phrase "right there" in a threatening discussion.*

[00:57:19] **Carl:** Oh, okay, but it—?

[00:57:20] **Walt:** *They* didn't want to go all the way to Portland. *It* was a baby— a woman with a baby.

[00:57:27] **Carl:** Oh, okay.

[00:57:27] **Walt:** Baby cried all the time.

[00:57:29] **Carl:** The baby cried all the time, as they always do on buses.

[00:57:32] **Walt:** Yeah.

[00:57:33] **Carl:** Yeah, okay. Uh, did the woman say anything at all other than hello?

[00:57:42] **Walter:** Yeah. Right there, *I* held the baby bottle right there when *she* was burping the baby. *Use of the phrase "right there" in a threatening discussion.*

[00:57:52] **Carl:** So she had to be a young woman.

[00:57:53] **Walt:** Yeah, *she* was, you know, *she* was young, but *she* wasn't good-looking.

[00:58:00] **Carl:** Yeah. *[laughs]* What— what— what were you thinking on— on the way there? *I* mean, was it, um—

[00:58:10] **Walt:** *I* think— *I* was thinking this is pretty fucking stupid.

[00:58:17] **Carl:** But you still kept going.

[00:58:19] **Walt:** Yeah.

[00:58:21] **Carl:** Let's go back let's go back to where you very first thought of this thing. I— I can't help but think that when— when you were wherever you were home in Hartline or wherever that— that, you know, I didn't just— I don't just wake up one day and say, "Oh, I'm going to go rob a bank or I'm going to go hijack an airplane." You have to have some sort of, uh, ah, an idea that, you know, I mean, what was it? Because if you hijacked an airplane, you could get more money than out of a bank?

[00:58:58] **Walt:** Uh, I'd seen some kind of, uh, a TV thing where people wanted to, uh, they were robbing something on television. I don't know what it was. And they got the money, then they wanted a bus, and then they wanted a plane. Well, I thought I could eliminate all that by just getting a plane. *[Carl laughs.]* Right?

[00:59:28] **Carl:** Right. *[laughs]* Yeah. That would do it. [Walt interjects: Yeah.] Then you don't have to ask anybody, you already got it.

[00:59:37] **Walt:** Yeah. I got everything there.

[00:59:38] **Carl:** *[laughs]* You went and drove to, uh, Spokane?

[00:59:42] **Walt:** Yeah. Oh, I took the bus out of Spokane, yeah.

[00:59:48] **Carl:** Right. And— and your— and ████ and the kids were staying at, uh—

[00:59:53] **Walt:** *They* had an apartment rented in Everett.

[00:59:55] **Carl:** In Everett? Okay. Oh, they had one rented there?

[00:59:59] **Walt:** Yeah.

[01:00:00] **Carl:** Was that wh—?

[01:00:07] **Walt:** *I* rented an apartment there. That was the only work around was at Grand Coulee Dam, and that's why *I* got that place in Hartline.

[01:00:12] **Carl:** Yeah. And— and— and but most of the time they lived in Everett?

[01:00:13] **Walt:** Yeah.

[01:00:15] **Carl:** Okay.

[01:00:21] **Walt:** Till, uh, till *I*, uh, after this happened, then *I* bought a home in Spokane.

[01:00:24] **Carl:** Yeah. Yeah

[01:00:26] **Walt:** 1207 Cleveland Street.

[01:00:32] **Carl:** Okay. And put a down payment on it from the from the Cooper money?

[01:00:32] **Walt:** Yeah.

[01:00:46] **Carl:** So— so to speak. How did you decide to drive to Spokane? Now, *I* can see on a map that that was a— a better bus ride going to, uh, Portland than probably anywhere else.

[01:01:02] **Walt:** Yeah, well, uh, that way *I* could say, uh, *I* was in Spokane at the Union Hall or something. <u>You know</u>, *I* don't— *I* don't remember exactly what, but *I* figured, that was the best way to do *it*.

[01:01:16] **Carl:** Okay. And did you— did you apply the, uh, the crazy glue in the car in your car in Spokane or in the bathroom or—?

[01:01:23] **Walt:** At the airport. <u>Right there</u>. First of all, *you* wash your fingers off with, uh, um, alcohol. *Use of the phrase "right there" in a threatening discussion.*

[01:01:24] **Carl:** Yeah.

[01:01:24] **Walt:** *You* wash your fingers out. See, all your fingers are coated with an oil.

[01:01:27] **Carl:** Uh-huh.

[01:01:28] **Walt:** And *it* wouldn't stick <u>right there</u>, uh, otherwise. Well, *it* would stick, but *it* wouldn't be, uh, a— as— as good stickwise <u>right there</u>. And then after *you* wash your hands off, get rid of that oil. Dry *it* off, and then *you* put the clazy *[sic]*— crazy glue— glue on *it*. And that was at the airport. *Use of the phrase "right there" in a threatening discussion.*

[01:01:47] **Carl:** Oh. That was at the airport in— in, uh, Portland?

[01:01:51] **Walt:** Yeah.

[01:01:53] **Carl:** Oh, okay. Uh.

[01:01:55] **Walt:** And *it*'s clear. Uh. *You* can even try *it* <u>right there</u>. Get an inkpad. And that's how *I* discovered *it* <u>right there</u>. *I* was putting something together one time, and *I* got crazy glue on *my* finger. And *I* just happened to, <u>you know</u>, tap on the inkpad a couple of times and then on paper. And there was nothing. There was like a, uh, blurry dot. Then *I* went further and further experimenting with *it*. *Use of the phrase "right there" in a threatening discussion.*

[01:02:19] **Carl:** Okay. When you went from— when you rode on the bus, uh, from, uh, Spokane to Portland, uh, you had the, uh, the briefcase.

[01:02:32] **Walt:** Yeah.

[01:02:32] **Carl:** And did you have anything else? Like you wouldn't have been wearing your insulated underwear then, would ya?

[01:02:38] **Walt:** Yeah.

[01:02:39] **Carl:** Oh, you wore it?

[01:02:39] **Walt:** Sure.

[01:02:41] **Carl:** So, *I* mean, even on the bus.

[01:02:43] **Walt:** Yeah.

[01:02:44] **Carl:** So you didn't have, you didn't need to have any other kind of a bag or suitcase or anything?

[01:02:49] **Walt:** No.

[01:02:51] **Carl:** Okay. Uh.

[01:02:53] **Walt:** *I* got the underwear still. The— the bottom piece.

[01:02:56] **Carl:** Yeah. Yeah. Uh.

[01:02:58] **Walt:** But *it* wouldn't fit anymore.

[01:02:59] **Carl:** Well, no. *[laughter]*

[01:03:02] **Walt:** Yeah. *[laughs]*

[01:03:03] **Carl:** So then when you, uh, the bus took you downtown, *I* suppose, or somethin'. Did you walk to that hotel, or how did you end up in that hotel you were at?

[01:03:12] **Walt:** Cab.

[01:03:14] **Carl:** Oh, Okay. So you took a cab from the Grey— from the Greyhound Station we'll say. And got there.

[01:03:20] **Walt:** *I*— *I* don't know the name of the hotel. But when I used to work out of Portland, you know, would go in there to work when there was no work around anywhere else.

[01:03:30] **Carl:** Yeah.

[01:03:31] **Walt:** Right there. Uh, *we* always stayed at that motel because *they* had a bar in the basement. Right there and *they* had girls that dressed up real nice, you know, shorts and nylons and all that, in the bar. *It* was like a businessmen's bar. And, uh, *they* invited us at different times over to their house for a barbecue and that. The wait— real, real nice-looking waitresses. *Use of the phrase "right there" in a threatening discussion.*

[01:03:54] **Carl:** Oh. So—

[01:03:55] **Walt:** So, *I* knew that was the, uh, motel *I* was going to. *It* wasn't like *I* just picked a motel out of *my* head. *I* knew where *I* was going.

[01:04:02] **Carl:** Oh. Okay. Uh, and, uh, so you— you got in there probably in the evening time or something or it doesn't matter. So anyway, you— you didn't have to leave the that . . . Was it a motel or a hotel?

[01:04:24] **Walt:** Uh, motel.

[01:04:26] **Carl:** It was a motel.

[01:04:28] **Walt:** Yeah. <u>Right there</u> <u>*you* know</u>— you know, drive your car beside the doors. And *it* had like a basement in there. Uh, a real nice— *it* was a businessman's bar. *Use of the phrase "right there" in a threatening discussion.*

[01:04:39] **Carl:** Yeah.

[01:04:39] **Walt:** <u>*You* know</u>. And, uh, the motel was above— above that.

[01:04:44] **Carl:** Then when you got there, do you remember anything you did while you were there? You probably had a couple of drinks.

[01:04:49] **Walt:** Yeah. *I* had a couple of drinks <u>right there</u>. Then *I* figured, uh, *I*'d better get <u>right there</u> up. Because *I* don't want a hangover. *I* want a clear head. Didn't have that much. And, uh, *I* still didn't know if *I* was going through with *it*. *Use of the phrase "right there" in a threatening discussion.*

[01:05:02] **Carl:** Yeah. And then that's where you applied the crazy glue.

[01:05:07] **Walt:** Yeah. In the restroom.

[01:05:09] **Carl:** Okay. And where did you get the alcohol, by the way?

[01:05:13] **Walt:** Rubbing alcohol. *I* carried *it* in a little bottle, like a mouthwash bottle.

[01:05:17] **Carl:** Oh, okay. So then once you put that on, did you just throw the stuff away?

[01:05:23] **Walt:** Yeah.

[01:05:24] **Carl:** Oh. Then ya, uh, then you uh went and bought a ticket, uh, with a twenty-dollar bill and whatnot and sat there and waited for the airplane. You don't remember whether you read or not.

[01:05:36] **Walt:** Uh. Maybe *I* had a newspaper in front of *me*, but *I* wasn't reading nothing.

[01:05:42] **Carl:** Yeah. Yeah.

[01:05:42] **Walt:** <u>*You* know</u>, *I* mean, *my* mind was racing.

[01:05:44] **Carl:** Yeah.

[01:05:45] **Walt:** A hundred miles an hour.

[01:05:46] **Carl:** Did <u>*you* know</u> even when you— when you left, uh, Spokane or any time, whi— what— how did you decide what airplane to get on to go to Seattle? *I* mean, was it just random?

[01:06:00] **Walt:** Just random. Whatever they sold me the ticket with.

[01:06:02] **Carl:** And so you— you didn't even know what kind of airplane you would be getting on.

[01:06:08] **Walt:** No.

[01:06:09] **Carl:** I that's what I told Michael. I said, "Knowing— knowing Walt. He, you know," I-I said, "Just any airplane." And he said, "He asked me— he said, "Well, can you open the door in the airplane?" I said, "Yeah. If you depressurize."

[01:06:25] **Walt:** Yeah.

[01:06:26] **Carl:** If it's not— if it's not pressurized. So, um, you— you really don't have to worry about— you wouldn't have had to went out that back door. I mean, I—

[01:06:35] **Walt:** I went out the side door.

[01:06:38] **Carl:** Yeah. Yeah. Your plans for this whole hijack were very basic. Um, as you got in your car at Hartline and started to drive to Spokane, what was going through your mind? Uh. Did you did you stop en route to eat? How many packs of—

[01:06:54] **Walt:** No.

[01:06:54] **Carl:** Uh, how many of cigarettes did you have? Uh, any clean clothes?

[01:07:00] **Walt:** No. Right there, uh, and, uh, how many packs of cigarettes? *Use of the phrase "right there" in a threatening discussion.*

[01:07:05] **Carl:** Yeah.

[01:07:06] **Walt:** Uh, *I* must have had, uh, less than a carton. *I*'d say maybe eight packs.

[01:07:12] **Carl:** Now where would you have put them?

[01:07:14] **Walt:** In *my* pockets.

[01:07:15] **Carl:** Your pockets were full of cigarettes?

[01:07:17] **Walt:** Yeah.

[01:07:18] **Carl:** Okay. All that— that makes sense. Uh, do you remember what kind of car you had?

[01:07:24] **Walt:** At that time?

[01:07:25] **Carl:** Yeah

[01:07:26] **Walt:** No.

[01:07:26] **Carl:** Okay. Do you remember what the weather was like?

[01:07:30] **Walt:** The weather? The weather was shining on *my* way to Spokane.

[01:07:36] **Carl:** It was— it was good weather.

[01:07:37] **Walt:** Yeah. Sunshine.

[01:07:39] **Carl:** Okay. Uh, and can you remember anything as you were driving along? Were you running this through in your mind what you were gonna do? And anything that you forgot, <u>you know</u>, and said *I* wished *I*'d have done this or brought this with me.

[01:07:54] **Walt:** No. *I* was keep—*I* kept on thinking <u>right there</u> this is a fucking stupid idea and, uh, I don't have to go through with this. *Use of the phrase "right there" in a threatening discussion.*

[01:08:06] **Carl:** Yeah. But nothing that nothing, uh, that you thought of then as you drove that, uh, I wished I'd have done something better. I'm gonna do it but, uh, I wish I'd brought this along or that along. Or did, uh, did you have any food? Did you think that maybe you were gonna land out in a, uh, in a forest and and—

[01:08:27] **Walt:** No. Nothing like that.

[01:08:28] **Carl:** And be three or four days in in the forest. Didn't have a candy bars or— or—

[01:08:32] **Walt:** No.

[01:08:33] **Carl:** Okay.

[01:08:34] **Walt:** I didn't have anything, but if I would have had anything I would have carried bouillon cubes with me.

[01:08:40] **Carl:** Okay, but but you didn't, though.

[01:08:42] **Walt:** No, I didn't.

[01:08:43] **Carl:** Yeah. Okay, there were a lot of things that could go wrong with this plan. Were there were you running anything like that through your mind?

[01:08:54] **Walt:** A lot of things that could go wrong with it?

[01:08:56] **Carl:** Yeah. You know, like uh—

[01:08:57] **Walt:** Yeah. I was running, I said, "This is fucking stupid." *[Carl laughs]* I was running that through *my* mind. *"I* don't have to go through with this. *I'*ll just go through the motions <u>right there</u> and see how *I* feel." *Use of the phrase "right there" in a threatening discussion.*

[01:09:12] **Carl:** Okay. *[laughs]* And you never thought that you might land out in the woods and die, or it'd end like that?

[01:09:20] **Walt:** No.

[01:09:20] **Carl:** At— at the motel in Portland. Do you do you remember what you did? In other words, did you get in in a afternoon off the bus and go to the bar or uh—

[01:09:32] **Walt:** Yeah that's a hotel <u>right there</u>. Motel, hotel whatever. *It'*s a, uh, *it'*s a businessman's, uh, luncheon place and after dinner *they* got good-looking attractive ladies there, <u>you know</u>, in short skirts and all. Uh, that's where *we* used to always when *we* went to work to Portland as ironworkers. *Use of the phrase "right there" in a threatening discussion.*

[01:09:53] **Carl:** Yeah. Yeah.

[01:09:54] **Walt:** *We* always stayed there and went down there and, uh, uh, the way—the waitresses all liked us, right, <u>you know</u>, the ironworkers—

[01:10:03] **Carl:** Yeah.

[01:10:03] **Walt:** —because everybody else was dressed, in suits and all that, and then *we'*d come in with old dirty work clothes and all that shit, <u>you know</u>.

[01:10:10] **Carl:** *[laughs]* Yeah. Yeah.

[01:10:11] **Walt:** And *we*'re talking to— and *they* even invited us one time to go to a party to their house, right, which, <u>you know</u>, *I* never did, <u>right there</u>. *I* said, *I* got to get back, <u>right there</u>, <u>you know</u>, to Everett, <u>right there</u>, *my* wife is— *Use of the phrase "right there" in a nonthreatening discussion.*

[01:10:23] **Carl:** Yeah.

[01:10:24] **Walt:** And, uh, some of the other guys wanted to go, but *I* had the vehicle so *they* had to go where *I* wanted to go—

[01:10:29] **Carl and Walt:** *[laugh]*

[01:10:34] **Walt:** But, *they* said, "At least *we*'re not phonies," <u>you know</u>, coming in with Carhartts soaking wet and full of fucking mud, dragging across the floor. The guys with suits would jump away from us at the bar.

[01:10:49] **Carl:** Did ya— did ya talk to anyone at the bar that day, or was there anything that happened?

[01:10:53] **Walt:** *I* talked to the girl, yeah.

[01:10:54] **Carl:** Yeah.

[01:10:55] **Walt:** <u>Right there</u>, the barmaid. *Use of the phrase "right there" in a threatening discussion.*

[01:10:56] **Carl:** But that's about— you don't remember any other—

[01:10:58] **Walt:** Yeah, and her name was, uh, *I* can't think of *it* now. Cindy.

[01:11:05] **Carl:** What— What was your last day like? In other words, uh, before you went out to Portland Airport. Did you sleep that night, or were you restless and tossing in bed or what?

[01:11:20] **Walt:** Uh, *I* had a hard time going to sleep, but *I* went to sleep.

[01:11:24] **Carl:** You— you eventually did go to sleep?

[01:11:26] **Walt:** Yeah, because *I* said, you know, "*I* don't have to do this."

[01:11:30] **Carl:** Yeah.

[01:11:30] **Walt:** *I* mean, there was two people in *my* head, you know.

[01:11:33] **Carl:** Yeah.

[01:11:35] **Walt:** Like, uh, the left shoulder would be the devil, the right shoulder would be the angel. You know, the devil made *me* do *it*.

[01:11:42] **Carl:** *[laughs]* So, you took the shuttle to the airport, did you— did you eat breakfast anywhere or did you eat at the airport or did you eat at, uh—

[01:11:49] **Walt:** No.

[01:11:50] **Carl:** —at— did you eat at the— breakfast before you went out there or anything?

[01:11:53] **Walt:** No, only coffee.

[01:11:54] **Carl:** Just coffee?

[01:11:56] **Walt:** Yeah.

[01:11:57] **Carl:** So, you really went quite a long while without eating through that whole— whole ordeal then?

[01:12:02] **Walt:** Yeah, *I* wasn't feeling like eating.

[01:12:03] **Carl:** Okay. Had you checked on— on the airlines that you were going to get prior to arrival or was just going out there or just all playing it by— by ear?

[01:12:14] **Walt:** Playing *it* by ear, that's all.

[01:12:15] **Carl:** So, you just got on the thing and went out there.

[01:12:17] **Walt:** Yeah, there was no— no plan, no nothing. *I* mean, really, nothing.

[01:12:22] **Carl:** Yeah.

[01:12:25] **Walt:** Uh, when *you* read— when *you* read about *it* in the papers, *you know*, "This was clever and that was—" there wasn't a fucking thing clever about the whole deal.

[01:12:33] **Carl:** *[laughs]* Okay, at the airport, did you see anybody there that— that— that was— looked unusual or looked, uh, *you know*, a big tall guy or a little fat— *you know*, anything that, at all, that was unusual?

[01:12:52] **Walt:** Naw, *I* was hunched in the corner. *I* would be the only person that'd be unusual out of that whole bunch, and *I* always thought people were staring at *me*, *you know*—

[laughter]

[01:13:03] **Carl:** But you just sat in a corner and, kind of looked at a paper?

[01:13:07] **Walt:** Yeah.

[01:13:07] **Carl:** Umm—

[01:13:08] **Walt:** Couldn't read *it*, *right there*, *you know I* was too busy, uh, being scared. ***Use of the phrase "right there" in a threatening discussion.***

[01:13:12] **Carl:** Now, how did you get on the airplane, wa-was— this was the old days, did you walk outside like and walk up a ladder, or did you actually walk up the back door of that 727, *you know*, the— the back tail thing?

[01:13:26] **Walt:** Yeah, *I* walked on a ramp, *you know*, a tunnel or whatever they got.

[01:13:30] **Carl:** Oh, you— they did have that tunnel in?

[01:13:33] **Walt:** Yeah.

[01:13:33] **Carl:** Just like the modern-day one, then.

[01:13:36] **Walt:** Yeah.

[01:13:36] **Carl:** So, you— you

[01:13:38] **Walt:** *I* mean, this isn't the last century this happened in.

[01:13:40] **Carl:** Oh, *I* know, but it was thirty, you know, now, you could— did you know what kind of airplane you were getting on?

[01:13:48] **Walt:** No.

[01:13:49] **Carl:** So, you had no idea, what— as you were getting on the airplane, what kind it was?

[01:13:54] **Walt:** There was no planning to anything, you know.

[01:13:56] **Carl:** So, how did you know that there was a tail that, uh, uh, that, uh, a door and a tail that went down then— because that was only on one airplane?

[01:14:07] **Walt:** Because *they* had a side door there that says, uh, "Red letters on *it* right there, open here," and *I* said *I* was going to open that right there, and *she* mentioned that "There's that tail door there," so *I* said, "Well, that's fuckin' good." *Use of the phrase "right there" in a threatening discussion.*

[01:14:19] **Carl:** Oh, really?

[01:14:20] **Walt:** Yeah.

[01:14:21] **Carl:** So, at first you were thinking about going out the side door?

[01:14:24] **Walt:** Yeah.

[01:14:26] **Carl:** And the stewardess actually talked you into going out the tail?

[01:14:29] **Walt:** *She* didn't talk *me*, *she* just mentioned *it*—

[01:14:31] **Carl:** She just mentioned it to you?

[01:14:33] **Walt:** Yeah. [Carl interjects: Yeah] Well, I don't have to fuck up the inside the airplane, you know. She could— at this time— she didn't know what altitude I was going to be going out at.

[01:14:44] **Carl:** *[laughs]* So, she thought maybe if you open that door, all— all the seats'd get sucked out or something?

[01:14:50] **Walt:** *[laughs]*

[01:14:52] **Carl:** Um, okay, was that the girl— was that Flo Schaffner you were talking to, you think?

[01:14:59] **Walt:** I don't know. I don't know their names, I can't, uh, I can't remember anybody's name.

[01:15:06] **Carl:** Okay.

[01:15:07] **Walt:** I can't remember. You know, everything's real vague.

[01:15:10] **Carl:** Yeah.

[01:15:12] **Walt:** Right there, uh— *Use of the phrase "right there" in a threatening discussion.*

[01:15:13] **Carl:** I'm just gonna make a note of that, uh, uh, you were gonna go out the side door, or, uh, or, um—

[01:15:28] **Walt:** It's all vague to me, Charlie, you know, the way it all happened right there, uh— don't 'member names or anything, uh— *Use of the phrase "right there" in a threatening discussion.*

[01:15:37] **Carl:** Yeah, Walter, *I* know.

[01:15:37] **Walt:** —been so long and, uh, *it* was something after *it* was done, *I* didn't wanna remember. <u>You know</u>, *it*'s—

[01:15:44] **Carl:** But you remember this gal— you must have had a conversation with her, and said, "Well, *I*'m gonna go out that door there," or something or she must have said that—

[01:15:55] **Walt:** Yeah, *I* already opened that door—

[01:15:57] **Carl:** She must have said how—

[01:15:58] **Walt:** —the instructions was right on *it*, how *you* gonna open that door, <u>*you* know</u>, how do *you* open that door?

[01:16:02] **Carl:** Yeah, and then that's when she said, "Well, you could go out the back door"?

[01:16:06] **Walt:** Yeah.

[01:16:07] **Carl:** Okay. Um, okay. Well, see that's— that's— *I*'m getting the stuff that, uh— umm, and this is something maybe the— maybe the FBI knows and— and, uh, they may be holding back with it or something like that. Um, so, okay—

[01:16:29] **Walt:** *I* think anything that the FBI would know would be just, some assertions, uh, nothing— their imaginations.

[01:16:40] **Carl:** *I*— *I*— *I*— *I* tend to agree with you.

[silence]

[01:16:54] **Carl:** Did you know that you told them where to park the airplane when you landed in Seattle? When that airplane landed in Seattle, it's— it had already been hijacked—

[01:17:07] **Walt:** Mm-hmm.

[01:17:07] **Carl:** —and when it landed, you told them where to position the fuel truck. Wh-why did that seem important to you?

[01:17:22] **Walt:** *I* don't know. Right there, probably— right there, where nobody could get a clear shot or come in. *I* had a reason, *I* know that, but *I* don't know what *it* was. *Use of the phrase "right there" in a threatening discussion.*

[01:17:36] **Carl:** Okay, what— the thing *I* was gonna tell you before is not important, you haven't read anything on it, but see the later airplanes, they put a switch on there, so that you could not open that door in-flight, and— and to tell you the truth, being a pilot, ex-pilot, *I* cannot imagine that— that those stairs would have been capable to open in-flight from the time they first made that airplane. In other words, *I* would have thought that, that that would have went on the gear switch, and if the gear was up, that you could not open that door.

However, *I* think what happened— *I* think what happened, 'cause that might be true, because when you— when you took, uh, after you, uh, hijacked the airplane and you were flying from Seattle-Tacoma, now you're gonna jump, you ordered them to have the gear down, on the airplane.

[01:18:34] **Walt:** Yeah.

[01:18:36] **Carl:** Flaps— flaps a quarter and gear down. Do you remember why that was?

[01:18:46] **Walt:** No.

[01:18:47] **Carl:** Well, it might have been— at the time, it might have been because you might have thought the controls for those stairs were were— were on the gear switch, and that might have been, it might have been. Now they have it— to where even if the gears were up or down, you can't put the gear— the door down in flight, and that switch is called the Cooper Switch. It's named after you. The Cooper Switch.

[01:19:09] **Walt:** Yeah, right there, well— the wheels down slow the aircraft down, and right there and the flaps right there is when we're jumping right there. You know, you give it flaps right there, cut power. *Use of the phrase "right there" in a threatening discussion.*

[01:19:18] **Carl:** Yeah, yeah.

[01:19:19] **Walt:** Wheels down there's drag right there, so I'm not gonna be hit—

[01:19:21] **Carl:** Well, you ordered them to fly at— at only two hundred miles an hour—

[01:19:25] **Walt:** Yeah.

[01:19:26] **Carl:** —yeah. Okay, you ordered, four parachutes, from— from McChord?

[01:19:33] **Walt:** Yeah, but they didn't come from McChord.

[01:19:35] **Carl:** Where'd they come from?

[01:19:37] **Walt:** Skyhomish *[sic—Snohomish]*. The jump center that's right next to the airport.

[01:19:43] **Carl:** Oh, okay, they came from where now? What was the name of it?

[01:19:46] **Walt:** Skyhomish *[sic]*.

[01:19:47] **Carl:** Kyhomish?

[01:19:49] **Walt:** Skyhomish *[sic]*, yeah.

[01:19:50] **Carl:** Sky-homish?

[01:19:51] **Walt:** Yeah, *it*'s right— that Skyhomish [sic] River, and, uh, that's where the Seattle Skydivers do all their jumping.

[01:20:00] **Carl:** Okay.

[01:20:02] **Walt:** *It*'s only a couple miles away.

[01:20:04] **Carl:** From the airport?

[01:20:07] **Walt:** Yeah.

[01:20:06] **Carl:** God. How— how could they be jumping that, uh, close to Seattle? *I* mean, just— just— just between you and me, as, ex-jumpers. *I* mean, you'd— that doesn't seem like it'd be that good to be just two or three or four miles from a major airport.

[01:20:23] **Walt:** *They* got the Skyhomish *[sic]*— well, maybe, <u>you know</u>, to *me*—what's a mile or this and that, <u>right there</u>? But *they*'re close to— *they*'re right, *they*'re right close to Seattle, *they* were Seattle Skydivers. *They* jump there and *you* got to be up at the tower all the time, right there with the— when *you*'re putting out people, *you* got to be on the radio, not like *it* was for us at Saginaw. **Use of the phrase "right there" in a threatening discussion.**

[01:20:42] **Carl:** Yeah. So, they're called Seattle Skydivers?

[01:20:45] **Walt:** Yeah.

[01:20:49] **Carl:** And that's where the chute *[sic— chutes]* come from?

[00:20:51] **Walt:** Yeah.

[01:20:49] **Carl:** And there was two main chute *[sic—chutes]*, two backpacks, and two reserves.

[01:20:58] **Walt:** Yup. And, uh— ah, ██████████, right there. ████████████████████████. Don't mention his name in this, though. **Use of the phrase "right there" in a threatening discussion.**

[01:21:07] **Carl:** No. No. Uh, okay. Um. Now, uh, why did you open the one parachute in the airplane?

[01:21:20] **Walt:** Seeing *it* wasn't tied off.

[01:21:24] **Carl:** Okay and it— was that reserve or main?

[01:21:27] **Walt:** *It* was a main.

[01:21:28] **Carl:** It was a main. So now you're down to the one main?

[01:21:31] **Walt:** Mm-hmm.

[01:21:32] **Carl:** And, did you wear a reserve when you did this?

[01:21:36] **Walt:** No.

[01:21:38] **Carl:** Y-you didn't? *I* didn't think you would. You did not wear a reserve, uh, but the reserve that was, the— the dummy chute was kicked out of the airplane?

[01:21:48] **Walt:** Yup.

[01:21:50] **Carl:** So why did you just toss? Why did you toss that one out?

[01:21:55] **Walt:** Oh. Wanted a lot of chutes in the area open, *you know*.

[01:21:59] **Carl:** You didn't open it when you tossed it out.

[01:22:03] **Walt:** No. *It*'ll open when *it* hit the trees.

[01:22:06] **Carl:** Okay. So you tossed it away before you jumped?

[01:22:11] **Walt:** Yeah.

[01:22:13] **Carl:** Oh, okay. Uh, did you see the reserve that you kicked out that had the— the dummy chute, that had a, may be the x's on it or something.

[01:22:22] **Walt:** No. *I* tossed *it* out. That's all. *You know*, just get rid of everything that *I* could.

[01:22:29] **Carl:** Okay, so, you didn't even examine that chute at all or even hardly look at it?

[01:22:33] **Walt:** No.

[01:22:35] **Carl:** N-now, did you— what did you do with the other reserve, the— the— the dummy reserve, and then there'd been a good reserve?

[01:22:43] **Walt:** Threw *it* out. Those were thrown out as well.

[01:22:46] **Carl:** But you did not wear a reserve?

[01:22:47] **Walt:** No.

[01:22:49] **Carl:** Okay.

[01:22:48] **Walt:** *It* was too bulky with the things in *my* raincoat.

[01:22:51] **Carl:** Yeah. Okay. Uh, *I-I* probably wouldn't of worn a reserve either, you know. Did you, uh, now, you did have a wrist altimeter?

[01:23:05] **Walt:** Mmmh.

[01:23:10] **Carl:** Wh-what happened to that?

[01:23:13] **Walt:** Wasn't a wrist— *it* was a, uh, stopwatch on *my* wrist.

[01:23:16] **Carl:** But you requested a wrist altimeter as well?

[01:23:20] **Walt:** That's what *I* got is a stopwatch.

[01:23:20] **Carl:** Oh, it was not a— they give you a stopwatch instead of a wrist altimeter?

[01:23:27] **Walt:** Yeah.

[01:23:29] **Carl:** Okay. Um—

[01:23:31] **Walt:** And then *they* had no wrist altimeters.

[01:23:32] **Carl:** Yeah. Steve Snyder had invented them, but they were new.

[01:23:37] **Walt:** Yeah.

[01:23:39] **Carl:** They were new. Did, when— when you figured this thing at all, I know you've told me a bunch of times, there wasn't any, uh, any planning but did you figure— did you— figure to have to time it, so it would be a night jump so that nobody on the ground at least would be able to see you jump?

[01:23:59] **Walt:** No.

[01:23:59] **Carl:** In other words, that was just luck of the draw as well.

[01:24:04] **Walt:** Yeah.

[01:24:06] **Carl:** It was not figured to— to be a night jump? Just whenever it happened?

[01:24:10] **Walt:** Just whenever it happened. First of all, <u>right there</u>, uh, in *my* sane moments, I believed it would never happen. It was just the thought. ***Use of the phrase "right there" in a threatening discussion.***

[01:24:21] **Carl:** Uh uh.

[01:24:23] **Walt:** So, when it happened it surprised me as much as it did everybody else.

[01:24:29] **Carl:** Yeah. So, um, uh, what did you do with the— the— the flare bot— the, you know, the satchel.

[01:24:41] **Walt:** I tossed that out.

[01:24:42] **Carl:** Yeah, that was tossed out as well.

[01:24:45] **Walt:** Mm-hmm.

[01:24:46] **Carl:** Uh, incidentally, the— we talked about this a couple of days ago. The tie clasp was a mother of pearl thing. They keep calling it a mother of pearl tie clasp. *I* don't know if that rings a bell with you or not, but they keep saying he left on the airplane a black tie which is, uh, wh-what they claim they have a little bit of DNA on. *You* know, eh, some. And, uh, uh, whether your nose dripped on it, er, er, whatever, *you* know.

[01:25:22] **Walt:** Yeah.

[01:25:24] **Carl:** Ah, um, and a mother of pearl tie clasp. So anyway, that's—

[01:25:27] **Walt:** *It* was a pin.

[01:25:30] **Carl:** Pin, a tie pin.

[01:25:32] **Walt:** Yeah.

[01:25:32] **Carl:** Yeah.

[01:25:32] **Walt:** Mother of pearl tie pin.

[01:25:34] **Carl:** Yeah.

[01:25:36] **Walt:** *I* still got 'em. Not that one but *I*— that's what *I* used all the time.

[01:25:40] **Carl:** Where, did— did you get a whole bunch of them? *I* mean were they from a, uh, were they from, uh—

[01:25:46] **Walt:** Haberdashery shop.

[01:25:47] **Carl:** Oh, okay, you just bought 'em?

[01:25:50] **Walt:** Yeah.

[01:25:52] **Carl:** They were— well, the reason *I*, *I*'m saying that they weren't like a Zantop Zippo Lighter that—

[01:25:56] **Walt:** No, no.

[01:25:56] **Carl:** *You* know, people were, *you know*, giving away and it— and, *you know*, said, uh, Ed's Haberdashery on it or something like that, *you know*.

[01:26:03] **Walt:** Yeah.

[01:26:06] **Carl:** Um, you actually bought them?

[01:26:06] **Walt:** Mm-hmm.

[01:26:07] **Carl:** Yeah. And— and do you still have one?

[01:26:11] **Walt:** Yeah. *I* got a couple pins.

[01:26:14] **Carl:** Were they bought at the same place?

[01:26:16] **Walt:** No. *They* were bought over the years, *you know*.

[01:26:19] **Carl:** Yeah, yeah.

[01:26:19] **Walt:** But that's what *I* always wore.

[01:26:22] **Carl:** Yeah. Do you remember anything that you, that you told the captain? You wrote notes. These are the where you wrote notes and you handed them to the, to, uh, the stewardess to take up to the captain, to tell him, for example, fly with the gear down and the flaps down and two hundred mile an hour, and what course and— and— and what altitude and— and, uh. Oh, and— and that you wanted four parachutes and you ordered— you— you said from McChord, but they ended up coming from the other place there, you know. Um, um, the— the— the jump thing and the wrist altimeter was actually a stopwatch.

[01:27:12] **Walt:** Yeah.

[01:27:12] **Carl:** Um, so they didn't have it but anyway, uh—

[01:27:16] **Walter:** Sure, because— *[clears throat]* okay, *you* say Steve Schneider invented *it*.

[01:27:20] **Carl:** Yeah.

[01:27:22] **Walt:** Right there. *He* invented *it* right there— what would the Air Force at McChord be doing right there with a wrist altimeter? The Air Force? *Use of the phrase "right there" in a threatening discussion.*

[01:27:31] **Carl:** Yeah.

[01:27:32] **Walt:** *They* didn't have *it*.

[01:27:34] **Carl:** Where did you— right, they didn't. Where did you tell them to get the parachutes from?

[01:27:39] **Walt:** Skyhomish *[sic]*.

[01:27:40] **Carl:** Oh, that's where you told 'em? You did not tell 'em McChord?

[01:27:44] **Walt:** No.

[01:27:44] **Carl:** See, this is some other misinformation put out by the FBI. This is more misinformation put out by the FBI, you know.

[01:27:57] **Walt:** Mm-hmm.

[01:27:59] **Carl:** And, uh, uh, okay. Getting back to the captain, um, did— um, do you remember anything on those notes at all?

[01:28:10] **Walt:** No.

[01:28:12] **Carl:** Now, did you ask for the notes back?

[01:28:17] **Walt:** *I* don't recall, Charlie.

[01:28:19] **Carl:** Well, yeah, they did. They give 'em back to you, but w-while they had 'em, they copied what was on 'em, you know, somebody wrote down, you know, the co-pilot or someone was— was writing down what they, what they said they were, um—

[01:28:34] **Walt:** See at this time, *it*'s a time of extreme excitement.

[01:28:37] **Carl:** Oh, *I* know.

[01:28:40] **Walt:** Yeah, so *I* mean, uh, not only *am I* dealing with somebody, you know, that divorced himself from the original personality right there. *It*— *it*'s an extreme excitement, you know, like, uh. *Use of the phrase "right there" in a threatening discussion.*

[01:28:55] **Carl:** Oh, *I* understand. [Walter interjects: Dr. Jekyll] It's just like— what according to our source was the exact wording of the typewriter note? In other words, when you write, wrote out the note on the typewriter that you give to the stewardess about this is a hijack, what— what do you remember pretty close to what it said, if not exact, do you remember what you said? In other words, what was, uh, what was the note about, you know?

[01:29:23] **Walt:** *I* can't remember <u>right there</u>. At best that *I* can, "This is a hijack and *I*'ve got explosives." ***Use of the phrase "right there" in a threatening discussion.***

[01:29:29] **Carl:** Okay.

[01:29:32] **Walt:** And that's about the best *I* can remember.

[01:29:34] **Carl:** Okay.

[01:29:35] **Walt:** And that was with one-finger typing.

[01:29:38] **Carl:** Yeah, yeah. Okay, well, that— that's— that's good enough. *I* mean that's— nobody can remember exactly, <u>you know</u>, somethin' forty years ago. Okay. Were there any other notes written on the plane or elsewhere, and what did they say? Were there any other notes written?

[01:29:39] **Walt:** *I* wrote something on a napkin, but *I* forgot what *it* was.

[01:30:03] **Carl:** On a napkin?

[01:30:04] **Walt:** Yeah, <u>you know</u> them napkins that *you* wipe your mouth with?

[01:30:08] **Carl:** Yeah.

[01:30:08] **Walt:** <u>Right there</u> that *they* give *you* when *they* give *you* a drink? *Use of the phrase "right there" in a threatening discussion.*

[01:30:10] **Carl:** Yeah. Okay, you wrote something on a napkin. Okay.

[01:30:16] **Walt:** Whether anybody picked *it* up or did *I* give *it* to somebody, *I*— *I* have no idea about that.

[01:30:27] **Carl:** But you did write somethin' on a napkin?

[01:30:28] **Walt:** Yes.

[01:30:29] **Carl:** Okay.

[01:30:31] **Walt:** 'Cause when *I* get nervous, *I* always scribble.

[01:30:33] **Carl:** Okay. That's good. That's all right. Did you have— did you have the stewardess write on a— a pad of paper, some kind or whatever it was, the instructions for opening that back door in-flight or anyway to open it? You had to know how to open that back— back door and, uh, and, uh, to lower the stairs.

[01:31:04] **Walt:** Yeah. But *it* had the— the directions written on the side of the door, for emergency use.

[01:31:14] **Carl:** It did, really?

[01:31:14] **Walt:** Yeah.

[01:31:15] **Carl:** So, that's where you got it. You read the— just read the directions?

[01:31:19] **Walt:** Yeah.

[01:31:22] **Carl:** Okay. Uh. Now, when you put that— started putting them stairs down— this isn't anything from anybody. *I*'m just— this is just— that had to be terrifying. That had to be terrifying when you're lowering— lowering those stairs, they had to be gruntin' and groanin' 'cause they are not made to go down in-flight and they had to be making noises and wind and all that shit like— like nothing that you have ever heard. Yeah, well—

[01:31:54] **Walt:** Yeah, well, <u>right there</u>, uh, when we go into Dr. Jekyll and Mr. Hyde, Mr. Hyde wasn't scared of shit, was *he*? ***Use of the phrase "right there" in a threatening discussion.***

[01:32:01] **Carl:** No.

[01:32:02] **Walt:** Yeah, well.

[01:32:06] **Carl:** Okay. Um, the parachute that you opened in the airplane did, uh, you did cut shroud lines off, you know.

[01:32:18] **Walt:** Yeah.

[0:32:19] **Carl:** And what did, what did you do with the shroud lines? 'Cause you did—

[01:32:23] **Walt:** *I* tied the money on to *me*.

[01:32:25] **Carl:** Okay, so that's what you tied the money onto you with?

[01:32:28] **Walt:** Yes.

[01:32:29] **Carl:** And you also tied some around your legs *I* think, too.

[01:32:33] **Walt:** Yeah.

[01:32:33] **Carl:** Uh. Did not wear a reserve— oh. Were you wearing long underwear?

[01:32:39] **Walt:** Yes.

[01:32:41] **Carl:** Okay.

[01:32:42] **Walt:** Mackinaw kind. Remember, what we used to wear in Saginaw?

[01:32:44] **Carl:** Them— them puffy ones?

[01:32:47] **Walt:** Yeah. *I* even got the, uh, the pair of pants right here now.

[01:32:52] **Carl:** The pair of pants? Oh, you mean the pants to the—

[01:32:53] **Walt:** The bottom part. Yeah.

[01:32:56] **Carl:** Really?

[01:32:57] **Walt:** Yeah.

[01:32:58] **Carl:** Um, hold on to 'em. Will 'em to me if you ever die.

[01:33:04] **Walt:** Yeah.

[01:33:04] **Carl:** Say, uh, put a note on them and for Willard and say, "Give these to Charlie. Uh."

[01:33:11] **Walt:** Pick *it* up.

[01:33:10] **Carl:** Okay. Is there anything that you think of that you can think of that you said to that girl, Flo Schaffner, or maybe anybody, uh, but— but somebody that— that had something to do with it that would— would, uh, in other words, is there something that you said that, um, that kind of struck a note or something that she said, something even that she said to you that— that— that struck a note?

[01:33:44] **Walt:** No, right there, because at the time, Charlie, right there, you know, I mean, I was numb. *Use of the phrase "right there" in a threatening discussion.*

[01:33:50] **Carl:** Yeah, yeah, yeah.

[01:33:52] **Walt:** You know, I mean, none of this, none of it was planned. Nothing.

[01:33:56] **Carl:** Yeah. Well, comes right back to the ten seconds to— to plan. You know, I mean, in— in the world, you know, uh, okay, so, um, so, you're on the airplane now, and, uh, and you passed these notes back and forth, you know, and you're— you're sitting there smoking cigarettes. How did you hook up the wires to the flares? Ah, was it a meticulous attempt at realism? In other words, if you looked into your little, uh, uh, hand-pouch, there, you know, the thing that, uh, the—

[01:34:36] **Walt:** You could see wires that I had, uh, tape around them right there, and I had the wire bent in as if it was going to a fuse, but I had it taped around the side. *Use of the phrase "right there" in a threatening discussion.*

[01:34:49] **Carl:** Okay.

[01:34:50] **Walt:** And, uh, the— the, and the things on the bottom, right there, where you're sticking around like a nail. *Use of the phrase "right there" in a threatening discussion.*

[01:34:58] **Carl:** Yeah.

[01:34:58] **Walt:** I had them cut off.

[01:35:00] **Carl:** Okay. That's good. Do you remember asking for non-military chutes to the stewardess after, uh. Well, do you remember asking for non-military chutes?

[01:35:19] **Walt:** I didn't use them. Course, I wanted the chutes to come out of Skyhomish *[sic— Snohomish]* right there because that's close by, and that's the jump center. *Use of the phrase "right there" in a threatening discussion.*

[01:35:28] **Carl:** Yeah, and that's where you wanted them from.

[01:35:31] **Walt:** Yeah.

[01:35:33] **Carl:** And you're sure that the chutes had D-rings— [Walt interjects: Yeah.] with D-rings on them. Okay. Uh, did you take the phone from the stewardess to talk to the cockpit at all? And, did the captain ever talk to you over the intercom? He— he did it one time to say, "Can we help you?" when you were back— by the back door? But I mean, did you ever— did you ever, uh, have a conversation over the intercom?

[01:36:05] **Walt:** I can't remember that, Charlie.

[01:36:06] **Carl:** Okay. Uh.

[01:36:12] **Walt:** *My* mind was going a thousand miles an hour at that time. You know, *it*'s, uh—

[01:36:19] **Carl:** Yeah.

[01:36:22] **Walt:** *I* was too busy praying to be thinking about anything too much.

[01:36:25] **Carl:** Do you remember the captain or stewardess trying to convince you to let the FAA man on board?

[01:36:34] **Walt:** No.

[01:36:35] **Carl:** You don't remember 'em even askin'?

[01:36:37] **Walt:** No. Right there, *they* ask right there. *You* go, "Of course not." ***Use of the phrase "right there" in a threatening discussion.***

[01:36:42] **Carl:** Yeah. Yeah. Did you ask anybody about how to lower the back door or did— or did, for example, did a, did a stewardess lead you back there? Did you say, "How do you open the door?" and she'd lead you back there and just pointed to the— the directions and say, "Follow those directions"?

[01:36:58] **Walt:** Yeah. Directions are written, right. *I* read that.

[01:37:02] **Carl:** Okay, but you don't remember stewardesses ever taking you back there and—?

[01:37:05] **Walt:** No.

[01:37:06] **Carl:** Could you see any goings-on as you waited for the parachutes and— and the plane to be refueled? Did there look like any funny business going on out there?

[01:37:18] **Walt:** No, *I* was concerned about snipers.

[01:37:20] **Carl:** Yeah. Okay, but could ya—

[01:37:23] **Walt:** *I* covered the window where I was sitting.

[01:37:25] **Carl:** Oh, okay. You did.

[01:37:27] **Walt:** With a newspaper.

[01:37:29] **Carl:** Okay. Do you remember anything *I* asked you this here before? Do you remember anything on how the parachutes arrived? Did— did you see anybody pull up with the parachutes or— uh, or, all of a sudden, did some guy would just carry 'em on the airplane or something?

[01:37:52] **Walt:** *They* were just bringing 'em on the airplane.

[01:37:54] **Carl:** Okay, and, uh, it was just like, um, wha— what kind of guy, what kind of uniform or in other words, what did he appear to be, uh, uh, like an airline worker?

[01:38:12] **Walt:** *I* don't know. *I* didn't want nobody in coveralls.

[01:38:14] **Carl:** You didn't want anybody in coveralls?

[01:38:18] **Walt:** No, 'cause *they* could hide a sawed-off shotgun or anything under that.

[01:38:22] **Carl:** Yeah. Now, how did you get the money? In other words, was it, was that carried back to you or did you have to go up to the front? You wouldn't have went up to the front of the airplane, you'd ordered it to been brought to you someway.

[01:38:33] **Walt:** *I* wanted everything brought to *me* where *I* was sitting.

[01:38:36] **Carl:** Okay. And— and, how— how did the parachutes get back to you? By a stewardess?

[01:38:43] **Walt:** *She* brought them back to *me*— the stewardess.

[01:38:46] **Carl:** The stewardesses brought 'em back?

[01:38:47] **Walt:** Yeah. 'Cause *I* had the windows covered with paper where *I* was sitting right around there.

[01:38:52] **Carl:** Yeah. Do you remember any other notes or any other information that you gave to anybody? Uh, for example, [Walt interjects: No.] when you said, "Well, when— when they bring the parachutes, don't have somebody in coveralls."

[01:39:11] **Walt:** What *I* said <u>right there</u>, everything was verbal. *Use of the phrase "right there" in a threatening discussion.*

[01:39:18] **Carl:** Okay.

[01:39:19] **Walt:** <u>You know</u>, when *they*— writing out these notes and all that, why would I type something out and then go to handwriting, <u>you know</u>, in the airplane?

[01:39:29] **Carl:** Yeah. Yeah. Do you ever remember taking your sunglass— glasses off well, in— in the airplane?

[01:39:37] **Walt:** *I* can't remember, but *I* probably did to wipe *my* eyes, *you* know, I always do that but *I* mean, *you know*—

[01:39:44] **Carl:** You didn't leave—

[01:39:44] **Walt:** Not for any length of time.

[01:39:48] **Carl:** Yeah. Um, so you could've taken 'em off to wipe your eyes and that— Now, you had to have communicated to the captain some way to tell him to fly with the, *you know*— keep the speed down at— at two hundred, *you know*. Flap's— flap's a quarter and— and, uh, don't go over ten thousand and— and, uh, keep the airplane, uh, uh, without pressure. *You know*, no— You had to— communicated to him somehow was that— just verbal to the stewardess?

[01:40:31] **Walt:** *I* believe *it* was verbal to the— because *I* didn't want nobody to see *me* too much.

[01:40:34] **Carl:** Yeah. And you didn't— And you're sure you didn't write that out on notes?

[01:40:41] **Walt:** No, because why would *I* type a note to give *it* to the— and then start writing everything on paper?

[01:40:49] **Carl:** Right. Well, that makes sense. And you did order— you did order a— an altimeter from Skyhomish *[sic—Snohomish]*.

[01:41:00] **Walt:** Yeah, but *I* got a stopwatch instead.

[01:41:03] **Carl:** Right. Right. *I*— *I* don't know, you know. *I*— *I* probably wouldn't have ordered the altimeter even if they had— would have had them then because *I*— *I* don't think *I* would have counted on doing any kind of a free fall there at night, you know. *I* think *I*'d a just said, well, *I*'m gonna go out and wait about five seconds, which is what you said you didn't pull. So the altimeter really— it— you couldn't see it at night, you know.

[01:41:32] **Walt:** Yeah. Couldn't see the stopwatch to see *it*.

[01:41:34] **Carl:** Yeah. Of course, it was daytime when you ordered them, and you might not have been thinking, "Well, it's gonna be pitch dark by the time that *I* do this thing," <u>you know</u>. So—

[01:41:43] **Walt:** There was no thinking involved in the whole situation.

[01:41:46] **Carl:** It was just a lot more of— of uh [Walt interjects: Yeah.] What— What you've done in the past and that type of thing, you know.

[01:41:56] **Walt:** *I*'d like *it* all to be written out like *I* was a fuckin' genius.

[laughter]

[01:42:05] **Carl:** By the note, you say it was typed, and *I* believe it was typed myself. But another book says it was a handwritten note.

[01:42:16] **Walt:** Well, *I* don't know if *it* was handwritten, somebody must of uh handwritten *it* because mine was on a rented typewriter.

[01:42:26] **Carl:** Okay. And you got that, as far as you can remember, from some kind of a stationery store.

[01:42:30] **Walt:** Yeah, *I* rented it.

[01:42:32] **Carl:** Yeah. Okay.

[01:42:33] **Walt:** *I* mean *my* typing wasn't that good either, <u>right there</u>, but *I* mean *it* wasn't bad because *I* learned to type at Zantop. *Use of the phrase "right there" in a nonthreatening discussion.*

[01:42:40] **Carl:** Yeah. So— so you ride the airplane on up to, uh, Seattle. And you can see the weather outside, and you can see it's pretty bad.

[01:42:52] **Walt:** Uh, yes, *you* can see *it* <u>right there</u> or *you* can anticipate that *it*'s pretty bad, but when *you*'re numb in the head from fear, *you* know, *you* don't seem to notice. The weather, the clouds, uh, <u>you know</u>. *Use of the phrase "right there" in a threatening discussion.*

[01:43:08] **Carl:** Okay.

[01:43:09] **Walt:** *You* don't notice things <u>right there</u> when *you* are scared. *Use of the phrase "right there" in a threatening discussion.*

[01:43:13] **Carl:** So how long do you think it was before the airplane took off? *I* don't think it was very long. Um.

[01:43:21] **Walt:** *I* have no idea—right there if *it* was five minutes or, uh, seven hours or three weeks right there. *It— it— it* wasn't in *me* to be thinking at this time. *I* had to f— freeze emotional thoughts.

[01:43:37] **Carl:** So you did hand her— hand her the note and, uh— and— and she kind, uh— She was busy doing other things and she kind of put it in her pocket like and— and then when she, uh—

[01:43:51] **Walt:** Came back.

[01:43:52] **Carl:** Came back, she was— Yeah. After the airplane actually took off, uh, she came back to you. And— and that's when she said, *"I* can't believe you're actually hi— hijacking this airplane."

[01:44:05] **Walt:** And *I* said, *"I* can't believe *it* neither, but *I'm* serious."

[01:44:08] **Carl:** Yeah. Um, then do you remember what she said?

[01:44:14] **Walt:** *She* stared at me for a little while.

[01:44:18] **Carl:** *[laughs]* *I* would imagine— That's what *I'da* done, too.

[01:44:24] **Walt:** Yeah.

[01:44:25] **Carl:** And— and— and then did you tell her anything like, "Well, take this note up to the captain," or anything?

[01:44:32] **Walt:** Told her that about three times.

[01:44:35] **Carl:** You told her to take the note up to the captain?

[01:44:37] **Walt:** Yeah.

[01:44:38] **Carl:** And what did she—

[01:44:39] **Walt:** *She* was just staring at *me*.

[01:44:41] **Carl:** Okay. So, but finally, she did, though.

[01:44:45] **Walt:** Yes.

[01:44:45] **Carl:** Or— or— Okay. At what point did you open the briefcase and show her the dynamite?

[01:44:51] **Walt:** Well, *she* wasn't paying no attention to *me*.

[01:44:54] **Carl:** Okay. Right.

[01:44:54] **Walt:** Just staring at *me*.

[01:44:55] **Carl:** Right then and there and then that's when she actually—

[01:44:58] **Walt:** Then— then *she* figured *it* was all the truth, <u>*you know*</u>.

[01:45:01] **Carl:** Yeah. Okay, so—

[01:45:03] **Walt:** *I*- mean *she* just— *She* was as scared as *I* was. *I* think *she* was petrified, and so was *I*.

[01:45:10] **Carl:** Okay.

[01:45:12] **Walt:** *We* both looked at each other.

[01:45:14] **Carl:** *[laughs]* Well, it doesn't happen every day, you know.

[01:45:17] **Walt:** Yeah, yeah. *It* is sort of unusual event.

[01:45:20] **Carl:** Yeah. Right. *I'd— I'd* say so, *[laughs]* really unusual. But—

[01:45:24] **Walt:** Yeah.

[01:45:25] **Carl:** Okay. So she goes up and she tells the captain and— and, uh— Then do you 'member, you know, she tells him. So then do you remember anything about what happened after that at all?

[01:45:41] **Walt:** Uh, *I* was smoking a lot of cigarettes.

[01:45:45] **Carl:** Yeah. Now.

[01:45:47] **Walt:** I got another drink.

[01:45:48] **Carl:** Right. What— Do you remember what you were drinking, by the way? *I* wouldn't. But you were drinking drinks. You weren't drinking beer. *I* know that. But you were drink—

[01:46:00] **Walt:** Yeah, *I* was drinking liquor.

[01:46:00] **Carl:** Yeah.

[01:46:03] **Walt:** And, uh, *I* never—

[01:46:03] **Carl:** What do you use— what do you— *I* know you don't—

[01:46:06] **Walt:** Scotch and water or somethin'. *I* don't— I don't— *I'm* not a liquor drinker, but *I* was drinking liquor.

[01:46:11] **Carl:** *I* know. Yeah. Um, okay. So you're— you're ordering, you know, the liquor type stuff and *I* know you had several of those so that— that had to kind of ah putting you back on your heels a little bit, you know, because you're not a liquor drinker.

[01:46:30] **Walt:** Yeah.

[01:46:31] **Carl:** Um, okay.

[01:46:33] **Walt:** *It* didn't settle *me* down any, though, Charlie. *I* was— *I* was too scared to— to get, you know.

[01:46:41] **Carl:** You practically didn't know you were drinking, in fact.

[01:46:43] **Walt:** No. Right there *I* mean *it* was, uh— *I* was so scared, *it* was false security, *you* know, like a baby takes a security blanket. *Use of the phrase "right there" in a threatening discussion.*

[01:46:54] **Carl:** Yeah.

[01:46:55] **Walt:** Right there. That was *my* security blanket, but *it* didn't do any good. *I* didn't feel very fuckin' secure. *Use of the phrase "right there" in a threatening discussion.*

[01:47:01] **Carl:** But— But you'd already started it by now, the— the process. When the airplane landed at, uh, Seattle-Tacoma there, there was a certain procedure that, um, that you had the gas truck pull up to a certain place on the airplane. Do you remember if you give any other orders, uh, to— to, uh, for what to do or what not to do at that time? Well, you had to have told them at that time, you had to have told them, probably some time before you landed about the parachutes and— and the money.

[01:47:38] **Walt:** Yeah. And also, *I* didn't want too many lights on in the plane.

[01:47:43] **Carl:** Okay. You wanted the plane kept pretty dark.

[01:47:46] **Walt:** Yeah. Didn't want no snipers coming in. <u>*You know*</u>.

[01:47:49] **Carl:** Okay. And you were wearing wraparound sunglasses.

[01:47:52] **Walt:** Yup.

[01:47:53] **Carl:** Okay. Um, uh, do you remember now, once the plane landed, uh, were they just free to open the door and everything, or what?

[01:48:08] **Walt:** *They* were looking at *me* and asking me.

[01:48:13] **Carl:** You mean the stewardesses were?

[01:48:15] **Walt:** Yeah.

[01:48:16] **Carl:** Okay.

[01:48:18] **Walt:** What to do? Fuck, *I* didn't know what to do. *I* said, "Do what *you* normally do when you got all these people here," <u>you know</u>. But—

[01:48:22] **Carl:** So but, they open, uh— So you were holding these people for ransom though, until you got the money.

[01:48:30] **Walt:** Yeah.

[01:48:31] **Carl:** Okay. So the door musta stayed shut.

[01:48:34] **Walt:** Yeah. Nobody jumped off right away.

[01:48:37] **Carl:** Okay. Do you remember how you told them about to get the parachutes and that stuff? Do you remember anything at all?

[01:48:46] **Walt:** Well, no.

[01:48:49] **Carl:** Note? Or did you tell them by—

[01:48:50] **Walt:** *I* checked the— the reason *I* found out that one chute was a sewed-off chute—

[01:48:55] **Carl:** Yeah.

[01:48:56] **Walt:** —because all reserve chutes right there have, uh, uh, rigger seal on *it*. That didn't have a rigger seal. So that's one of them training reserve chutes. *Use of the phrase "right there" in a threatening discussion.*

[01:49:07] **Carl:** But it also *I* think, it had X's on it. *It would have been nice if Carl hadn't contaminated the "X" issue since the evidence suggests there was an "X" on the training reserve chute. However, Walt focuses on the lead seal: there was no lead seal, which tells Walt the chutes came from McChord AFB.*

[01:49:09] **Walt:** *I* didn't look at X's right there. I looked at the uh— at the uh, seal, no lead seal. *Use of the phrase "right there" in a threatening discussion.*

[01:49:18] **Carl:** Oh, okay. Uh, but that's the only chute that you found that was, uh—

[01:49:24] **Walt:** Yeah.

[01:49:25] **Carl:** —uh, out of the ordinary. All the rest of 'em looked— looked okay.

[01:49:30] **Walt:** Yeah. Now, how could *they* say that the chutes come from McChord? I didn't request them from McChord, and if *it* comes from McChord, *it* wouldn't have D-rings on *it* to hook the reserve onto.

[01:49:41] **Carl:** Well—

[01:49:42] **Walt:** So that's—

[01:49:43] **Carl:** Right.

[01:49:43] **Walt:** —So that's— *They*'re wrong.

[01:49:44] **Carl:** Right. See. *I* told that to Michael. *I* said, "Look it, Michael, just because you read something that doesn't mean it's so, because don't forget the FBI is laying traps here." In other words, they're putting out false information, uh, to— to —to see who corrects it, *you* know. In other words who— who— who really would know, who— who does it correct, *you* know. But you ordered the— the— the parachutes from somewhere else?

[01:50:16] **Walt:** Skhomish *[sic—Snohomish]*.

[01:50:17] **Carl:** Yeah. Okay. Uh, and you had to wait, uh, for a while now. Once time passed, let's say a couple of hours, and they got the money together. Um, how did they bring you the money? Did they bring you the money separately from the parachutes or— or did— did— did they say, "Well, okay. We've got the stuff up here, um—"

[01:50:44] **Walt**: The chutes come first.

[01:50:45] **Carl**: The chutes came first.

[01:50:47] **Walt**: Yeah.

[01:50:48] **Carl**: Okay. Then how did you actually get the money? *I* mean, did a— did a stewardess bring it to you or— It would not seem to me that— that you would want a guy to bring—

[01:51:03] **Walt**: No. Yeah. No, there was no— no— nobody that was— no mechanics in suits or anything like that that brought *me* the money right there. *It's*— *they* brought *it* to the front right there, and then *I* got *it*. *It* was brought back to *me*. ***Use of the phrase "right there" in a threatening discussion.***

[01:51:20] **Carl**: Okay. And who brought it back to you?

[01:51:23] **Walt**: One of the ladies, the stewardess.

[01:51:25] **Carl**: Okay. One of the ladies brought it back. Oh, okay. Now, it's getting to—to where it's time to go an— and you tell the— you tell the, um, uh, stewardesses that, uh, you tell them what?

[01:51:45] **Walt**: Tell them *we're* going to Reno.

[01:51:48] **Carl**: Well—

[01:51:50] **Walt**: Oh, and what else to— to fly?

[01:51:52] **Carl**: Well, But *I* mean the people got off.

[01:51:55] **Walt**: Yeah. Happy Thanksgiving.

[01:51:57] **Carl:** Right. Uh, did— did you make kind of an issue out of that, or did you just— just say, "Well, this is where the people get off," or, "This is where we part company," or—?

[01:52:12] **Walt:** No, *I* was asked, "Can they get off?"

[01:52:14] **Carl:** Okay. And you said yes?

[01:52:19] **Walt:** "Yeah, Happy Thanksgiving."

[01:52:20] **Carl:** Yeah. Um, and at what point did you offer something?

[01:52:29] **Walt:** What, the four thousand dollars?

[01:52:30] **Carl:** Yeah.

[01:52:32] **Walt:** Right there. *I* don't know how much *it* was right there. *It* was a handful of money and *I* just offered *it* to a stewardess. *Use of the phrase "right there" in a threatening discussion.*

[01:52:38] **Carl:** Yeah. And you said the same thing that you said on the Eight Mile Road job.

[01:52:46] **Walt:** Yeah, the insurance'll cover *it*.

[01:52:50] **Carl:** Uh, didn't you say something like, uh, "You've been nice to me"?

[01:52:57] **Walt:** Yeah, kindness.

[01:52:59] **Carl:** Huh?

[01:53:00] **Walt:** Well, polite and kindness.

[01:53:03] **Carl:** Uh, Okay. An—, and she wouldn't take it and you told her the insurance would cover it?

[01:53:10] **Walt:** Yeah.

[01:53:12] **Carl:** Uh—

[01:53:12] **Walt:** The one on Eight Mile Road took *it* *[clears throat]*.

[01:53:15] **Carl:** Yeah, yeah. And they took it back from her, too, though, you know.

[01:53:19] **Walt:** No.

[01:53:19] **Carl:** Oh, they didn't?

[01:53:21] **Walt:** Uh-uh. *She* said, uh— *I* said, "Here." And *it* was a hundred dollars or more, <u>*you* know</u>.

[01:53:28] **Carl:** Uh-huh.

[01:53:29] **Walt:** And, uh, *she* tucked *it* down in her brassiere. So later on, what— what come out in the newspapers that, uh, uh, that *I* even offered *her* a ten-dollar tip, but *I* know *it* was over a hundred.

[01:53:47] **Carl:** Yeah. Okay.

[01:53:47] **Walt:** So *she* could disprove of what *I* said, <u>*you* know</u>.

[01:53:51] **Carl:** Yeah.

[01:53:53] **Walt:** <u>Right there</u>— but *she* kept *it*.
Use of the phrase "right there" in a nonthreatening discussion.

[01:53:55] **Carl:** Okay. Didn't she come and visit you in jail?

[01:53:59] **Walt:** Yeah.

[01:54:03] **Carl:** Yeah. Did she say anything then?

[01:54:07] **Walt:** Nothing about the money right there. *She* said, "*I* wish *I* could have met *you* under different circumstances." *Use of the phrase "right there" in a nonthreatening discussion.*

[01:54:12] **Carl:** Yeah. Okay. Um, okay. Can you think of anything up— up to this point that, uh— that we've missed? *I* mean something that pops into your head that— that you did or said or somebody else said or— or somebody on the airplane did something, can you 'member any— anything?

[01:54:34] **Walt:** No.

[01:54:34] **Carl:** Nothing about, on the airplane, that was at all unusual or that somebody said or that the stewardess said or anything like that?

[01:54:43] **Walt:** No.

[01:54:45] **Carl:** Okay. *[clears throat]* So now—

[01:54:47] **Walt:** *I* can't— *I* can't remember that much. Right there, uh, on that Eight Mile Road job right there, *I* had everything under control, you know. *I* knew *I* was gonna go out in the car. *I* was gonna drive off and, uh, uh, everything right there. *I* can remember that better because *I* wasn't as scared. *Use of the phrase "right there" in a nonthreatening discussion.*

[01:55:06] **Carl:** Yeah.

[01:55:06] **Walt:** Over here, right there, fuck. *Use of the phrase "right there" in a threatening discussion.*

[01:55:11] **Carl:** Okay. *[laughs]* So now, the airplane takes off—

[01:55:15] **Walt:** *I* thought *I* had bit off more than *I* could chew.

[01:55:18] **Carl:** Uh, yeah. *I* can— *I* can understand that, you know. *I* mean that's— that's what *I*'m saying. *I*— *I* don't think you understand how— how, uh, big this— this actually was, you know. People just thinking about ju-ju-just what had happened, it just seemed like it was beyond human capability, you know.

[01:55:44] **Walt:** Yeah, *it* was beyond my comprehension.

[01:55:49] **Carl:** *[laughs]* Yeah. Okay. So—

[01:55:51] **Walt:** Like *I*'m gonna wake up and *it*'s, *I*'m a dream.

[01:55:54] **Carl:** Yeah. So they get the airplane, they're getting ready. They take off, and they've changed stewardesses now. There's, there's just one stewardess on the airplane.

[01:56:11] **Walt:** *They* all looked the same to *me*, Charlie.

[01:56:13] **Carl:** Yeah.

[01:56:13] **Walt:** But there was, there were just the one. And, uh, um, anyway—

[01:56:19] **Walt:** Told 'em all, "Get forward. Go in the cockpit."

[01:56:22] **Carl:** Yeah. She's the one that, um—she's the one that, uh, told you, uh, or walked back to the back door and said, "Well, maybe—" *I*—*I*— *I* don't know what she said, "To open it just follow those instructions," er— or whatever else.

[01:56:40] **Walt:** Yeah. *It*'s written right on the door.

[01:56:41] **Carl:** Yeah. Um, Okay. So, it's— *I*— *I* guess it's dark now or getting— getting dark. And, uh, the airplane's taken off and uh, um, you—you— she takes you back there and shows you how to open that door or where the directions are. And you start— Now, what— what's your first thing that you do that you can think of, first thing that, uh, you can remember doing?

[01:57:17] **Walt:** Put a rubber band around *my* glasses to hold them on *my* head.

[01:57:22] **Carl:** Oh, okay. Where did you get the rubber bands from?

[01:57:25] **Walt:** From *my* pocket.

[01:57:26] **Carl:** Okay.

[01:57:29] **Walt:** So *I*'d have goggles going out.

[01:57:31] **Carl:** Yeah. Um, by the way, did they stay on?

[01:57:36] **Walt:** No.

[01:57:39] **Carl:** *[laughs]* Okay. Um, all right. So um, you did that, now at some point you start examining the, uh, the parachutes or the money or something. Um, did you even open the bag and look in to see if there was money in it?

[01:58:01] **Walt:** Yeah.

[01:58:02] **Carl:** Well, yeah.

[01:58:02] **Walt:** Put some in *my* uh, put— took *my* belt from around *my* waist, tied *it* around *my* raincoat, put the money in there, *I* buttoned *it* all the way up to *my* neck.

[01:58:15] **Carl:** And then put the parachute on?

[01:58:17] **Walt:** Yeah.

[01:58:19] **Carl:** Um, and— but you'd already, um, opened the, uh— opened the other chute, too.

[01:58:28] **Walt:** Yeah.

[01:58:30] **Carl:** And, um— Okay. So, uh, um, nobody from the cockpit had ever come out of the cockpit, other— other than the stewardesses going in and out? None of the— none of the men, you never seen any of the pilots or co-pilots or anything like that?

[01:58:53] **Walt:** *I*'m quite sure *they* were peeking out, <u>you know</u>, *I* mean for that.

[01:58:56] **Carl:** Yeah. Well, they might have been. Yeah.

[01:58:58] **Walt:** Yeah.

[01:58:59] **Carl:** *I* wouldn't be surprised. Um, and when you took off, you had to have told them where to take the airplane?

[01:59:09] **Walt:** Yeah.

[01:59:12] **Carl:** And you give 'em instructions for how high and other things, right?

[01:59:17] **Walt:** Yeah.

[01:59:19] **Carl:** Uh, how did you do that?

[01:59:22] **Walt:** *I* asked, "How slow can *you* fly this?"

[01:59:26] **Carl:** Okay.

[01:59:27] **Walt:** "What— what stall speed?" *you know*.

[01:59:28] **Carl:** Yeah.

[01:59:30] **Walt:** "Wanna go above that."

[01:59:31] **Carl:** Yeah. But not— not very much?

[01:59:35] **Walt:** Yeah.

[01:59:35] **Carl:** Yeah. Did you— did you actually ever use the intercom, for example— *I*'m just giving you examples. Uh, did you—you— did— you nev— you never talked personally, you said, to the cockpit crew?

[01:59:49] **Walt:** No, *I* talked to the, uh, stewardess and stewardess relayed the message to the cockpit.

[01:59:53] **Carl:** And— and they were always verbal?

[01:59:56] **Walt:** Verbal, nothing was written.

[01:59:58] **Carl:** Okay. But one time, you said that you wrote something on a— on a napkin.

[02:00:02] **Walt:** I scribble when I'm nervous.

[02:00:04] **Carl:** Oh, okay. But *I* mean, was it— you were just scribbling on a napkin, but was it actually about the hijacking or you were just—

[02:00:10] **Walt:** Nothing. Just scribbling.

[02:00:11] **Carl:** Oh, you were just doodling on the napkin?

[02:00:13] **Walt:** Yeah.

[02:00:14] **Carl:** Okay. So you don't even know what it was.

[02:00:18] **Walt:** No.

[02:00:19] **Carl:** Okay. Anything since we've talked on how you told 'em to get the parachutes and the money, uh, you wanted the— the money in twenty-dollar bills and— and what not?

[02:00:33] **Walt:** Used. Used twenty-dollar bills.

[02:00:36] **Carl:** Oh, you wanted all used ones.

[02:00:38] **Walt:** Yeah.

[02:00:38] **Carl:** Okay.

[02:00:40] **Walt:** *I* didn't get all used ones. But *I* got uh— a lot of 'em were used.

[02:00:45] **Carl:** Did you actually order the wrist— the wrist altimeter when you ordered the—?

[02:00:51] **Walt:** *I* got a— *I* got a stopwatch.

[02:00:53] **Carl:** Yeah, but— but did you tell 'em to send a wrist altimeter, or was this just somethin' they sent ya, the stopwatch?

[02:01:00] **Walt:** Uh, *I—* *I* can't recall that, Charlie.

[02:01:02] **Carl:** Okay.

[02:01:04] **Walt:** <u>Right there</u>, but *I* did get a, uh— a stopwatch. *Use of the phrase "right there" in a threatening discussion.*

[02:01:06] **Carl:** Yeah.

[02:01:07] **Walt:** *I* don't know where everybody's coming up with an altimeter because, uh, *I* had no faith in them.

[02:01:14] **Carl:** Did you see— did you see any passengers or anything that— that looked funny to you? <u>You know</u>, like— like in the— in the restaurant there, the cowboy hat and the suit, and they drove away in a dump truck. Was there anything at all that you remember on the airplane that— just even for an instance, you said—

[02:01:33] **Walt:** Charlie, *I* saw but *I* didn't see.

[02:01:36] **Carl:** Okay.

[02:01:36] **Walt:** *You* know, *I* mean, uh—

[02:01:38] **Carl:** Oh, that's all right. No, that—

[02:01:39] **Walt:** The vision— vision was just— people were unimportant.

[02:01:45] **Carl:** And— and the only thing you were carrying is a raincoat and a briefcase.

[02:01:49] **Walt:** Yeah.

[02:01:51] **Carl:** Now, where did you carry your typed note? In your suit pocket or—?

[02:01:57] **Walt:** Inside pocket of the suit.

[02:01:58] **Carl:** Inside pocket of the suit.

[02:02:01] **Walt:** Yeah.

[02:02:02] **Carl:** Uh, now, when you gave that note to the stewardess, that was Schaffner was her name, was that the hardest thing that you had done so far, because that starts the whole thing?

[02:02:16] **Walt:** That— that committed me.

[02:02:17] **Carl:** Yeah, right. In other words that— that— Yeah, you know, you were always saying, "Well, I can back out now," but by the time that, uh, you did that or when you did it, uh, backing out was getting a little bit late right then.

[02:02:31] **Walt:** Well, what was going through my mind all this time right there is smoking cigarettes, uh, scribbling on the napkin, and if I get killed, am I gonna go to hell? *Use of the phrase "right there" in a threatening discussion.*

[02:02:42] **Carl:** How did you order the parachutes? Did you say, "I want four parachutes"? Or did you order two reserves and two backpacks?

[02:02:50] **Walt:** Two reserves and two backpacks.

[02:02:52] **Carl:** Okay. So they give you what you wanted?

[02:02:55] **Walt:** Yeah.

[02:02:55] **Carl:** Basically, one of them was just a— a dummy thing. When you got to Sea-Tac, cuz that's only a twenty-five-minute trip, *you know*, from Portland. Uh, they— they, um, did you tell them to circle until they got the stuff ready or what? Because you— you had to circle while they were getting the money and getting the parachutes and stuff.

[02:03:20] **Walt:** Yeah. *I* just was, uh, was wishing, *I* was hoping that, Ar— that *it* wasn't a guy like, Art was, the pilot.

[02:03:27] **Carl:** Why is that?

[02:03:29] **Walt:** *It*'d be a kamikaze flight—

[02:03:32] **Carl:** *[laughs]* Oh, you mean he was— Yeah. *I*'m gonna crash the airplane and kill everybody on board?

[02:03:39] **Walt:** Right. *[laughs]* One time, *I* asked Art many, many years ago before all this happened, *I* said, "What would happen if somebody hijacked *you*, *you know*, in the airplane?"

[02:03:51] **Carl:** Uh-huh.

[02:03:52] **Walt:** And Art told *me*, *he* said, "That guy would be in a lot of fuckin' trouble."

[laughter]

[02:04:00] **Carl:** Why? Because he was gonna— he was gonna take her down with all hands on—

[02:04:04] **Walt:** Yeah.

[laughter]

[02:04:10] **Carl:** So you— you— you thought of— actually thought of that?

[02:04:14] **Walt:** Yeah, in the back of *my* mind, yeah.

[02:04:16] **Carl:** Did the stewardesses ever look scared to you?

[02:04:20] **Walt:** No, *they* were well composed.

[02:04:23] **Carl:** They— they— Okay, they were well composed. Okay. Um, wha—

[02:04:30] **Walt:** *I* think *it* surprised *them* as much as *it* did *me* that this had happened.

[02:04:33] **Carl:** And you didn't know their names, so what did you call them, you were— when you wanted them to— when you wanted to say something to them, how did you— how did you address them?

[02:04:41] **Walt:** Young lady.

[02:04:43] **Carl:** Young lady?

[02:04:43] **Walt:** Yeah.

[02:04:44] **Carl:** Okay. Did— did you do that every time?

[02:04:48] **Walt:** Yeah.

[02:04:50] **Carl:** And you're not sure if you ordered a wrist altimeter 'cause you really didn't trust them?

[02:04:55] **Walt:** No, *I* didn't trust them.

[02:04:56] **Carl:** But— but for some reason or other, they sent you a stopwatch *[crosstalk]*.

[02:05:00] **Walt:** A stopwatch. But *I* would— would of liked to have an altimeter now. But *I'm* thinking of *it* now.

[02:05:08] **Carl:** Yeah.

[02:05:09] **Walt:** <u>Right there</u> because *I* could check the altitude before *I* exited the aircraft.
Use of the phrase "right there" in a threatening discussion.

[02:05:13] **Carl:** Yeah, that's about all it would be good for—

[02:05:15] **Walt:** Yeah.

[02:05:15] **Carl:** —is— is knowing if they really were at ten thousand and— and, uh, <u>you know</u>, and the elevation down there was, uh, <u>you know</u>, seven—eight hundred feet or whatever. <u>You know</u>, that— that's all it would have been good for. After that here, you couldn't see the thing out there anyway.

[02:05:32] **Walt:** Yeah.

[02:05:33] **Carl:** You're circling over Sea-Tac there and finally they say, "Okay, uh, we got the— got the parachutes and the money," so now you gotta land and— and fuel up and, uh, yeah. Had you already told them by this time that you gotta go to Mexico?

[02:05:52] **Walt:** Uh, *I* don't remember.

[02:05:54] **Carl:** Okay.

[02:05:56] **Walt:** Uh, but *it* come up somewhere in the conversation.

[02:05:59] **Carl:** Yeah, and while you were on the airplane, all you did was drink booze and smoke cigarettes.

[02:06:06] **Walt:** Yeah, a lot of cigarettes.

[02:06:08] **Carl:** Yeah. Um, okay. So the airplane, now they tell you they're— you're gonna land. Did you ever remember giving instructions to where they should park the— the fuel truck?

[02:06:21] **Walt:** No.

[02:06:22] **Carl:** You don't remember that?

[02:06:24] **Walt:** *I* couldn't remember *I* had a brown suit 'til the next day, and *I* even got one hanging in my closet.

[02:06:29] **Carl:** Yeah. *[laughs]* Well, *I* told ya. *I* says *I* saw a picture of you wea— and you're wearing a brown suit, but then— then you talked me out of it because *I*'m color-blind. And *I*— *I* thought myself, "Well, you know, it looked brown to me, but maybe it wasn't," you know. *[laughs]*

[02:06:48] **Walt:** Yeah. *[laughs]*

[Long pause 02:06:53]

[02:07:05] **Walt:** And there's a lot of things, too, right there that, uh, *I*'m quite sure. Because *I*— *I* haven't followed it at all right there. Once— once *it* was over, *it* was out of *my* mind totally.

Use of the phrase "right there" in a threatening discussion.

[02:07:16] **Carl:** Yeah.

[02:07:16] **Walt:** <u>Right there</u>, *I* mean totally out of *my* mind.

[02:07:19] **Carl:** Did you—

[02:07:19] **Walt:** And there's one thing that, uh, *I*'m quite sure of, <u>right there</u>, that the, uh, government itself that investigated this put a lot of disinformation into that. *Use of the phrase "right there" in a threatening discussion.*

[02:07:30] **Carl:** Oh, *I* think they did, too. *I* think they did, too. They say none of the money was ever spent, and you were dead. And *I* think they did this to egg people on. <u>You know</u>, somebody with an ego and call 'em up and say, "Hey, *I*'m Cooper, and *I*'m not dead." <u>You know</u>, what *I*'m say— *I* think that's why they, um— How long did you think— do you think you were at the truck stop? It took— it took Don a while to get there. He had to be a hundred— a hundred and fifty or two hundred miles away, right?

[02:08:03] **Walt:** Yeah. <u>Right there</u>. How long was *I* there? At least two and a half to three hours. And— and this is a rough guess, though. *Use of the phrase "right there" in a threatening discussion.*

[02:08:09] **Carl:** Yeah. Oh, *I*— *I* know, yeah.

[02:08:11] **Walt:** Yeah. *I* had no wristwatch that went off.

[02:08:16] **Carl:** Yeah. Okay. Hey, here's something *I* thought of. *I* don't— don't even have it wrote down. *I* was thinking the other day, um, you know the guy that, um, uh— the guy with— that was playing in the band and had the dump truck. When you called him over to— to give the— the directions to Baker *[sic—Brennan]*, did— weren't you listening to what he told Dave *[sic—Don]*? You know *I* mean on— on, uh—

[02:08:44] **Walt:** No.

[02:08:46] **Carl:** You weren't?

[02:08:47] **Walt:** No. Right there. *I* didn't know where the fuck *I* was. *It* wouldn't make no difference. **Use of the phrase "right there" in a threatening discussion.**

[02:08:51] **Carl:** Yeah.

[02:08:54] **Walt:** Directions wouldn't mean anything to *me.*

[02:08:56] **Carl:** But like you did hear, uh— you did hear him say it. You just forgot, because you must have been standing right there.

[02:09:01] **Walt:** Yeah. Uh, *I* mean *I* was uninterested, *you* know.

[02:09:05] **Carl:** Okay.

[02:09:07] **Walt:** *I* was just— uh, *I* got the phone back, *I* just was talking to Don, right there. *I* said, "Did *you* understand everything?" You know. **Use of the phrase "right there" in a threatening discussion.**

[02:09:13] **Carl:** Uh-huh.

[02:09:14] **Walt:** Because *he* still didn't believe what was going on.

[02:09:16] **Carl:** Still didn't?

[02:09:17] **Walt:** No-o.

[02:09:21] **Carl:** *[laughs]* What else— what else— In other words, did you have to tell him, "Now look, this is true. Don't— don't go back to sleep er— er," you know, I mean, "come down here for sure and get me"?

[02:09:34] **Walt:** Yeah. Well, *he* was gonna come back, you know. *He* was gonna get *me*, but *he* still couldn't, uh, you know— I said *I* did *it*, and *he* said, "*You* did what?" You know, I said that's when *I* talked to *him* at first. But *he* was gonna come and get *me* as if *my* car broke down or something.

[02:09:51] **Carl:** Yeah. Yeah. Was— was your leg throbbing?

[02:09:55] **Walt:** Oh, everything, yeah. *I* mean *my* leg, *my* head, uh. *My* hands are shaking. *My* sore leg right there as *I* could feel *it* swelling up.

Use of the phrase "right there" in a threatening discussion.

[02:10:05] **Carl:** Yeah. Did you have to take your shoe off, or would it still be on?

[02:10:10] **Walt:** No. *I* never take *my* shoe off because then *you* couldn't get *it* back on.

[02:10:13] **Carl:** Oh, okay.

[02:10:15] **Walt:** Then *you* draw a lot of attention, you know, walking around barefooted in November.

[02:10:20] **Carl:** Yeah. And *I* keep going back— *I* keep going back to the— the truck stop, where— where you walked into. Um, was there— w-w-was there a bar in that truck stop by any chance?

[02:10:38] **Walt:** No. *It* was a restaurant.

[02:10:40] **Carl:** Just— just a plain truck stop with a restaurant.

[02:10:43] **Walt:** Yeah. Oh, another thing <u>right there</u> before *I* forget, <u>right there</u>. <u>You know</u> how a beet looks? *Use of the phrase "right there" in a threatening discussion.*

[02:10:50] **Carl:** A beet?

[02:10:53] **Walt:** Yeah, *you* know when *you* peel a beet, how red *it* looks?

[02:10:55] **Carl:** Yeah.

[02:10:56] **Walt:** That's the way *my* face looked when *I* looked in the mirror. After— after *it* all happened, right, with that— that fuckin' hit— that rain hitting *me* in the fuckin' face.

[02:11:05] **Carl:** You mean, when— when you were in the, um, in the bathroom in the airport— or wait a minute. You mean—

[02:11:13] **Walt:** No, no. When *I* ended *it* in the aircraft.

[02:11:15] **Carl:** Yeah. And *I* mean you looked that way when you got to the, uh, uh— what do you call— the truck stop?

[02:11:22] **Walt:** That restaurant there. Yeah.

[02:11:24] **Carl:** Did anybody say anything?

[02:11:26] **Walt:** Uh, yeah, *it* was mentioned *I* think, *they* said, "Your face is real red," <u>you know</u>?

[02:11:31] **Carl:** Uh-huh.

[02:11:32] **Walt:** And *I* didn't pay any attention. <u>You know</u>, *I* mean *I*— *it*'s a question *you* don't answer.

[02:11:38] **Carl:** Yeah. Yeah.

[02:11:40] **Walt:** *You* can't say, "Well, *I* jumped out in the fuckin' rain," or something.

[02:11:48] **Carl:** *[laughs]* Yeah. Um, was it raining as you walked to the— to the truck stop?

[02:11:52] **Walt:** Yeah and misty— like a mist.

[02:11:56] **Carl:** More mist than— than hard rain?

[02:12:09] **Walt:** Yeah.

[02:12:02] **Carl:** Okay. Was the wind blowing down on the ground, like a— <u>you know</u>—?

[02:12:08] **Walt:** *It* wasn't a calm day.

[02:12:11] **Carl:** Could you see when you were gonna hit the tree? *I* mean, were you really moving over the ground?

[02:12:17] **Walt:** *I* couldn't notice that— that— that much.

[02:12:21] **Carl:** But did you s— did you see— see the tree before you hit it?

[02:12:25] **Walt:** No. *I* hit the tree first.

[02:12:27] **Carl:** You hit the tree first?

[02:12:29] **Walt:** Yeah.

[02:12:30] **Carl:** *I* know *I*, uh— in— in— a night jump, *I* never seen anything till *I* hit the ground, you know?

[02:12:34] **Walt:** Yeah.

[02:12:35] **Carl:** Maybe— maybe *I* seen something six feet before *I* hit it but, *I* mean it— it— *you*'re talking about a quarter of a second or somethin', you know. Um, okay. So now, you're— you're plowing down through this tree. Limbs breakin' and all that crap.

[02:12:52] **Walt:** Yeah. The only fuckin' dead tree in the forest, and *I* happen to get to *it*. *[laughs]*

[02:12:55] **Carl:** *[laughs]* Was it hilly, where you hit, or just kind of flat?

[02:13:02] **Walt:** Flat.

[02:13:03] **Carl:** Pretty flat.

[02:13:04] **Walt:** Yeah.

[02:13:06] **Carl:** Okay. So when you, uh— when you walked out, it wasn't too really— too bad a walkin'.

[02:13:12] **Walt:** No, not bad at all right there. *I* mean there was a little rise right there when *I*— *I* mean not a big rise. You know what *I* mean?
Use of the phrase "right there" in a threatening discussion.

[02:13:20] **Carl:** Yeah.

[02:13:20] **Walt:** But when *I* got to the rise, *I* could see the lights on the highway. You know? Cars going.

[02:13:25] **Carl:** Yeah. Um— Okay, um. And you could see the cars, though, before you landed on the ground, right?

[02:13:37] **Walt:** Yeah.

[02:13:39] **Carl:** It— it's a wonder you knew which way you were going, though.

[02:13:42] **Walt:** *I* didn't. <u>Right there</u>, *I* seen cars. *I* seen, <u>you know</u>— there was in the distance.
Use of the phrase "right there" in a threatening discussion.

[02:13:48] **Walter:** Yeah.

[02:13:51] **Carl:** So, how did you know which way to even walk in the first place?

[02:13:56] **Walt:** <u>Right there</u> towards the direction <u>right there</u> where *I* assumed the cars were going. *It* was like a little knoll. <u>You know</u>?

[02:14:02] **Carl:** Yeah.

[02:14:03] **Walt:** Yeah, no bigger — *It* was a slope— slope of the ground. *I* just got up there and then— about no higher than a little fuckin' tree stump, <u>you know</u>.

[02:14:10] **Carl:** Yeah.

[02:14:11] **Walt:** And then *I* could see in the distance, <u>right there</u>, traffic.

[02:14:15] **Carl:** Holy mackerel, that was, um— that's amazing.

[02:14:20] **Walt:** Yeah.

[02:14:22] **Carl:** You see— you see if you'da landed— if you'da jumped two minutes before you did, you would have been in— right in the middle of a huge forest.

[02:14:31] **Walt:** *I* woulda been in somethin'. *[laughs]*

[02:14:33] **Carl:** Yeah, yeah. You— you've landed now and you— *you know* your leg is in bad shape, uh, twisted ankle or something. *You know— you know* it's gonna be, *you know—*

[02:14:45] **Walt:** Yes, broke.

[02:14:47] **Carl:** Yeah. Uh, could you tell it was broke or—?

[02:14:49] **Walt:** Yeah, *it* hurt.

[02:14:51] **Carl:** Okay. Um, uh, so then, you— you, um— you buried your chute.

[02:15:01] **Walt:** No.

[02:15:05] **Carl:** So you didn't bury it?

[02:15:06] **Walt:** No, *I* just gathered it all up right there and put *it* like in the backpack and left *it* there with the broken trees. Threw a few branches on top of *it*. *Use of the phrase "right there" in a threatening discussion.*

[02:15:15] **Carl:** Well, that's what *I* mean, You— you didn't bury it by digging a hole. You just threw— threw what was there on top of it.

[02:15:22] **Walt:** Yeah.

[02:15:23] **Carl:** So, um— um— okay. So now, you, uh, uh— is the— when you're walkin' out to begin with, is the money still like, uh, uh, around your chest and your raincoat on?

[02:15:39] **Walt:** No. *I*— *I* had to, uh, clean off myself off, took the raincoat off, put the money in the raincoat.

[02:15:46] **Carl:** Okay.

[02:15:47] **Walt:** Had like a bundle.

[02:15:48] **Carl:** Yeah. And, uh, were your— were your pants or anything, torn or anything from hitting all those tree—dead limbs?

[02:15:56] **Walt:** No.

[02:15:57] **Carl:** Really?

[02:15:58] **Walt:** Yeah.

[02:15:59] **Carl:** That was amazing.

[02:16:01] **Walt:** Not really, right? Dead trees— how can *you* tear? Anything *you* hit, *you* break.

[02:16:06] **Carl:** Oh, yeah. But if they were a big limb, somethin' could get caught under there and, uh, you know, under there— well anyway, um, so you walk out and you get to the road and you remember at one point seeing cars going across the bridge, some place.

[02:16:28] **Walt:** Yeah.

[02:16:31] **Carl:** Um—

[02:16:33] **Walt:** The— the, a neon light there at the restaurant.

[02:16:37] **Carl:** Okay.

[02:16:38] **Walt:** *It*'s dark but, you know, *you* can tell and *it*— *it*'s not a town or anything.

[02:16:42] **Carl:** Yeah.

[02:16:43] **Walt:** You know, *it* was just a restaurant there.

[02:16:45] **Carl:** Yeah.

[02:16:46] **Walt:** Maybe a quarter of a mile away.

[02:16:48] **Carl:** Yeah. Okay, now you're walkin' along. You're walkin' along to the restaurant.

[02:16:56] **Walt:** Yeah.

[02:16:57] **Carl:** And you get there, and do you remember anything or you just find a door and go in? Er—

[02:17:03] **Walt:** Yeah, *I* find the door and *I* go in. *I* ordered a cup of coffee. *My* hand's shaking real bad right there. *It*'s spilling right there, so *I* didn't want nobody to see *it*. *Use of the phrase "right there" in a threatening discussion.*

[02:17:13] **Carl:** Uh-huh.

[02:17:14] **Walt:** And *I* got some change from the waitress right there and *I* asked *her* where the telephone was and *I* called up Don. And *I* said, *"I* done *it."* *He* said, *"You* done what?" [Carl interjects: Yeah.] *I* had discussed *it* with *him* before. *Use of the phrase "right there" in a threatening discussion.*

[02:17:28] **Carl:** Did you have to go to the bathroom or anything?

[02:17:32] **Walt:** Oh, fuck yeah. *[laughs]* Yeah, *I* mean *I* was pissing in the woods coming out.

[02:17:42] **Carl:** Oh, yeah.

[02:17:43] **Walt:** Yeah.

[02:17:46] **Carl:** Yeah. Um, okay and there's nothing you can remember. Somebody said your—your face is beet red.

[02:17:52] **Walt:** Yeah. [Carl interjects: Um]

[02:17:53] **Carl:** Um— Do you remember any music playing in that truck stop or anything?

[02:18:00] **Walt:** No. Um, *I* was incoherent pretty near at that time.

[02:18:08] **Carl:** Yeah. Um, boy it's a wonder that when they heard about it, that they didn't say, "Hey, <u>you know</u> somebody seen a guy come in here that, uh," <u>you know</u> it was— <u>you know</u>, yeah, it's almost a wonder that they didn't report somethin'.

[02:18:27] **Walt:** Nobody would believe *it*, Charlie.

[02:18:31] **Carl:** Well, *I* mean.

[02:18:33] **Walt:** *I* couldn't believe *it* myself.

[02:18:36] **Carl:** Yeah, but *I* mean after it— it had happened, <u>you know</u>, every— everybody in the world believed that it happened after it happened.

[02:18:44] **Walt:** *It* just wasn't that noticeable.

[02:18:48] **Carl:** What made you think— just— just what made you think you were at Steven's point and, uh, Cashmere between there, *I* mean what— what gave you the idea that, that's where you were?

[02:19:02] **Walt:** *I* don't know, <u>right there</u>. *I* just figured that's where *I* was, but *I* guess *I* wasn't. *Use of the phrase "right there" in a threatening discussion.*

[02:19:08] **Carl:** But you had to get directions from the— from somebody in the, um, in— in the restaurant in— in the, uh, the truck stop. You had to get directions to tell Don where to come and pick you up.

[02:19:23] **Walt:** *I* give *it* to the guy with the tru— uh, with the dump truck— the telephone. *He* give *him* the directions.

[02:19:29] **Carl:** Oh, he gave you the directions?

[02:19:31] **Walt:** *He* give *it* to Don.

[02:19:33] **Carl:** Ohh. Oh, um—

[02:19:37] **Walt:** That's how come *I* remember *him* good, too, with his fuckin' guitar, cowboy hat, Western gear <u>right there</u> at, uh— *Use of the phrase "right there" in a threatening discussion.*

[02:19:43] **Carl:** Oh, how— how come he was by the, um— how come he was by the telephone?

[02:19:48] **Walt:** 'Cause *I* called *him* over.

[02:19:49] **Carl:** Oh, just to tell him where you were? You just said to, "Come and get me," yeah.

[02:19:52] **Walt:** Yeah, because *I* don't know where *I* was. *He* knew where *we* were.

[02:19:56] **Carl:** Well, yeah, yeah. What's, uh— so you sat there and drank coffee for two and a half hours.

[02:20:03] **Walt:** Yeah, right about that. *It* could have been two and a half hours <u>right there</u>. *Use of the phrase "right there" in a threatening discussion.*

[02:20:07] **Carl:** Yeah.

[02:20:08] **Walt:** *It* could have been an hour, <u>you know</u>—

[02:20:11] **Carl:** Yeah. Well, it had to be, if he lived in Everett at the time.

[02:20:15] **Walt:** No. *He* didn't live in Everett.

[02:20:17] **Carl:** Where did he live?

[02:20:19] **Walt:** Pardon, *he* lived in Seattle.

[02:20:23] **Carl:** Oh, oh, Don lived in Seattle at the time?

[02:20:26] **Walt:** Yeah.

[02:20:27] **Carl:** Oh, okay. So— but it was still a two-hour drive at least down there.

[02:20:32] **Walt:** Yeah.

[02:20:33] **Carl:** Yeah, it was a two-hour drive. It— Do you remember what kind of a car he had at all?

[02:20:40] **Walt:** No. Not at all.

[02:20:43] **Carl:** Okay. Did he— did— did you see him pull up from out? You could see outside and see him pull up, or did he actually have to come in the place and look for you?

[02:20:54] **Walt:** *He* come in the place.

[02:20:56] **Carl:** Okay. And you seen him after he walked in the door?

[02:21:02] **Walt:** Yeah. *He* seen *me* and come walking over to *me*.

[02:21:04] **Carl:** Yeah. Did he order a coffee or anything or he just, uh—?

[02:21:09] **Walt:** *I* don't think— *I* couldn't see— *I* was just staring and numb. *You know* what *I* mean? Staring at the— the, *you know*— they got a menu overhead. *You know* like hotdogs, hamburgers, or whatever *it* is, and *I* was like mesmermized *[sic]* by just staring at that sign.

[long pause 02:21:24]

[02:21:38] **Carl:** How— but how did you— in other words, *I* just— *I* just didn't wake up today and say, "Well, *I* think *I*'ll go to the airport and hijack an airplane," you know. There had to be some— some process that you were thinking about.

[02:21:50] **Walt:** *You* know, well, how did *I* think about hanging *my* tomato plants upside down? *You* know, *it* just come to *my* mind and *I* did *it*.

[02:21:59] **Carl:** But there— there— there was some planning because you handed the first note.

[02:22:05] **Walt:** I didn't even know if I was going— *[crosstalk]*

[02:22:08] **Carl:** *I* know but—

[02:22:09] **Walt:** — if *I* was going to—

[02:22:10] **Carl:** —but you did have a note. You did have a hijacking note, and it was typed. So you had— you had to have typed the note.

[02:22:19] **Walt:** But that still didn't make the— *I* still didn't know if *I* was going through with *it*.

[02:22:24] **Carl:** Well, *I* know, but *I* mean there had— there was a— there was a process.

[02:22:29] **Walt:** There wasn't any process.

[02:22:33] **Carl:** Well, if you typed the note, there had to be something.

[02:22:34] **Walt:** No, *I* would have been better prepared if there was a process.

[02:22:39] **Carl:** But you had— you— you had a note that was typed. You had to go— if you don't type or if you don't have a typewriter, you had to go somewhere and get a typewriter and type that note, even if it was at work, in the office, *you know*, or where you were working you had to say, "Hey, can *I* borrow your typewriter for a minute or something?" *You know*?

[02:22:58] **Walt:** Yeah, *I* rented a typewriter *[clears throat]*.

[02:23:00] **Carl:** You rented—?

[02:23:01] **Walt:** *I* didn't want no typewriter layin' around the house.

[02:23:04] **Carl:** Okay. So there— there is a process. So you— you— you know, you went and you got a typewriter and rented it and you typed the note.

[02:23:13] **Walt:** Yeah, 'cause *I* could—uh, *I*'m not a good typist.

[02:23:16] **Carl:** Well, *I* know.

[02:23:17] **Walt:** But *I* learned typing for Zantop.

[02:23:20] **Carl:** Yeah.

[02:23:20] **Walt:** *You* know, *I* did two-finger typing.

[02:23:22] **Carl:** Well, that's— that's, uh— *I* mean it's a short note. All— all the note said was, uh, um, "*I*'m hijacking this airplane," or something, you know, *I* mean of that effect. But— but you had to have done that. You know *I* mean there had to be a process to where you said— to where you decided and said, "Well, even though *I*'m kind a screwed up," and— it, there ain't a lot of— "*I*'m gonna hijack an airplane." There had to be a point where you decided to do it even if you said, "Well, *I* might back out," but there had to be a point at one— because then you went and you drove your car hundred and fifty miles to Spokane and got a bus ticket, so there had to be some process here.

[02:24:08] **Walt:** *I* was still unaware, Charlie, right there, *I* was just numb in the head. Am *I* gonna do this or aren't *I* gonna do *it*? *Use of the phrase "right there" in a threatening discussion.*

[02:24:19] **Carl:** Yeah.

[02:24:22] **Walt:** Uh— 'cause *you*'re dealing with two personalities. One that does *it* and one that don't want to do *it*.

[02:24:31] **Carl:** Well, one— one that wants to do it and one that— that thinks that it would be prudent not— *[laughs]* not to do it, probably.

[02:24:42] **Walt:** Right, yeah. *[laughs]* Put it that way.

[02:24:43] **Carl:** You know. Yeah. Um—

[02:24:45] **Walt:** In other words, one personality *is* divorced from the other when *you* get into something like this.

[02:24:53] **Carl:** Okay. But one personality, *I* mean, there are two personalities but one of 'em was doing something, because one of 'em rented the typewriter, took it back, <u>you know</u> typed the note, got in the car, drove to Spokane, parked the car there. So see, Walt, there was a thought process here.

[02:25:16] **Walt:** Okay. Well, *you*'ve got *it* then.

[laughter]

[02:25:20] **Carl:** But *I* mean, you see what *I*'m talking about? You're— you are doing things that make sense to do and the— there has to be a thought process here. Um, now what did you do with the, um— the, uh, um—

[02:25:35] **Walt:** *You*'re— *you*'re trying to analyze something that wasn't there. *[laughs]*

[02:25:41] **Carl:** Well, there—there is something there. *I* mean it isn't a baboon doing this. You're doing it, <u>you know</u>? And they—

[02:25:46] **Walt:** Yeah, <u>right there</u>. <u>Right there</u>. *I* mean the individual that did *it*, <u>you know</u>, that's another personality, that had an IQ of minus fifteen. *[laughs]* **Use of the phrase "right there" in a threatening discussion.**

[02:25:57] **Carl:** Well, you can't say that because it worked. You know, *I* mean—

[02:26:03] **Walt:** *[laughs]*

[02:26:06] **Carl:** It's, uh— you know *I* mean it was good enough to work. You did see— you did see the composite picture that was drawn of— of— of Cooper?

[02:26:14] **Walt:** Yeah. *I-I* was real skinny then.

[02:26:18] **Carl:** But that picture doesn't— didn't look anything like you. It looked like Kevin Costner.

[02:26:23] **Walt:** *[laughs]*

[02:26:24] **Carl:** That's who the picture looks like. It— it didn't look like you at all. It had a real high, uh hairline.

[02:26:34] **Walt:** Yeah. And how— how can *you* get a good, uh— good drawing of somebody <u>right there</u> in a dark light? **Use of the phrase "right there" in a threatening discussion.**

[02:26:41] **Carl:** Well, it wasn't always dark, in the airplane. It was— it was dark when you took off at night. But *I* mean before that, it was— it was all daylight.

[02:26:52] **Walt:** Yeah.

[02:26:55] **Carl:** But anyway, just— all— all they had was what the girl described.

[02:27:00] **Walt:** Yeah.

[02:27:02] **Carl:** *You* know, so, um, her description of you wasn't that good. *I* guess.

[02:27:06] **Walt:** No.

[02:27:07] **Carl:** *I* mean didn't— when you looked at it, you— it didn't— that's the one thing that Loretta said, she said, "Well, they couldn't be that far off on the, uh, uh, on— on— on the drawing," and *I* said, "They're always off." *I* said, "Don't you see these drawings and then they catch the guy and the— and the person doesn't look anything like it?" *You* know?

[02:27:27] **Walt:** Yeah. That— that's on television. *You* see that all the time.

[02:27:29] **Carl:** *I*— That's what *I* told her. *I* said— *I* said, "*You* know, they, people, you— you wouldn't believe it." *You* know, their— their eyewitness description is the— the worst kind, *you* know. [Walt interjects: Yeah.] Um, but, anyway, what—

[02:27:42] **Walt:** Just recently, *I* was watching a detective story, and *he* said that eyewitnesses accounts, uh, uh— accounts are the most unreliable.

[02:27:51] **Carl:** Absolutely, and they are, they are. Uh, what color was your suit that you wore that day? Do you remember going way back, what color suits that you had, you know about that time?

[02:28:07] **Walt:** Dark gray, I believe it was.

[02:28:12] **Carl:** Did you— did you ever have a dark brown suit?

[02:28:16] **Walt:** Yeah.

[02:28:19] **Carl:** Could it have been dark bro— brown?

[02:28:22] **Walt:** Sure. 'Cause I know— I remember right there— I bought a pair of, uh, dark, uh, brown shoes to match the suit. *Use of the phrase "right there" in a threatening discussion.*

[02:28:30] **Carl:** Oh, okay.

[02:28:32] **Walt:** So that's the way I remember I had one.

[02:28:34] **Carl:** Okay. Did you know the jumper, E. C., who ultimately found the chutes to be delivered to the plane? In other words, somebody with the initials E. C., I don't know who that is, found the chutes that they took out to the plane?

[02:28:53] **Walt:** Yeah, right there, but it wasn't no E. C. right there. It was L. H. *Use of the phrase "right there" in a threatening discussion.*

[02:28:59] **Carl:** Okay. And did— did you ever talk to him after that, at all? After the, uh, event took place, did— did you and him ever talk? And did he say, "Whatever happens, leave me out of this," or anything— anything like that, for example?

[02:29:18] **Walt:** No.

[02:29:20] **Carl:** You never talked to him since then?

[02:29:21] **Walt:** Uh-uh.

[02:29:22] **Carl:** Okay. How do _you know_ that it was him that— that actually located the— the chutes? How— how did _you know_ that?

[02:29:30] **Walt:** Because _he_'s the one that runs the sports center.

[02:29:33] **Carl:** Okay.

[02:29:37] **Walt:** Because everything was unknown.

[02:29:39] **Carl:** Right. And you never one time, as far as you can remember, seen anything on TV because you didn't have TV at Hartline or you never read anything about it in a newspaper, or— or— or a book or anything like that?

[02:29:59] **Walt:** No.

[02:30:00] **Carl:** And, you—

[02:30:03] **Walt:** _I_ had to drive twenty miles to get a loaf of bread in Hartline. Ya know, _it_'s twenty miles one way and twenty miles back—

[02:30:09] **Carl:** Yeah.

[02:30:11] **Walt:** —right there. *I* mean, *I* wouldn't drive twenty miles for a twenty-five-cent newspaper. *Use of the phrase "right there" in a nonthreatening discussion.*

[02:30:16] **Carl:** Yeah, yeah. Did— Did— Did you ever hear people talking about it? When you went to work on the dam project, did—

[02:30:25] **Walt:** No.

[02:30:26] **Carl:** You never heard anybody say, uh, "God, did you hear what happened, uh, Thanksgiving?" You know?

[02:30:33] **Walt:** Naw. The only thing *they* talked about, right there, *is*, uh, cows. A lot of 'em were ranchers and *they* had cows, and *they* all bought Charolais cows 'cause *they* could, uh-uh, stand the weather. The winter? *Use of the phrase "right there" in a nonthreatening discussion.*

[02:30:48] **Carl:** Uh-huh.

[02:30:48] **Walt:** But then *they* couldn't sell 'em and get a price on 'em 'cause the Charolais right there *is* a big-boned cow. *I* know more about fuckin' cows— *Use of the phrase "right there" in a nonthreatening discussion.*

[02:30:56] **Carl:** *[laughs]*

[02:30:56] **Walt:** —learned at lunchtime than the fuckin' cowboys in the old Western days.

[laughter]

[02:31:06] **Carl:** So, you never really— Is it fair to say, it's hard— This is hard to believe. Is it fair to say that you never knew what a legend that Cooper was?

[02:31:17] **Walt:** No.

[02:31:18] **Carl:** You never knew?

[02:31:21] **Walt:** No, not at all. Why— *I* mean, uh— just, uh, <u>you know</u>.

[02:31:30] **Carl:** Okay, how did you find out even that they were calling you D.B. Cooper?

[02:31:38] **Walt:** Oh, that <u>right there</u>, uh, uh, *I* don't know. ***Use of the phrase "right there" in a threatening discussion.***

[02:31:46] **Carl:** But you— But you did—

[02:31:47] **Walt:** *I* didn't sign on as D.B. Cooper.

[02:31:49] **Carl:** No, *I* know, but you did know, eventually— Eventually at some point of time that somebody, through some way had— had— had changed it to D.B. Cooper.

[02:32:01] **Walt:** Yeah, *it* was a long time afterwards, <u>right there</u>, when *I* just ran across an article in the paper. <u>Right there</u>, and that was, oh shit, maybe six months later or something. [Carl interjects: Yeah.] So, *I* didn't— ***Use of the phrase "right there" in a threatening discussion.***

[02:32:16] **Carl:** Did— Did you read that article?

[02:32:19] **Walt:** Did *I* read *it*?

[02:32:20] **Carl:** Yeah.

[02:32:21] **Walt:** No, *I* glanced through *it*, right there. *I* wanted all that shit out of *my* mind. *Use of the phrase "right there" in a threatening discussion.*

[02:32:25] **Carl:** You just wanted to forget it?

[02:32:28] **Walt:** Yeah.

[02:32:29] **Carl:** Uh. Where were you when you played poker with some of the money? 'Member you said one time you played a little poker somewhere where— *I* thought you said in Idaho?

[02:32:40] **Walt:** Yeah, uh, Wallace, Idaho.

[02:32:43] **Carl:** Wallace, Idaho?

[02:32:44] **Walt:** Yeah.

[02:32:45] **Carl:** How come, uh— How come you still had money then?

[02:32:53] **Walt:** Uh, *I* didn't put everything in the bank. Right there, Wallace, Idaho, right there, uh, all the bars had, uh, three or four poker tables all the time in the back in Idaho. And *I* was going someplace, uh— *I* don't know where the fuck *I* was goin'—goin' to work somewhere in Idaho, right there. Or was *I* going to Montana? Right there— But anyhow, uh, that was, uh, Wallace *is* before *you* cross the, uh, Fourth of July Pass. *Use of the phrase "right there" in a threatening discussion.*

[02:33:25] **Carl:** Okay. Um, did you know any of the guys you were playing poker with or just—

[02:33:32] **Walt:** No.

[02:33:34] **Carl:** You just stopped in there?

[02:33:35] **Walt:** Just come in. Stopped in <u>right there</u>, and, uh, ordered a hamburger and a fuckin' beer. Poker game's going on, *I* says, uh, "*You* got room for one more?" and *they* said, "Yeah," and *I* sat in there. ***Use of the phrase "right there" in a threatening discussion.***

[02:33:48] **Carl:** Oh, okay. Did you win or lose?

[02:33:53] **Walt:** Oh, *I* don't think *I* won anything.

[laughter]

[02:33:57] **Carl:** Okay, uh, and that was about six months or so, did you say after?

[02:35:05] **Walt:** Yeah, right about there.

[02:34:07] **Carl:** Yeah. Are there any slip-ups you made, uh— other— <u>you know</u>, other stuff you did, like writing, uh "Copper" instead of "Cooper," can you think of any slip-ups that you made or something that somebody might remember or, uh— or would be, uh, an unusual, uh, uh, event— <u>You know</u>, like— like the doodling on the napkin, <u>you know</u>, something— Is there any other, um, *I* don't know of what to use— the word "slip-ups," but just, uh— yeah, *I* suppose slip-ups is a good word, if you're writing a thing wrong, or just something that you did or seen somebody do or anything in connection with this thing while you were in the airplane that—that, uh, would be, uh, noticeable?

[02:34:54] **Walt:** No.

[02:34:56] **Carl:** Okay.

[02:34:57] **Walt:** And on that ticket, right there, where *I* wrote "Copper," uh, that wasn't on the airplane ticket, that was on the ticket that *I* was gonna— when *I* carried *my* briefcase aboard. *Use of the phrase "right there" in a threatening discussion.*

[02:35:10] **Carl:** Oh, that ticket? *I* was going to ask you—In fact, *I* think *I* got it in another question. Wh-what do they mean the ticket on carrying the briefcase aboard? What—

[02:35:20] **Walt:** They got little things there— right there when *you* got luggage. Right there— to write your— write your name on something, right there, your carry-on and all that, you know? A little tag. Right there, and that's when *I*, you know, *I* was nervous and *I* put "Cooper" *[sic—in the previous paragraph Walter said Copper, but here he said Cooper]* on the tag, put *it* on *my*, uh, briefcase on the handle. *Use of the phrase "right there" in a threatening discussion.*

[02:35:39] **Carl:** But you never checked it, you held that with you?

[02:35:41] **Walt:** Yeah.

[02:35:43] **Carl:** Well, did the thing go about as you pictured it or, when you— When you first thought of this, did— did— In other words, did you have any image of how this was supposed to go?

[02:35:54] **Walt:** Did *it* come out the way *I* pictured *it*?

[02:35:55] **Carl:** Yeah, yeah.

[02:35:56] **Walt:** Of course not.

[02:35:57] **Carl:** *[laughs]* How did you picture it?

[02:36:01] **Walt:** I didn't know, right there, uh, I had no concept of how it was gonna come out, you know, but I pictured— I just I don't know how I pictured it, but, no, anything that happened to me, and that happened to the plane and the FBI and everything was just, uh— it was— it was as new to me as it was to them. *Use of the phrase "right there" in a threatening discussion.*

[02:36:27] **Carl:** *[laughs]* But— But you had to know that if you hijacked an airplane, you had to jump out of it?

[02:36:31] **Walt:** Yeah, the jumping was nothing, you know.

[02:36:33] **Carl:** Yeah, yeah.

[02:36:35] **Walt:** That night I jumped in, uh, uh Saginaw. Uh, I made—That— that was my third jump that night, and I went over to, uh, what is it, the anemometer that, uh, Sadie had in, uh, his hangar over there, with the wind was blowing, and it was blowing forty-five miles an hour and gusting. So the wind, uh, never bothered me, you know what— what the outside wind's gonna be, you know when I make— 'Cause I made that one and survived it.

[02:37:07] **Carl:** Yeah, of course, you broke a leg, too.

[02:37:09] **Walt:** Yeah, a couple of 'em.

[laughter]

[02:37:10] **Carl:** Yeah, yeah, two of 'em.

[long silence]

[02:37:25] **Carl:** How— How long did you sleep with the money under the bed in Hartland *[sic— Hartline]*? *I* mean, how many days or a week or—

[02:37:33] **Walt:** About two weeks ~~right there~~, till *I*, uh, was able to get up ~~right there~~ and walk around and go— ~~You know~~, *I* didn't know what *I* was gonna do with *it*, till *I* decided ~~right there~~, *I* better go to Vancouver— **Use of the phrase "right there" in a threatening discussion.**

[02:37:45] **Carl:** Uh-huh.

[02:37:47] **Walt:** —and, uh, when *I* crossed— Not— *I* didn't cross the border at Blaine, there was another place east of Blaine, where *you* cross the border, where there's no, uh, custom agents. *You* just go across the border and that's at Sumac *[sic—Sumas?]*.

[02:38:09] **Carl:** That was just a deal that only the locals knew about.

Walter: Yeah.

[02:38:12] **Walt:** *I* couldn't believe *I* did *it* ~~right there~~. *I* pulled out the money and *I* looked at *it* looked at *it* put *it* and *I* still couldn't believe *I* did *it*. *I* had to pull *it* out again. *[*Added via video.]* **Use of the phrase "right there" in a threatening discussion.**

[02:38:15] **Carl:** Yeah. Um— Well, *I* tell you there was three people that— that *I* know, uh, that believed you did it, me, Loretta, Zephie, and McCusker—*I-I* didn't know about Zephie till you told me a couple of days ago, but— but, um— So, that's what— that's what kind of impact that you made on people that— *I* don't know how many other people, *I* only know those three and there might have been others, but— but, *I— I— I* never heard anybody else use anybody else, but your name. In other words, uh, everybody thought that— Well, course these are people that *I* know, too, *you know*, but *I* didn't know Zephie.

But, anyway, uh, McCusker and Loretta and me, when we heard it, *I* said, "That was Peca, that had to be Peca," *you know*, but then *I* didn't do anything with it for years. *I* didn't even know you were there, *you know*, at all until *I* found out that you were there at that time and that and— *I* said, "God damn," *you know*. Maybe, it was, and then other things started, *you know* falling into place and shit like that, but, um, uh—Well, how long did the— after that did the— was it before the dam project stopped or you weren't working there anymore?

[02:39:37] **Walt:** No, soon as work broke anywhere else *right there*, *I* quit the dam, and they're fuckin' terrible places to work. ***Use of the phrase "right there" in a nonthreatening discussion.***

[02:39:44] **Carl:** Oh, it was?

[02:39:45] **Walt:** Oh, yeah, there's— fuckin', uh, water up to your ankle all the time, to curing the concrete *right there*, and, uh, there's carpenters twelve inches on center, *you know* and *you*'re trying to drag a lead <u>right there</u> to do some welding across all that shit <u>right there</u>. *It*, uh, wasn't— Dams are no good to work on. A lot of people like dams because *it*'s steady employment. ***Use of the phrase "right there" in a nonthreatening discussion.***

[02:40:10] **Carl:** Uh-huh. Now, last, yeah, the— they last seven, eight years.

[02:40:15] **Walt:** Yeah.

[02:40:15] **Carl:** A lot of times, so, yeah. Ah, okay, so, as quick as other things would happen, you'd— you'd go to work other places.

[02:40:25] **Walt:** Yeah.

[02:40:26] **Carl:** Then— then, did you ever— did you come back and work on the dam, some more or—?

[02:40:29] **Walt:** Yeah.

[02:40:30] **Carl:** Oh, okay. They'd let you come back and work again?

[02:40:34] **Walt:** Sure, <u>right there</u> *they* had to call in the hall for men, *you know*. ***Use of the phrase "right there" in a nonthreatening discussion.***

[02:40:37] **Carl:** Yeah.

[02:40:37] **Walt:** And there was no work nowhere else. Then, *you*'d go out to the dam. *We* had our own dry shed on the dam. *You know*, the Iron Workers.

[02:40:45] **Carl:** Yeah.

[02:40:46] **Walt:** So, uh, one time *I* walked in there, and *they* said, uh, "Things must be, uh, tough at the hall, Walt's back here again."

[02:40:55] **Carl:** *[laughs]* Okay, that's— that's—

[02:41:00] **Walt:** *I*—

[02:41:01] **Carl:** Huh?

[02:41:02] **Walt:** Here's something that happened at the dam, too. Uh, over there, *they* got what *they* call bell boys. The cranes are Worleys, <u>*you* know</u>, big cranes.

[02:41:10] **Carl:** Yeah.

[02:41:11] **Walt:** The bell boys signal the crane, how *you* want **it** in, 'cause the operator can't see.

[02:41:14] **Carl:** Uh-huh.

[02:41:14] **Walt:** *They* got the bell boys doing this.

[02:41:16] **Carl:** Uh-huh.

[02:41:17] **Walt:** And, *they*— *they* did *it* in, uh— The crane and the bell boys work for— Oh, shit, different trades, <u>*you* know</u>. So, this foreman tells *me* *I* got a welding machine on this one tier. And *he* says, uh, "Get the welding machine outa there." Well, *I* couldn't get the bell boy, <u>*you* know</u>, 'cause *they* had other commitments at the time.

[02:41:36] **Carl:** Uh-huh.

[02:41:38] **Walt:** So at lunchtime *he* says, "*I* told *you* to get the crane duh— uh— that welding machine over to another tier." So, *I*'m sitting there, thinking *it* sort of pisses *me* off. So, after lunch *he* says, "Don't *you* forget to do that now." *I* says, "No, *I* won't forget *it*." *I* pushed the fuckin' welding machine off the fuckin' tier into the Columbia River.

[02:42:00] **Carl:** Oh, geez. *[laughs]*

[02:42:02] **Walt:** *I* moved *it* like *he* asked.

[02:42:05] **Carl:** *[laughs]* So, then, what did he say?

[02:42:07] **Walt:** Nothing. *He* thought *it* was moved to the other tier, <u>you know</u>. What the fuck.

[02:42:11] **Carl:** Oh.

[02:42:14] [laughter]

[long pause]

[02:42:26] **Carl:** *I* wouldn't call that— that one at Warsaw an embarrassment. *I* don't know what *I* call it. *[laughs]* <u>You know</u>, but, *I*— *I* don't see any— *I* don't see anything embarrassing about it. In other words, you were— a— and at the— and you told me, you said, "*I*'d have done it for nothing."

[02:42:44] **Walt:** Yeah. And the guy lived, though— that's a— Maybe *I* was too much in a hurry to get out of the place.

[02:42:53] **Carl:** Well, those— those bullets that you showed me, they— they didn't look like they would— *I*— *I*— *I*'m not quite— *I* wouldn't really do this, but *I* was looking at those bullets, and *I*'d say, "Well, *I*'d let Walt put five of those into me." You know? *[laughs]* *I* really wouldn't. *I* really wouldn't, but— but they— they didn't look like anything that would— Oh, you bought 'em on the black market.

[02:43:16] **Walt:** Yeah.

[02:43:16] **Carl:** You're lucky they even exploded, you know.

[02:43:19] **Walt:** Yeah.

[02:43:19] **Carl:** But, um, ah, that was—

[02:43:22] **Walt:** Did *you* ever see that, uh, movie Enemy at the Gates?

[02:43:26] **Carl:** Uh—

[02:43:28] **Walt:** About the Russians in a— Where was *it*, Stalingrad <u>right there</u>, about the snipers? Well, at the beginning of the movie, *they*'re sending all these Russian soldiers over to the front. *Use of the phrase "right there" in a nonthreatening discussion.*

[02:43:40] **Carl:** Yeah.

[02:43:41] **Walt:** And *they*'re on this boat, and a lot of them don't want to get off— off the boat to assault these Germans, and that was the pistol *they* were shooting everybody in the head with that wouldn't get off the boat.

[02:43:55] **Carl:** Yes. That same little pistol.

[02:43:58] **Walt:** Yeah.

[02:43:59] **Carl:** Yeah.

[02:44:38] **Walt:** Yeah, Enemy at the Gates, that's the name of *it*.

[02:44:01] **Carl:** Yeah, yeah. But that— But that didn't seem to be an embarrassment. *I* mean, *I*— It— It— It— *I* think that one— *I* don't know about any of the rest, but *I* think that one, you told me you— you'da done it for free.

[02:44:19] **Walt:** *I* would've.

[02:44:20] **Carl:** That was— When— when *I* told you that that guy lived, did you— did you know that before, or is that the first time ever?

[02:44:29] **Walt:** That was the first time that *I* heard that *he* lived.

[02:44:31] **Carl:** You kidding me?

[02:44:33] **Walt:** No.

[02:44:36] **Carl:** Holy cow. Wow. Nobody told you?

[02:44:43] **Walt:** Yeah. Nobody told *me* nothing, right there, and *I* felt, uh, uh, disappointed.
Use of the phrase "right there" in a nonthreatening discussion.

[02:44:50] **Carl:** Well, yeah, yeah, but *I* mean, it seemed *[crosstalk]*

[02:44:52] **Walt:** Because if anybody deserves the change of address from this world to the next, *it* was *him*.

[02:44:55] **Carl:** Yeah.

[02:44:57] **Walt:** *He* was a butcher.

[02:44:58] **Carl:** Yeah. Oh, yeah. Yeah. 'Cause he had, there was other things that he did other than that— that, um, uh, the— the—the, uh, Olympic thing, you know. There were other things that— that guy did too, *you know*. But, uh, *I*'ll be darned. *I— I* didn't— *I* thought maybe you were kidding me, *you know*, when you said, "*I* didn't know it," because it seemed like, *you know*, the— the— um, your buddy in Poland would've known it, it would seem like.

[02:45:30] **Walt:** Oh, *we* don't talk about *it*.

[02:45:34] **Carl:** Well, *I* know, but *I* mean it seemed like when— when— when you go to— to do something like that, and it doesn't work out, it seems like— like somewhere somebody would say, "Hey, *you know*, uh, this thing here didn't work out the way we— we planned it," you know. Uh—

[02:45:56] **Walt:** Well, something like that happens, right there, nobody talks about *it* afterwards. *You* acknowledge nothin', *you* don't say nothin'. *Use of the phrase "right there" in a threatening discussion.*

[02:46:01] **Carl:** Well— But they paid you in full.

[02:46:05] **Walt:** Yeah, in Amsterdam.

[02:46:07] **Carl:** Yeah. Yeah.

[02:46:09] **Walt:** But *I* didn't even, *you know*, nobody mentioned nothing there. *I* picked up *my* money and— Where did *I* go then? *I* think *I* went home to Joni, then, uh. Or did *I* go to Saudi?

[02:46:22] **Carl:** *I* don't know.

[02:46:25] **Walt:** Gotta figure that out. Where'd *I* go? Well, *I* went to Jo— *I* went to, ah, went back to the States and—

[02:46:32] **Carl:** Yeah, yeah.

[02:46:35] **Walt:** <u>Right there</u> and then, *I* only was there for a week, and from there *I* went to, uh, back to Saudi. ***Use of the phrase "right there" in a nonthreatening discussion.***

[02:46:49] **Carl:** Yeah. Yeah. *I*'ll be darned. But anyway, you— <u>*You* know</u>, you've had an interesting life. *I*— *I* wouldn't classify some— Some of it, *I*'m sure *I* would, but *I* wouldn't classify everything as an embarrassment. <u>*You* know</u>, *I* mean, some of it might have been dumb shit stuff but not an— not necessarily an embarrassment, <u>*you* know</u>. And a lot of it—

[02:47:07] **Walt:** *I* think some of *it* was such a dumb shit stuff, *it* is an embarrassment.

[02:47:11] **Carl:** Well, *I* know. *I* know. *I* think—

[02:47:13] **Walt:** *Why* couldn't *I* think better than do that, <u>*you* know</u>. Here's the way *I* could have done *it*, <u>*you* know</u>, but *I* didn't, <u>*you* know</u>.

[02:47:19] **Carl:** Yeah. Like *I* say, you made it, and a lot of these people that do things like you did, didn't make it. They never got any— They never got half as far as you got, you know.

[02:47:33] **Walt:** Yeah.

[02:47:34] **Carl:** *I* mean and a lot of them got killed by their own people too, you know.

[02:47:39] **Walt:** Yeah.

[02:47:40] **Carl:** Just like that ▮▮▮ guy out there at Hammett *[sic? possibly Hemet]*, you know, or wherever it was that you met him.

[02:47:46] **Walt:** Oh, ▮▮▮▮▮▮▮.

[02:47:47] **Carl:** Yeah. Yeah. You know, they— they become what they call expendable and that guy that— that— that Art knew that, Bob Hall, you know. They become expendable, you know, they— Either that or they see something that somebody thinks they shouldn't see or whatever, you know. But, um, well—

[02:48:07] **Walt:** They drink too much, too, a lot of people.

[02:48:08] **Carl:** Yeah.

[02:48:09] **Walt:** Right there— Especially at the bar, right there— He did, uh— This happened to me once, right there— Somebody took me to the bar, right there, he said he was a tea salesman. Uh, selling Lipton's tea to the supermarkets and all that. We got talking on different things, right there— *Use of the phrase "right there" in a nonthreatening discussion.*

[02:48:29] **Carl:** What country were you in?

[02:48:26] **Walt:** Here, in the States.

[02:48:33] **Carl:** Oh, oh.

[02:48:35] **Walt:** And then they had some girl sit down next to me that she— he introduced me to the girl. And she was edging *[sic]* me on some questions, you know.

[02:48:44] **Carl:** Yeah.

[02:48:45] **Walt:** And, uh, *I— I— You know*, *I* just played ignorant, *you know*. And I had *my* drinks *right there* and *I* told *him*, uh— Told the guy, *I* says— *"You* watch her, *she* might try to get into your wallet," *right there*, and *I* said, *"I*'m going home now," and *I* left *right there*. But, uh, *they* were fishing. The both of them. *Use of the phrase "right there" in a nonthreatening discussion.*

[02:49:06] **Carl:** Uh-huh.

[02:49:07] **Walt:** That was above the, uh, pizzeria. That got hit with Jewish lightning [02:49:11].

[02:49:16] **Carl:** Oh, yeah. Yeah. Well, that would've been— that— that was around Detroit, then?

[02:49:22] **Walt:** Yeah.

[02:49:26] **Carl:** Yeah. It was prob— It was probably locals, though it— it wouldn't have been, uh— it wouldn't have been the feds. *I* would [crosstalk]

[02:49:35] **Walt:** Probably fire inspectors or something.

[02:49:37] **Carl:** Yeah.

[02:49:39] **Walt:** Or some agency right there. But, *I* mean that's the way *it* works *right there*, *you know*. People, *you know*, they get a few drinks in them, and *they* get loose, *you* always got to be on your guard. Stay away from bars. *Use of the phrase "right there" in a nonthreatening discussion.*

[02:49:51] **Carl:** But you went to bars?

[02:49:55] **Walt:** Yeah. Yeah, *I* did. *I* cut that off then afterwards. When *I* was young, *I* went to the bars a lot of times.

[02:50:03] **Carl:** Oh, really, when you were— when you were really doing this other stuff, you— you'd just go to a bar occasionally, and you wouldn't get that sloshed up or anything?

[02:50:13] **Walt:** No, no, <u>right there</u>, if *I* was going to do any drinking, *I*'d drink at home. ***Use of the phrase "right there" in a nonthreatening discussion.***

[02:50:18] **Carl:** Yeah, yeah. So you— So you had the sense, somewhere— somewhere you acquired the ability to be real good at what you did, somehow. In other words, you seemed to have the— *I* don't— *I* don't even know what the word for it is, the expertise, to do what you did in— in— in the field that you were in and do it as good or better than anybody else that may ever have done it.

[02:50:57] **Walt:** Yeah, well—

[02:50:58] **Carl:** There aren't that many people— there aren't that many people that— that— that do it, that are retired and getting up in the morning now and drinking their coffee.

[02:51:10] **Walt:** Yeah, that's true.

[02:51:11] **Carl:** There aren't. And *I*— Well *I* mean, *I* don't know all the people that were in that, but you hear time and time and time again where— where a guy that was in that, <u>you know</u>, doesn't make it, <u>you know</u>—

[long pause 02:51:22—02:51:35]

[02:51:36] **Carl:** What— What did you think all through life— All through life, how— how did you feel? I— I— I'm— I don't even know how to ask this really, because this— this is such a unique thing. How do you feel, knowing that you were D.B. Cooper and nobody'd ever caught you or even got close?

[02:51:59] **Walt:** Never give *it* a second thought.

[02:52:01] **Carl:** You never give it a second thought?

[02:52:03] **Walt:** No, right there *it* was done and *it* was done, you know, and right there and, uh— *Use of the phrase "right there" in a threatening discussion.*

[02:52:10] **Carl:** Was there a time in life where you— where you nearly forgot that you were D.B. Cooper?

[02:52:16] **Walt:** Yeah, almost right afterwards. I— I— I thought of putting the money in a bank, I had that all figured out, I was concerned about the money in the bank, I had family, you know, to take care of and overseas jobs come up right there and— *Use of the phrase "right there" in a threatening discussion.*

[02:52:32] **Carl:** But you didn't think it was— then that big a deal, it was no more than— than robbing a bank like you'd done in the past or something?

[02:52:40] **Walt:** No, *it* wasn't— *It* was no deal really. *It* was done, you know?

[02:52:44] **Carl:** Yeah.

[02:52:46] **Walt:** *It* was done, and *I* lived through *it*.

[02:52:49] **Carl:** Oh, what was the closest that you've ever been to that frame of mind before possibly when you went through the— the thing smuggling diamonds out of— out of Sierra Leone? *I* mean, that had to be practically just as bad or just as bad or worse, because—

[02:53:06] **Walt:** *I* controlled everything, *you know*, with the diamonds *I* had— *I* planned. This— this was totally unplanned, *you know*—

[02:53:15] **Carl:** Yeah.

[02:53:16] **Walt:** *It* was like, uh— uh— How *my* mind was at the time, *I— You* can compare *it* to a poached egg, and *my* mind at that time was like a scrambled egg.

[02:53:26] **Carl:** Yeah, you just couldn't hardly think of anything—

[02:53:30] **Walt:** No.

[02:53:31] **Carl:** You were just walking along almost like an out-of-body experience.

[02:53:35] **Walt:** Yeah, like a fuckin' zombie.

[02:53:38] **Carl:** And yet— And yet, you had the wherewithal to pull it o—*[laughs]* to pull it off—

[02:53:43] **Walt:** Yeah.

[02:53:44] **Carl:** —*you know*— That's— that's the hard part, *you know*, that's the hard part to

imagine. Thi— this was— this was pretty much a—
a— a daze, you know— um.

[02:53:57] **Walt:** Yup. What was *I*— 'cause *it*'s a
scary situation from the time *I* committed myself
on the plane.

[02:54:04] **Carl:** Was— was— was this— Was this—

[02:54:07] **Walt:** *I* was scared.

[02:54:07] **Carl:** A lot— This was a lot scarier
than— than— than the diamond smuggling.

[02:54:11] **Walt:** Oh, of course.

[02:54:12] **Carl:** And do you think that your mind
kind of like a guy oh—ah— Anytime you have a
traumatic experience, people— they— they can't
think of it, you know. In other words, uh,
they say, "*I* can only remember about two days
before it happened and— and two or three days
or a week after," but they can never remember
their traumatic experience because it was too
traumatic.

[02:54:36] **Walt:** Yeah. Right there, *I* mean, the—
I mean the fear was really in *me*. ***Use of the phrase***
"right there" in a threatening discussion.

[02:54:42] **Carl:** Yeah, you couldn't get any more
scared?

[02:54:46] **Walt:** No. If *I* did, *my* heart would
have stopped.

[02:54:50] **Carl:** Right. *[laughs]* *I*— *I* believe
it. *[laughs]*

[Beginning of a new phone call.]

[02:54:59] **Walt:** Hello?

[02:55:00] **Carl:** D.B., is that you?

[02:55:02] **Walt:** Who?

[02:55:03] **Carl:** D.B.

[02:55:04] **Walt:** D.B.?

[02:55:05] **Carl:** This is Charlie.

[02:55:08] **Walt:** Charlie? Let's see, do *I* know a Charlie or not?

[02:55:11] **Carl:** Yeah.

[laughter]

[02:55:15] **Walt:** *I* never talked about this to anybody but *you*—

[02:55:17] **Carl:** Right.

[02:55:18] **Walt:** Yeah.

[02:55:19] **Carl:** Okay. Well, look it— Uh, we're taping now, it's, um, November 7, 2008.

At this point, one tape ends and another begins in a different time period. As I mentioned earlier, although these cassette tapes were recorded from October 2008 through late December 2008 or early January 2009, the tapes had no dates or titles.

[02:55:26] Okay, basically what you told me in the last few days is, um— is— The reason that you done this— this thing was more for your kids than for yourself.

[02:55:39] **Walt:** Yeah.

[02:55:39] **Carl:** And you never wanted them to go through the hunger and— and hardships and stuff that you did. Um— uh—

[02:55:48] **Walt:** What *I* wanted is a future for 'em.

[02:55:51] **Carl:** Yeah.

[02:55:52] **Walt:** Yeah, and, uh—

[02:55:56] **Carl:** And— And even though you tried to provide a future for 'em, uh—

[02:56:00] **Walt:** *They* turned *it* all down.

[02:56:01] **Carl:** They— They turned everything down. The— the college—

[02:56:03] **Walt:** *I* got them a car, *I* paid them to go— *I* paid them to even go to school.

[02:56:06] **Carl:** Yeah, yeah. Plus their tuition and everything or—

[02:56:10] **Walt:** Yeah.

[02:56:11] **Carl:** So it didn't— Wouldn't cost them nothing and they all— Every one of them turned it down?

[02:56:15] **Walt:** Yeah.

[02:56:16] **Carl:** You thought of other plans before you executed the— the Cooper hijacking. In other words—

[02:56:21] **Walt:** Oh, yeah.

[02:56:23] **Carl:** You— You thought, well, bank robbery is— is out because you don't get enough money for that and— and you even thought of an, uh—

uh—armored car— [Walt interjects: Supermarket] and the one in the supermarket was kinda neat where you were gonna call from across the street and tell him you were the cops and give the guy the money and that— Did— Wa—Was there any other things that you can think of?

[02:56:45] **Walt:** No, that and the armored car with a smoke grenade or a tear gas grenade— Just walked up with the cash and checks as if *you* are gonna cash the checks and push *it* through the window.

[02:56:56] **Carl:** Yeah. Okay, so— So that's— But you come up with the Cooper one because you thought there was the most money in it, and you already had the airplane for the getaway—

[02:57:06] **Walt:** Yeah.

[02:57:08] **Carl:** —basically.

[This seems to be the start of an entirely new conversation.] *I* was always under the impression that rather than— When— when— when those two guys met you in that bar and said, "Well, you work for us now," *I* was always under the impression that they got you from the Teamsters, rather than for the other thing that you did, you know?

[02:57:27] **Walt:** Yeah.

[02:57:28] **Carl:** *I* mean, *I* couldn't prove either one of 'em, but *I*— *I* just— *I* just always thought that— that— that it would be easier to catch you for the Teamster thing because there— there— there was a lot more people involved with the

Teamster where the other thing was a one-man deal.

[02:57:50] **Walt:** Yeah.

[02:57:51] **Carl:** And if they didn't catch you <u>right there</u> doing it, there was nobody to rat on you, nobody to squeal, um, that's— that's just my thinking, <u>*you* know</u>. In other words, if— if— My thinking was, if they didn't catch you, that they— that you did that— that thing, that other one, then how the hell would they catch you? That's my— That's my thinking on it. You know what *I*'m saying?

[02:58:17] **Walt:** Yeah. *[crosstalk]*

[02:58:21] **Carl:** How— How would they— How would they trace?

[02:58:22] **Walt:** *I* don't even think about *it*, Charlie.

[02:58:23] **Carl:** Well, *I* know, but *I*— *I*—

[02:58:25] **Walt:** That's the problem. If *you* start thinking about things like that, *you*'d never go to sleep at night.

[02:58:32] **Carl:** *[laughs]* Well, let me tell you, *I*'m writing this friggin' book and— and *I* want— *I* want you to know *I*'ve spent some sleepless nights, you know, thinking about this stuff and trying to put what happened, when and how could this be, because that's what writing a book is.

[02:58:53] **Walt:** Yeah.

[02:58:54] **Carl:** You know, that's— that's what it is. I— I— I've gotta figure this stuff out more, you— you— you have the luxury of just— just— [laughs] forgetting about it, you know, but if— if you're writing a book, uh, you gotta—

[02:59:07] **Walt:** Then *you* gotta connect the dots.

[02:59:09] **Carl:** I gotta connect the dots and— and the dots that I've connected are that I— I still don't think today that they know what you did. I— I think they got you for the Teamsters, because don't forget there's a lot of guys on the Teamsters that'll squeal. You know, I mean—

[02:59:32] **Walt:** Yeah.

[02:59:33] **Carl:** And— And, uh— So they could say, "Well, this guy did this and this guy did that," because they're trying to get themselves off, but there wasn't anybody on this other deal to— ta— ta— ta do it and if— if they didn't catch you the day you did it and got home and all that, then how are they gonna catch you? That— that's— And I still believe that. I still believe that.

[02:59:59] **Walt:** Don Brennan called *me* yesterday. *Always take note of unsolicited information. It is insightful that Walt freely offers to Charlie that Don Brennan still calls him. Don Brennan is an important witness. Walt wanted Charlie to know this. Why? Brennan is still alive at the time of this discussion.*

[03:00:01] **Carl:** No kidding.

[03:00:02] **Walt:** Yes. *He* calls *me* about once a month. *We* talk.

[03:00:06] **Carl:** He still won't— He still won't, uh— You never did ask him where you were, did you?

[03:00:15] **Walt:** No. *I— We* don't even talk about that.

[03:00:19] **Carl:** *I* know it. *I* know.

[03:00:21] **Walt:** 'Cause if *I* did <u>right there</u>, *he*'d never call again. *Use of the phrase "right there" in a threatening discussion. Also, Walter provides further information about Don Brennan's reluctance to talk about the hijacking—because of his paranoia, as noted below.*

[03:00:22] **Carl:** Really?

[03:00:23] **Walt:** Yeah.

[03:00:25] **Carl:** You're kidding me.

[03:00:27] **Walt:** Why not?

[03:00:29] **Carl:** He's that paranoid?

[03:00:30] **Walt:** Yeah.

[03:00:32] **Carl:** Well— God, he ought to know better because, <u>you know</u>, *I* mean what— what— You're not gonna— You're not gonna do anything to— to, uh, um, put him in— in hot water.

[03:00:52] **Walt:** Uh, *he* calls *me* once a month. *We* talk about some of these guys that *we* worked iron together, and that, <u>you know</u>, and that's about *it*.

[03:00:59] **Carl:** Yeah.

[03:01:02] **Walt:** So *I* mean there's no— no nothing, *you know*. Oh, no, or about *[unintelligible 03:01:08]*. *We* were parachute jumping up there.

[03:01:09] **Carl:** Yeah. Well, he must know, uh, Sinclair, too, doesn't he?

[03:01:12] **Walt:** Oh yeah. Bob knows *him*, too.

[03:01:15] **Carl:** Yeah. Yeah. *I*'ll be darned, but— He won't even talk to you about that. [Walt interjects: No.] *I*'ve never heard of anybody being so scared of anything in all my life.

[03:01:30] **Walt:** Yeah. *He*'s very cautious.

[03:01:34] **Carl:** Or cautious. What— What— Whatever you wanna call it. *You know*. Yeah. *I*'ve often thought about calling him, but— but, uh, you told me, you said, "Well, you can call him, but don't— don't mention that, or he'll hang up on ya," ya know, and so *I* said— *I* just figured what— what's the point? Ya know and, uh—

[03:01:55] **Walt:** Plus scare the old man. *He*'s a year older than *I am*.

[03:02:01] **Carl:** Who? Donnie is?

[03:02:02] **Walt:** Yeah.

[03:02:04] **Carl:** Yeah.

[03:02:05] **Walt:** *He* was born September the 22nd. *I* was born September the 20th. *I* was born in '33, *he* was born in '32.

[03:02:13] **Carl:** And— And when were you born? You were in September.

[03:02:21] **Walt:** Yes, September the 20th, '33.

[03:02:24] **Carl:** Okay. Yeah. Yeah you're— You're exactly six months older than *I* am, ya know.

[Seems to be start of a new conversation.] Give me some ideas on what you want me to do with this thing, because *I* wanna do it like as close as *I* can to what you want me to do, you know?

[03:02:51] **Walt:** Charlie, whatever it is *you're* gonna come up with right there is gonna be a winner. *Use of the phrase "right there" in a threatening discussion.*

[03:02:57] **Carl:** *[laughs] I-I*'ll try.

[03:03:03] **Walt:** That's what Art and *I* always said about *you* right there. "Whatever Charlie does right there, *it* will come out good." *You're* the only one that has any sense out of all of us. *Use of the phrase "right there" in a threatening discussion.*

[03:03:13] **Carl:** Yeah, but if that's the case, why did *I* get in so much trouble?

[03:03:17] **Walt:** A lot of associations, Art and mine.

[03:03:25] **Carl:** Gee, did *I* tell you what Loretta and *I* had— *I* think *I* did. *I* told you what we're gonna do on this. Um. We're— We're gonna wait, uh— We're gonna wait until you die— And *I* may die ahead of you, who knows? But Lo— Loretta might— What— Whatever. This is the plan. And then we're not publishing until then anyway.

[03:03:46] **Walt:** Yeah.

[03:03:47] **Carl:** These guys are getting old and dying off and stuff, it's just like our Billabog, you know. *I* mean probably five years from now, there won't be one. *You* know.

[03:03:57] **Walt:** Yeah and just, uh, uh, like when Willard and *I* used to have poker games. There's nobody left.

[This seems to be a new tape; definitely a new topic.]

Walt: Now what *it* is, right there, *I*'m overwhelmed, uh, uh, and—and hope that—Because *I* never thought *I* was like doing anything like this— was— well, *it*'s just like an everyday event right there— *Use of the phrase "right there" in a threatening discussion.*

[03:04:21] **Carl:** Walt.

[03:04:22] **Walt:** Taking his lunch box and going to work every day.

[03:04:25] **Carl:** Walter. Other people— Other people sell real estate and work in mattress families and, uh, and work in Jiffy stores and—and they're a clerk for Kmart. *I* keep tellin' ya this.

[03:04:44] **Walt:** Just, uh— Every op-opportunity that came *my* way, *I* grabbed *it*. That's all, you know.

[03:04:51] **Carl:** Yeah, but they don't. People that work in Kmart, they go work there every day and retire after thirty years or some darn thing. *You* know, *I* mean, other people didn't have a life like you did. Believe me. *[laughs]* Oh, believe me. But, uh, you had a life. Believe me. If you didn't think you did, uh, everybody else will when they read the book. You know. That's what's important.

[03:05:21] **Walt:** Yeah, well, I'm amazed at that, you know, because— uh, well, I told ███ a long time ago [clears throat] when we first got together, "Always keep your own counsel, ███. Don't tell nobody nothin'."

[03:05:35] **Carl:** Keep your own what?

[03:05:36] **Walt:** Counsel.

[03:05:38] **Carl:** I— I didn't hear. Counsel?

[03:05:42] **Walt:** Yeah. You know when you counsel somebody?

[03:05:46] **Carl:** Oh, okay.

[03:05:47] **Walt:** Yeah, keep your own counsel.

[03:05:50] **Carl:** Yeah yeah. Oh, yeah, yeah. Well— See, this is what makes it so— I don't— I don't just know how to— You know. This is what makes this— this story so unique. It's just so unique. It's— It's just one in a— one in a kind of— of history, believe me. And, uh, I'm glad I've— I'm glad I've had a— I've been able to be a part of it. I mean, it's really been a— a very, uh— It's been a very positive thing in my life. I— I enjoy doing it and not only that, but, um, I— I even— Here— This is a funny thing. I'm a guy that's never— never swiped anything in his life, and, uh, uh and *I– I* didn't like that part. But *I*'ve come to– to see the whole big picture on this and, uh, *I– I– I–*

I know it sounds crazy, *I*'ve taken your side of it a hundred percent, ~~you~~ know. And *I* know that there's things that– that you did that *I* don't even know a hundred percent and everything like that, but, *I– I* even understand that part of it. ~~You~~ know, in other words, uh, uh– *I*'ve seen guys, like *I* say, in– in my lifetime that *I*'d like to see go away, ~~you~~ know, and, uh– So, uh, putting it politely, *I* guess, so– *I– I– I* can understand that and– and– and it doesn't bother me one iota, ~~you~~ know.

So, the analysis shows several things. Walt's voice inflections, volume, pronunciations, and articulation were consistent throughout all 3.5 hours of audiotapes. Walt consistently uses the "I" pronoun, which connotes possession, responsibility, and the accountability of his statement. He consistently communicates in the past tense, using the active voice. His communication patterns are consistent, with no discernible difference noted when in the nonthreatening and the threatening question areas. He uses his unique and favorite colloquialism ("right there") throughout the discussions, whether in the nonthreatening or the threatening question areas. He answers the questions directly and even corrects the assumptions in the questions by providing detailed information only the hijacker would know. Finally, he makes several admissions that constitute a confession to all the legal elements of hijacking. Walt's statements here are consistent with truthful statements.

Chapter 8

ANALYSIS OF JEFF "COWBOY" OSIADACZ'S STATEMENTS

(Taken and obtained by Vern Jones,
on July 26, 2016, in Teanaway, Washington.)

LEGEND:

Pronouns (and pronoun-like articles)

Analysis

Important word/phrases

Description Consistency

⟶ follows consistency in "man."

⟹ follows consistency in "raincoat."

Jeff Osiadacz's statements are crucial in determining whether Walt Peca was D.B. Cooper. Mr. Osiadacz was named the honorable King Coal of 2017 in Kittitas County, Cle Elum, Washington.[22] Jeff's account surfaced many years after Walt provided the information to Carl in the 2008–2009 recordings (beginning in 2008, when Walt admitted being D.B. Cooper to Carl, which eventually resulted in the previous transcripts). Jeff's identity was unknown to Carl

---

22 *Northern Kittitas County Tribune*, Thursday, September 21, 2017, page B1,
    Col. 64, #38, Cle Elum, Washington.

or Walt at the time of Walt's responses to Carl. The only thing Carl learned from Walt was the following:

"[02:19:23] **Walt:** I give it to the guy with the tru— uh, with the dump truck— the telephone. He give him the directions.

[02:19:29] **Carl:** Oh, he gave you the directions?

[02:19:31] **Walt:** He give it to Don.

[02:19:33] **Carl:** Ohh. Oh, um—

[02:19:37] **Walt:** That's how come I remember him good, too, with his fuckin' guitar, cowboy hat, Western gear right there at, uh—

Carl then, with incredible perseverance and ingenuity, found the probable drop area, the since-destroyed Teanaway Junction Café, and finally "the guy with the dump truck," Jeff Osiadacz, hereinafter affectionately called "Cowboy." In his statements, Cowboy effectively corroborates all the essential details that Walt provided to Carl about what happened when Walt says he jumped out of the airplane. Jeff even provides a note from a former employer confirming that he, Cowboy, drove a "dump truck" in or around 1970. And he identified Walt as the man he remembered seeing in the Teanaway Junction Café on the night of November 24, 1971. His identification of Walt was the result of Carl sending a known photograph of Walt to Jeff (photo below). While this is not a forensically sound method for identification, it nonetheless offers more corroborative evidence. For an investigator, this kind of corroboration is monumental in determining whether Walt Reca was D.B. Cooper. (The date the picture was taken is unknown.)

Jeff: [00:00:00] Yeah, when I saw it, the man walking alongside the road in a dark suit, he was approximately— Oh, maybe about four hundred yards from the Wenatchee overpass *up here*. *"Up here" is an unusual phrase. He uses it only once more in this*

statement. It's a habitual and unique informal idiosyncrasy that suggests comfort. Comfort is consistent with truth-telling—the same with his use (37 times) of the word "here." These are all indicators of his consistent comfort level and truth-telling. The same follows for all the 57 "you know" phrases. The "you know"s are sprinkled fairly evenly throughout this whole statement, showing consistent comfort and little stress—again, indications of truth-telling. And he came across the road, oh— right about in that area right there, and he was walking east, going this way. *The pronoun "he" is the "man."* I was driving a dump truck, I had my music equipment in it, 'cause the wife had the car, and I wasn't allowed to pick up hitchhikers, 'cause I didn't have a seat on the other side anyway. *Jeff tells us he wasn't about to pick up hitchhikers, even if he had room in his truck. Jeff speaks directly, describing a past event using simple sentences and past tense language— both consistent with true recollections.* And I drove on to the Teanaway Junction, which is probably about another mile and a half, two miles down the road here.

After I'd seen this gentleman walking, like I said, it was dark, raining, snowing, blowing. It was cold. I stopped down here, and the old Teanaway Junction Café used to set right about in this area, which it burned down, and they built a fire station after that. Anyway, I— I parked the truck out here, I came in, I was sitting down, drinking a cup of coffee *[clears throat]*, and this man walks in with a black suit, white shirt, black penny loafers, his raincoat rolled up under his arm, he looked like a drowned rat. *The man now* becomes a gentleman. *Is this change explainable? Under the circumstances, I think so since Mr. Osiadacz hadn't met him yet. Mr. Osiadacz thereafter consistently calls him a "man" (follow the faint arrows showing his consistency). Also note the articles before "man." They are "the," "a," "this"—all consistent with the same man. Now, follow the heavier arrows to see how consistent he is in describing the "raincoat" or "trench coat" rolled up under "his" arm. In a later written statement, Mr. Osiadacz will describe it as a "large bundle." While this description in his written statement is different than the "raincoat" in this transcribed statement, it is not significantly inconsistent or contradictory. There is a reason for the description change. It could be he tired of calling it a "raincoat or trench coat" and chose to call it a "large bundle" to eliminate the need for that distinction. The written statement was obtained more than a year after this transcribed statement. The difference in these descriptions doesn't threaten the veracity of his statement.* His hands were beet red, he was shaking, and, <u>uh</u>, I told him, I says, "I'm sorry I didn't pick you up, but," I said, "I can't have hitchhikers," <u>you know</u>, with the dump truck. He says, "That's okay, kid." He says, "No problem." *He still talks in the active voice past tense (we always know who the "actor" is when we see a lot of "I," "they," and "he" pronouns. Again, the passive voice hides the "actor," and thus, it is frequently used to deceive). "Cowboy" continuously talks in the active voice in the past tense—traits consistent with truth-telling.*

So, we ordered a cup of coffee, and we talked a little bit. And he says, "If I give you— If I dial a phone number," he says, "can you give this friend of mine directions how to come over <u>here</u> to pick me up?" I said, "Sure." I says, "No problem." So, he went into the back room there where the telephone was, an old dial crank-on-a-wall phone. He dialed a number, and he says, "Uh, they got this guy over _here_ that lives _here_," he says. "Gonna give you directions how to get over _here_ to pick me up." So, the, uh— the guy on the phone says, "Where you located?" *[00:02:00]* I says, "Well, I'm at the Teanaway Junction." He says, "Where's that?" I said, "It's over by Cle Elum." I says, "Which way are you coming from?" *Notice he talks now in the present tense ("I says . . .") since he's recreating or reliving the conversation. This change in tense is not unexpected.*

"I's, "You gonna come over Snoqualmie Pass, you coming up over Stevens and Blewett, how you gonna get _here_?" He says, "Well, I'm gonna come up over Blewett." So, I gave the man directions how to get _here_, and I handed the phone back to this guy in the suit, and I went and sat down on the counter and drank my coffee, you know? And then I had to go out to the Grange Hall, which is about another four miles out of town to play music for a Grange function. And, uh, I told the guy, says, "You gonna be okay?" I says, "I'm not sure what time they close." He says, "Oh, my buddy'll be _here_ pretty soon," he says. "No problem."

He says thanks for giving him directions how to get _here_, he says, "I'll go ahead and buy your coffee." I says, "What a guy. Thank you." I shook hands with the man, got in my truck, and left. Uh, Teanaway Junction, it was the hot spot for all the locals around _here_. They used to come _here_ to get their gas, they used to come _here_, they had the best chicken-fried steaks and burgers. All homemade pies, there's two ladies of— that were of English descent, and they spoke, <u>you know</u>, kind of an English accent, and they were the best cooks, and I mean, the service was good, the food was great. You couldn't have— and the price was— you couldn't believe it. The price of the food, it was great. It was all good home cooking, there was none of this prefab stuff like you get nowadays.

It burned down, I'm guessing probably— Oh, it's been at least ten years. Say, ten, twelve years since it burned down. Ballpark: <u>somewheres in there</u>. I don't remember exact dates, but I suppose if a guy wanted, he could look up the local newspaper and get exact dates. Name is Jeff _[unintelligible 00:03:42]_ I was born and raised _here_ in Rawson, Washington. In the Rawson-Cle Elum area. <u>Uh</u>, I grew up, went to school _here_. My first job outta high school was working in a No. 9 Coal Mine where my family had— <u>you know</u>, my— my dad, _[00:04:00]_ my grandfather, three uncles, all of 'em worked in the mines. *There are 30 "uh"s in this statement. They are sprinkled fairly consistently throughout his statement. "Uh" is a filler, a habitual and unnecessary word. We use "uh" when we're uncomfortable, like when we're giving a speech. If I found this more prominent in one area, I would want to analyze that area and compare the content to other areas. However, the "uh"s in this statement are consistent and throughout this statement and appear whether he's talking about his history or the D.B. Cooper history. Thus, I find no problem with his use of "uh"s.*

And jobs were scarce, so that was one of the first jobs I had. Then in 1962, they decided to close the mines, and I got laid off, and, uh— then I went to work in some gyppo *[00:04:18]* sawmills around *here*. Then, I finally managed to find a job working in the woods logging, setting chokers, which was big money back in those days, it was like $2.50 an hour. And, uh, it was hard work. And then I graduated, you know, up to where I was driving logging trucks and dump trucks, start running some heavy equipment. You know, building logging roads, and, uh— when the logging started closing down in the area, I was lucky enough to get on with the police department.

I spent six years with those, uh— I was, uh— uh, acting chief, I guess you would say, for Rawson Fire— uh, Police Department. I was a reserve officer for Cle Elum Police Department. I was a reserve deputy for the Kittitas County *[00:05:04]* Sheriff's Department. And then, one thing led to another, and I wound up getting a divorce, and you know, when you get a divorce, everything falls apart. So, then I just— I moved on, and I moved to Ellensburg, and I worked in a packing house down there *[00:05:21]* on the kill floors, cutting locker beef and doing stuff like this. Then, I wound up working for Safeway for three years. Got laid off there because they were cutting back on man hours, so it seemed like— everything I grabbed a hold of, I ended up with nothing, <u>you know</u>? Just— everything was short term.

So, somebody said, "Well, how come you had so many jobs?" Well, they're— In this area, it's all seasonal, <u>you know</u>? There's just— you might work for two months, you might work for six months, you might work for a year. You just— You don't know. When you're raising a family, you take whatever jobs you can find in this area. Yeah, I played music a little bit. I did it for about forty years. I, <u>uh</u>— I got started with an old, *[00:06:00]* broken down Silvertone guitar, and my dad always wanted me to learn how to sing tenor. Ten or twelve miles from the house.

[laughter]

So, anyway, I, <u>uh</u>— I ended up getting a couple other guys, <u>you know</u>, that wanted to play music, and we struck up a little band, and we started getting' going and everything. And, <u>uh</u>, I played with some of the big names, Ferlin Husky, <u>you know</u>? When he'd come to town, we were the house band for him. And, <u>uh</u>— I've sang with Bonnie Guitar down at the Ellensburg Moose Lodge when she'd come in and perform, <u>you know</u>, do a show. And when I'd spend some time up in Alaska driving a hot oil tanker, out of Alas— <u>uh</u>, of Anchorage up there, we'd go to Kenai, down to Nikiski down <u>in there</u>, load up with hot oil, take it back up to the batch plants.

I got to meet and play music with some other big names, like Buddy Knight, was Merle Haggard's bass guitar player, Johnny Collinsworth was a lead player for Glenn Campbell. Julio Suzuki was a Japanese kid, he was on the *Hee Haw Show*. I just got to meet a whole— Frank Bernard, he was a guitar player for Ernie Tubbs. Now, I got to meet all these great guys, _you know_, great, fantastic musicians. And I had a lot of fun up there. And then, my dad had a towing service down _here_ in a wrecking yard, as I said earlier, and, _uh_, he had a stroke, and he couldn't run the towing service, so Mom got on the phone and singing the blues, _you know_, "Didn't nobody down _here_ to run the business," so I left Alaska, came back down and ran my dad's business for a while 'till he passed away. Then, my nephew took it over, 'cause I had enough of it, I didn't want no more.

And, _uh_— then I went to work for Suncadia Resort _up here_, big golf resort, and, _uh_, I've been with them now ten years. And I still play music once in a while, and people are always hounding *[00:07:56]* me, "When you gonna put a band back together?" Well, I don't wanna put a band back together. *[00:08:00]* I just wanna sit in with some of the other bands that's already established. And they know all the good, standard, _you know_, country songs that I used to do, and— Now, my son, he started playing in my band when he was twelve and a half, thirteen years old. He was playing the drums because my drummers would either end up drunk, forget to show up, or they were messed up with dope back in those days. So, I just got him to where he would play the drums in the band.

And after four years, he put his own band together, and now he's got another band that he— It's called Rusty Cage. It's a Johnny Cash tribute band, and— when, the first time I heard him sing, I almost— they almost called an aid car for me. I almost had a heart attack, because the kid sounded exactly like Johnny Cash. And I told him, I said, "Son," I said, "You sound like Johnny Cash." "No, I don't, Dad." I says, "Yes, you do." I says, "I'm gonna ask you one question, I'm gonna shut up." He said, "What?" I says, "Where were you when Johnny Cash was your age?" He wasn't even born, you know? I mean— Don't tell me what Johnny Cash sounded like. He was a big name when I was a kid, going to high school, growing up around _here_. So I know what the man sounded like.

And he— Everybody around _here_ just loves the band. I mean, they're really a success, doing great. Yeah, you're— doing some kind of documentary thing or something, you wanna hear stories. Okay. *[laughs]* So, Evidently, you're ta— wanna do a story on this guy that I met. Uh, which I found out later after how many years, he was D.B. Cooper. I didn't even know who the man was, but as I said, I played music and it was a three-piece band, there was a accordion player, a drummer, and a guitar player. Well, the guitar player couldn't make it that night, so he asked me to fill in out at the Teanaway Grange for a Grange Function. It was right close to Thanksgiving. And I said, "Sure," I said, "I'll go out there and do it." Well at that time I'd been driving dump truck, and my wife had the car, she went to work, so I called my boss, asked him if I could use the truck, <u>you know</u>, *[00:10:00]* to— to go out there.

He says, "Sure, no problem." He says, "But don't be picking up any hitchhikers." "Well, that's okay, because I didn't have a seat in the passenger side of the truck anyway." So on the way out there, I just passed the Wenatchee Overpass just outside of Cle Elum, about a mile. I noticed a man standing on the side of the road, hitchhiking, and he had a suit on, but I couldn't pick anybody up and it was— It had been raining and snowing— <u>you know</u>— mixed. It was cold, November, and I felt sorry for the guy, but I couldn't pick him up so I just kept going till I got to the Teanaway Junction, which is a little service station and a restaurant— <u>you know</u>— combination thing.

And I stopped <u>in there</u> for a cup of coffee 'cause I was running a little bit early. I said, "Well, I'll have coffee and then I'll, I'll go on out to the Grange Hall, out to Ballard Grange in Teanaway, and this man comes walking in. He looked like a drowned rat, he had black slicked-back hair, had on a black suit, a white shirt, penny loafers, soaking wet. And had his trench coat or raincoat rolled up under his arm. I thought, "Man, I guess it takes all kinds to make this world go round." I never said nothing. He—

We sat there and had a cup of coffee, and he says, "You live around _here_, kid?" And I says, "Yeah." He says, "Can you do me a favor?" I says, "Well, I— I'll try," I says, "I can guarantee nothing."

He says, "If I dial a phone number for you," he says, "will you tell this friend of mine how to come over _here_? Where I'm at and how to pick me up." He says, "Why we—" He says, "Where am I?" I says, "You're just outside of Cle Elum at the Teanaway Junction Cafe." He says, "Okay." So he went back there and had an old pay phone with a dial thing on it. Drops some money in it, made a phone call, handed me the phone. He says, "Yeah, Carl"— (***I contacted Jeff Osiadacz on his use of "Carl" here, and he said he knew no names at the time he gave directions to the guy on the pay phone. By the time of this interview, however, he had talked to Carl and told me this was an inadvertent slip.) Er, he says, "this guy wants to— directions, _you know_, how to get _here_." I says, "Okay." I said, "Which way you coming? You coming up over Snoqualmie Pass or you gonna come up over Stevens and Blewett? _[00:12:00]_ How you gonna, _you know_, where you coming from?"

He says, "Well I'm gonna come up over Blewett," and he says, "How far is it from Blewett Pass," he said, "to up where you're at?" I said, "It's probably about a half hour." I said, "It's just about four miles outside of Cle Elum, called the Teanaway Junction." And, _uh_, he's, "Okay, fine, thanks." So I handed the phone back to the guy in the suit. Went and sat down and finished my coffee and he came back over and he says, "Well, thanks for telling him how to get _here_." And he says, "Don't worry about it, kid," he says, "I'll buy your coffee." I said, "Well, thanks." _You know_, shook hands with the man, got in my truck, and went on out to the Ballard Grange and played music.

My big night, $2.50, he was alongside the road, yeah. And I thought, _you know_, then I says, "Why is this guy in a suit walking alongside of the road?" Maybe car broke down or something, _you know_, I— I don't know. I didn't have a clue. It's just, _uh_— What really stood out to me is _here_ stands a man, soaking wet, looks like a drowned rat, and he's got a— a raincoat, trench coat, whatever you wanna call it, rolled up under his arm. Somebody says, "Well, didn't you ever wonder what was in that trench coat?" I says, "He coulda had a dog _in there_," I says, "Got a— I have no idea," _you know_. And I said, "He coulda had, _you know_, some change of clothes or something that he didn't want to get wet." _You know_, that he just— If his car broke down, maybe he just grabbed a few items out of his car, rolled em up in that because he didn't have nothing else.

Just wanted to take something with him, _you know_. I said, "I have no idea." I said what people do is none of my business. _You know_, I said, "The guy wants to roll up stuff in his raincoat and get soaking wet, I guess that's up to him." _Uh_, it was maybe a few days before Thanksgiving. The exact date I'm not real positive on, I think it was right around maybe the 21st or somewhere's right in there, 'cause they were having a function out at the Grange Hall where all the farmers get together and they have a— have *[00:14:00]* a get together.

They had a meeting and they had kind of a dinner, I guess what you would call it, and we just got hired to play music for— for a while and I said, "Man," I said, "this is a lousy night to be having a function." You know, cold, windy, wet.

'Kay, I'll tell you, uh, I never met the man face-to-face. But I stopped at the Shell station here in Cle Elum, which I used to work at, you know, when I was in high school, and the owner's son told me that there was a guy looking for me. And I says, "A jealous husband?" You know, I mean, what is he? You know, I have no idea.

He says, "No," he said, "this guy's from Florida." I says, "I don't know anybody from Florida." I says, "What's the deal," you know, "what's he want?" He says, "Well, this guy's name's Carl, he left me a— a card, he said— said to give it to you." I says, "What's he want to talk to me for?" I said, "I don't know anybody down there." He says, "Well," he said, "he stopped in here and asked me if I knew anybody that drove a— drove a dump truck, wore a cowboy hat and played country music." He says, "You're the only one around here that did that."

I see— so he said, "I told him, Well, I'll give you the information, he wants you to call him." I says, "Okay," I said, "I'll call the guy." I said, "Whatever, I got nothing to lose." So I called him up and we got to talking, and he says, "Do you remember such such a thing, <u>you know</u>, that night, <u>you know</u>, blah-blah-blah-blah." And he says, "Can you just—" He says, "Do you remember anything about that?" And I says, "Holy cow, so that's over forty years ago." I says— I said, "I think, <u>uh</u>— Let me think a minute <u>here</u>." So I hung; I paused for a minute. I says, "Yeah."

I says yeah— I said, "I remember something, <u>you know</u>, just before Thanksgiving," I said, "about forty years ago <u>somewhere in there</u>." And I said, "I saw a guy walking on the side of the road, hitchhiking." And I said he wore a suit, *[00:16:00]* and I didn't pick him up, I just went straight on down to Teanaway Junction, <u>you know</u>, and had a cup of coffee. This man walks in." "What'd he look like?" And I said, "Well, he had slicked-back, <u>you know</u>, black hair, a white shirt, it was either charcoal gray or a black suit." I said, "It was soaking wet so it's hard to say, <u>you know</u>."

And I said, "He had penny loafers on." He said, "What kind of penny loafers?" I said, "Black, with white socks." He says, "You noticed anything unusual?" I says, "Yeah, he had his raincoat rolled up under his arm and he's soaking wet." *[laughs]* I says, "Which I thought was kinda goofy." Then

he says, "Do you have any idea who that was?"
I says, "No." I said, "I never asked names or
anything." I said, "The man asked me to give a
friend of his directions how to get to where he
was to pick him up." And I said, "That was it. I
had coffee with the man, shook hands, and left."

I says— He says, "Well, do you know who that
was?" I says, "No, I don't have a clue." He
says, "That was D.B. Cooper." I says, "D.B. who?
D.B. Cooper who?" I said, "I don't know no D.B.
Cooper." Well, this happened, I guess, evidently
the day that he jumped out of that plane. And
there was nothing on the news, you know. I mean,
it could have been Harry Schwartz, you know, as
far as I know that walked in there. And he says,
"Well, that was D.B. Cooper." And I says, "Who's
D.B. Cooper?" He says, "Well, he just hijacked a
plane out of Seattle."

I says, "And?" I says, "There's no jet air—
airports around here for jets to land." He says,
"No, this guy jumped out of the airplane." I
says, "Okay." [laughs] I'm not gonna argue, I
don't know nothing. And he says— After a few
other conversations, he asked me if I knew what
was rolled up in that raincoat. I says, "No." I
says, "It's none of my business," I says, "what
a man does." I said, "He could've had a dog in
there, he could've had a shaving kit." I said,
"I don't know what he had in there. That's his
business, none of mine." I said, "I don't get
personal, I don't ask questions."

I didn't notice any scratches or anything like that on him. *[00:18:00]* <u>Uh</u>, he wasn't bleeding anywhere that I noticed. If he was, it was underneath his coat where I— where it wasn't obvious, <u>you know</u>, for me to see. I know his face and his ears and his hands were beet red from being out there in the cold, but that's just anybody, <u>you know</u>. Other than that, I didn't notice anything unusual that he was soaking wet and that was it. No, he says, "That your dump truck out there, kid?" I says, "No," I said, "it belongs to my boss." Then I says, "He let me use it." I says, "I'm on my way out to play music." But I says, "I seen you walking up there on the side of the road, <u>you know</u>, maybe hitch hiking." I says, "But I'm not allowed to stop and pick up any hitch hikers or anything like that." I says, "It's company policy."

I said, "Besides, I didn't have a seat on the other side anyway." He said, "Well, that's okay," he said, "don't worry about it." He says, "I'll get your coffee for you." And I shook hands with the man and left. There was just one other person <u>in there</u>, I don't know if he was a truck driver or what he was. Just one other guy sitting <u>in there</u>. Had his back to us. That was it. And as I said earlier, I spent six years law enforcement, and one of the things they teach you is you look, you observe, and if you guys were to leave <u>here</u> right now and somebody a month later comes back and says, "What were you wearing? What color shirt did you have on? What color of tennis shoes did you have?"

<u>You know</u>, you learn to observe people, what they're wearing, what they look like, <u>you know</u>, how tall are they? <u>Uh</u>, what color hair do they have, do they have any hair? <u>You know</u>, I mean, just— just different things, <u>you know</u>, that you learn to— It just gets in your mind, and you just keep it there. Yeah, I have no idea what gave him an impression other than that I played country music, <u>you know</u>, and I was a singer. Um, I don't know why he would be, <u>you know</u>, bringing my name up and Carl says that— told me that every time he mentioned my name, Walter would just— <u>you know</u>, he'd be like this, <u>you know</u>, nervous.

[00:20:00] Well, like I said, I didn't know who he was. I says, "What's he got to be nervous about?" Out past Monroe, <u>somewheres</u> out there, there's a gold bar— Not gold bar, <u>uh</u>— Oh God, it's got a funny name, I can't think of it. It's just a little town out of, out of Monroe—

Interviewer: Okay.

Jeff: —east of Monroe. I can't think of the name of the town. My son used to live there. I should know it. I can't remember the name of the town.

Interviewer: All right.

Jeff: I just asked him. I says, "How you getting <u>here</u>?" And he says, "Well, I'm coming over," Say, "like from Monroe." He said, "I'll be coming over, <u>you know</u> Stevens and Blewett Pass." And he said, "I'll come down there." And he says— he's, "How long do you think it'll take me to get there?" I was, "Well, if you're coming from where you're coming," I said, "you're at least— You're a good half hour from where we're at to the top of Blewett Pass." Then I says, "From where you're at, so you're probably looking at about two and a half hours. Ballpark, <u>somewhere in there</u>. To get <u>here</u> from when you're coming from, <u>you know</u>, that direction."

Interviewer: Yeah.

[00:20:57] [END OF AUDIO]

Jeff (Cowboy) Osiadacz's previous statement is consistent with a truthful one. I see no deceptive language, patterns, or indicators. My review of the audiotape shows he is very comfortable and consistent in his recollection of events, as reflected in his speaking voice, voice inflections, and word pronunciation. He provides unprompted details and speaks in the active voice and in the past tense, which are traits of truth-tellers. He is also consistent with his previous statements to Carl and Vern and with the statements that follow. I am confident Jeff Osiadacz is telling the truth.

To continue, let's look at Jeff's written statements, below. The first is Jeff Osiadacz's unanalyzed written statement; the second shows my analysis.

As stated before, his written statement is generally consistent with his transcribed one, above, and is straightforward and precise. Notice the continuing active voice in the past tense. I do note that in his transcribed statement, he refers to the rolled-up "raincoat" or "trench coat" under his (D.B. Cooper's) arm. In his written statement, below, he refers to the "large bundle" "under one arm."

One of the difficulties in linguistic analysis is "contamination." I discussed "contamination" earlier. By the time of this written statement, several people (Carl, Dirk, and Vern) had talked to Jeff. Jeff is a former police officer, police chief, and pillar of his community, as evidenced by his being named 2017 King Coal of Kittitas County, Washington. When I first talked to him over the phone, I found him to be quick and consistent in his responses. When I asked him how he remembered the date as November 24, 1971, Jeff stated, "I remember the date because the next day I learned about the D.B. Cooper hijacking."

And, as noted in the complete timeline, "Jeff was the lead singer and lead guitar of several Country-Western bands over the years, performed locally nearly every weekend, wore cowboy attire while performing, and worked as a dump truck driver for several years."

While this description in his written statement is different than the "raincoat" in this transcribed statement, it is not significantly inconsistent or contradictory. Again, there is a reason for the description change. What is it? It could be he tired of calling it a "raincoat or trench coat" and selected "large bundle" to eliminate the need for that distinction. The written statement was obtained more than a year after this transcribed statement and eight years after Walt's admission to Carl. I conclude that this difference ("raincoat" to "trench coat" to "large bundle") is not fatal and is probably due to time elapse and contamination through unknown and unstructured discussions with other people at various times. I remain confident Jeff Osiadacz provided us with statements consistent with the truth of his memories and observations from the night of November 24, 1971, an event occurring almost forty-seven years ago.

My Name is Jeff Osiadacz.

I am a life long Resident of Roslyn and Cle Elum Washington.

I was in the Teanaway Junction Cafe The Night of November 24th 1971 when The Man on The Reverse Side walked in Dripping wet, wearing a Dark Suit and wearing Black loafers. He Had a Large Bundle under one arm. He asked me where He was and if He made a Phone call would I Give His friend Directions How To Get There To The Cafe and Pick Him up. Which I Did. He Thanked me Said He would Buy My Coffee and I left To Go Play Music.

I Don't Know His Name or who He was.

Po Box 617 So Cle Elum WA 98943

Jeff Osiadacz.

This 7th day of August, 2017
June B. Legg-Agterty
Kittitas County, Washington

My Name is Jeff OSIADACZ

I am a life long Resident of Roslyn and Cle Elum Washington.

I was in The TEANAWAY JUNCTION CAfe The Night of November 24th 1971 when The MAN on The Reverse Side walked in Dripping wet, wearing A DARK Suit and wearing Black loafers. He HAD A LARGE Bundle under one ARM. He Asked me where He was and if He MAde A Phone CAll would I Give His friend DIRECTIONS How To Get There To The CAfe and PICK Him up. which I DID, He Thanked Me SAID He would Buy My Coffee and I left To Go Play Music.

X   I DON'T KNOW His NAME or who He WAS.

Po Box 617 So Cle Elum WA 98943

Jeff OSIADACZ.

Jeff Osiadacz

This 7th day of August, 2017
Tena B. Legg-Afferty
Kittitas County, Washington

About 1970 Jeff came
to work, for my father
Bob Lumsden, owner of
Lumsden Logging as a
dump truck driver I also
drove with him.

Dave Lumsden

$1 THURSDAY, SEPT. 21, 2017 • NKC TRIBUNE

Jeff Osiadacz named KING COAL 2017

In the mines it was a risky O-Dark-Thirty all day long

CORONATION CANCELLED

Author's Note: King Coal 2017 Jeff Osiadacz was to be crowned in Roslyn on Sunday, Sept. 3, but the event was cancelled due to smoke, heat, concerns for public safety and the need to keep roads open for firefighters assigned to the Jolly Mountain Wildfire. The ceremony was rescheduled for Saturday, Sept. 30, 5 p.m., at Hawthorne Hall in Ronald – but due to an unforeseen booking conflict at Hawthorne Hall the coronation was cancelled last week for good. Heritage Club officials said Osiadacz would be crowned and recognized in a private, informal ceremony at some point in the near future. The following story pays tribute to Osiadacz, his family, and to Upper Kittitas County coalminers.

by Jim Fossett
jim@nkctribune.com

SOUTH CLE ELUM – It is a tragedy so many died in the mines or died later in life because of them. It is a miracle some did survive the terrible ambushes awaiting miners in deep, dark places where the cry for help was easily smothered. King Coal 2017 Jeff Osiadacz began his story with the blows the mines dealt him, his father and his grandfather a thousand feet or more below the grounds where today we build our homes, work our jobs and mow our lawns. They are the grounds on which Upper County mothers and fathers raise their children.

Rockfall, cave-in, explosion

"My dad and I were down 1,200 feet or so," Osiadacz began, "about halfway to the bottom of the shaft, when a big rock broke

shook it off and went back to work.

"My dad came back to the mines because he didn't want me to be down there alone. He worked in the No. 3 and Patrick's Mines. It was in the No. 3 he got caught in a cave-in. It crushed his left hip and pelvis.

"There were two other miners with him at the time. One of them took off running. The other, Sam Craven, told dad he wouldn't leave him behind.

"Sam was a big man, a giant at over six-feet tall.

"He got some jacks to free my dad from the rubble, then he carried him out.

"The Cravens: I got nothing to say but good things about that family."

Osiadacz's grandfather worked in the Shaft Mine behind Roslyn City Hall, 200 yards from the turnoff to Carek's Meat Market. The slag piles there are

KING COAL 2017 Jeff Osiadacz with the miner's helmet and lamp, like the one he wore back in the day. This one is on display at Swiftwater Cellars Winery, site of the old No. 9 Mine, where he worked.
Photo courtesy of Osiadacz Family

---

23   Photo of page B1 of *NKC Tribune*, purchased September 21, 2017.

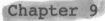
MORE EVIDENCE, D.B. COOPER AND WALT RECA COMPARISONS, ABBREVIATED TIMELINE

D.B. Cooper sketch   **Walt Reca**

This photograph (date unknown) of Walt is the one Carl Laurin sent to Jeff Osiadacz. Using this photo, Jeff identified Walt as the man he saw in the Teanaway Junction Café, Cle Elum, Washington, on the night of November 24, 1971. Jeff later stated he didn't have a mustache the night of November 24, 1971 and the early 1972 photo below shows Walt without a mustache.

This is Walt Reca in early 1972.

OPTIONAL FORM NO. 10
MAY 1962 EDITION
GSA FPMR (41 CFR) 101-11.6

UNITED STATES GOVERNMENT

Memorandum

TO : SAC, ALBANY   DATE: November 30, 1971

FROM : SAC, SEATTLE (164-81)(-P-)

SUBJECT: UNKNOWN SUBJECT, aka Dan Cooper;
NORTHWEST AIRLINES
FLIGHT #305,
PORTLAND TO SEATTLE,
11/24/71,
CAA - HIJACKING; EXTORTION
OO: SEATTLE
BUfile 164-2111

     Enclosed for each office is one artist's conception
of the captioned subject. The Bureau is preparing a circular
for field-wide circularization concerning captioned case and
will include an artist's conception of the hijacker. The Bureau
has been asked to prepare a sketch showing the unknown subject
without glasses. Additional distribution will be made from
time to time to parachute clubs, flight instruction schools and
airports, etc., in an effort to identify the unknown subject
which undoubtedly will result in various field divisions receiving
calls on this case.

     For the assistance of all offices in conducting
investigation and to evaluate complaints from citizens, the
following information is furnished.

     The unknown subject boarded captioned flight at
Portland, Oregon, using the name DAN COOPER. As the plane   b6
was taxiing toward the runway, Stewardess [   ]   b7C
occupied the seat reserved for the stewardesses on the right
side of the plane and behind the last row of passenger seats.
The unknown subject, who occupied the center seat in the last
row of three seats, turned and handed her an envelope
which she did not open for a few minutes until he glanced
at her several times. She then opened the envelope and read
the enclosed note which said: "Miss - I have a bomb here
and I would like you to sit by me." At this point Stewardess

2 - All Offices (Encl 1)
3 - Seattle (164-81)
CEF:klb

164-91-7

SEARCHED ___ INDEXED ___
SERIALIZED ___ FILED ___

**The FBI's All Office Report on the Hijacking,
November 30, 1971**

SE 164-81

[_____] came toward the rear of the plane and [_____]
handed [____] the note. [____] then called the pilot on the intercom.

Stewardess [_____] then sat next to the hijacker
who opened a black attache case' and showed her what he said
was a bomb. She described the contents of the attache case
as a bundle of red sticks, which she believed was dynamite.
The bundle consisted of six or eight red colored sticks
approximately six to eight inches long with no writing on the
outside. The hijacker was holding in his hand a wire which
lead to the bundle of sticks and indicated that he could
detonate the bomb by touching the wire to a contact. Also in
the attache case was a cylindrical shaped battery about eight
inches long.

At first the hijacker asked for $200,000 and two
parachutes.

After [_____] left her stewardess seat and gave
the note to [_____] sat beside the hijacker who, after
showing the contents of the attache case, told her to,
"Take this down." From her purse she obtained a pen and note
pad and he dictated the following message:

"I want $200,000 by 5:00 PM in cash. Put
it in a knapsack. I want two back parachutes and two
front parachutes. When we land, I want a fuel truck ready
to refuel. No funny stuff, or I'll do the job."

At the Seattle-Tacoma International Airport (Sea-Tac)
in answer to his demands, the hijacker was provided with the
four parachutes and $200,000 in 20 dollar bills in a canvas
bank bag. When the plane landed at Seattle at 5:45 PM (PDT)
he instructed Stewardess [_____] to go after the money
which she did. He opened the bag; inspected the money and then
told them that the passengers as well as the two other
stewardesses could leave the plane. They did deplane. The
remaining crew members were the three male members of the
flight crew as well as Stewardess [_____]

[_____] then made several trips out of the
plane to obtain the parachutes which she brought to the subject.

The hijacker instructed that he be flown to Mexico
City and also told the pilot that he wanted the plane flown at
not more than 10,000 feet with the flaps at 15 degrees, the landing
gear down and the rear steps of the plane also down. The
plane involved was a Boeing 727, a Tri-jet with stairs at
the rear which lowered for passengers. The hijacker finally

SE 164-81

agreed to having the steps raised and a flight plan was
arranged from Seattle to Portland and down south to Red
Bluff, California and then to Reno, Nevada for refueling.

The plane departed Sea-Tac with the three crew
members in the cabin and [   ] in the rear with the
hijacker. Within minutes after take off at 7:36 PM, the
hijacker had the stewardess show him how to lower the steps
and he then ordered her to go to the first class section
which she did, and she then continued on to the cabin.

b6
b7C

At 8:05 PM the captain was in touch with the
hijacker by the intercom. This was the last communication
he had with the hijacker. Just prior to this communication,
the captain had a signal indicating that the stairs had been
lowered. At 8:12 PM, the captain experienced "oscillation"
in the plane and thought perhaps the hijacker had departed
the plane.

Air Force fighter planes were escorting the craft
but because the 727 was flying at 170 knots, the fighter jets
were too fast. Further, the weather was overcast and
visibility extremely low.

When the plane arrived at Reno, the hijacker was
gone and two of the parachutes were still in the airplane.
The attache case also was not in the plane and has not been
found.

Extensive search of the southwestern part of
Washington State, which was indicated by the 8:12 PM oscillation,
has been conducted but with negative results to date.

Subject is described as follows:

Race: White
Sex: Male
Age: Mid 40s
Height: 5'10" to 6'
Weight: 170 to 180 lbs.
Build: Average to well built
Complexion: Olive, Latin appearance,
                 medium smooth

3.

GETTING THE TRUTH

Hair:	Dark brown or black, normal style, parted on left, combed back, Sideburns, low ear level
Eyes:	Possibly brown. During latter part of flight, put on dark wrap-around sunglasses with dark rims
Voice:	Low, spoke intelligently; no particular accent, possibly from Midwest section of the United States
Characteristic:	Heavy smoker of Raleigh filter tip cigarettes
Wearing Apparel:	Black or brown suit; white shirt; narrow black tie; black rain-type overcoat or dark top coat; dark briefcase or attache case; carried paper bag 4"x12"x14"; brown shoes

Leads should be set forth by telephone or teletype and, to facilitate handling at Seattle, each incoming communication should be sub-captioned with the name of the suspect.

THIS INDIVIDUAL IS BEING SOUGHT IN CONNECTION WITH THE EXTORTION OF $200,000 FROM NORTHWEST AIRLINES BY THREATENING THE CREW OF THE AIRLINE WITH A PACKAGE WHICH HE STATED CONTAINED A BOMB. HE SHOULD BE CONSIDERED DANGEROUS.

To: / All Offices Except
     Seattle, Portland, Las Vegas

From: Director, FBI (164-2111)
       NORTHWEST   164-91*
UNSUB; NORTHEST AIRLINES
FLIGHT 305, 11/24/71
CAA - HIJACKING
OO: SEATTLE

       Enclosed for each receiving office are two copies of an
artist's conception of captioned unsub.

       Shortly after 3:00 p.m. Pacific Standard Time (PST)
11/24/71, a lone white male traveling from Portland, Oregon, to
Seattle, Washington, on captioned flight displayed the contents of
his brief case to a stewardess indicating to her it was a bomb
which would be exploded unless his demands were met. The hijacker
indicated his willingness to exchange the safety of the 36 passengers and crew for $200,000 in cash and four parachutes. He
instructed that the plane circle the Seattle airport until his
demands were met at which time the plane landed. Once the money
and parachutes were loaded and the plane was being refueled, the
hijacker allowed the passengers and two airline stewardesses to
deplane leaving a flight crew of three males and one female and
the hijacker aboard. The hijacker indicated a desire to fly to
Mexico City and instructed the plane to take off flying at a low
altitude and slow speed, maintaining a southerly direction. Upon
demand the hijacker was instructed on lowering the rear passenger
door while the aircraft was in flight. He was last seen in the
aircraft by crew members at 8;05 p.m. PST, when he instructed

Enclosures (2)

164-91-8

DEC 2 1971

Sent Via _____ M   Per

DB Coop

GETTING THE TRUTH

the hostage stewardess to go forward to the first class section and close the curtains behind her. Stewardess complied, going through first class section into pilot's cockpit and locking door behind her. Prior to departing from passenger cabin, hijacker told stewardess the money bag was not in accordance with instructions and to cut up one of the parachutes to rewrap the money, which was done. When the aircraft landed at Reno, Nevada, for refueling, the hijacker, two parachutes, the ransom money, and the vinyl brief case had disappeared.

Investigation determined that the hijacker had purchased his ticket at the Portland Airport shortly before the plane's departure. Upon arrival at Seattle, all passengers were accounted for except a white male using the name Dan Cooper. There were no sky marshals aboard this flight and at no time did subject show any firearms.

From information available, the subject is described as white male, mid 40's, 5'10" to 6', 170 to 180 pounds, average to well built, olive or swarthy complexion, medium smooth, dark brown or black hair parted on left side, combed back, sideburns to low ear level, dark eyes, probably black or brown. Subject wore a dark suit, white shirt, with narrow black tie. He wore dark glasses with plastic rims (possibly prescription lenses) most of the time. He had dark overcoat and was described as cool and calculating. His voice was low. He spoke intelligently and was a heavy smoker of Raleigh filter tip cigarettes.

All leads should be handled immediately and set out telephonically and confirmed by teletype. The Bureau must be kept advised of all pertinent developments as they occur. A list of the loot is being prepared and will be disseminated. Consider subject dangerous.

D.B. COOPER AND WALT RECA COMPARISONS

FBI Identifiers on Cooper and Walt Reca

	D.B. Cooper	Walt Reca
Race	White	White
Sex	Male	Male
Age	Mid 40s	38 yrs. at time of hijacking
Height	5'10" to 6'	5'10"
Weight	170 to 180 lbs.	
Build	Average to well built	Average to well built
Complexion	Olive, Latin appearance, medium smooth.	Walt was probably suntanned due to his outside work with the ironworkers.
Hair	Dark brown or black, normal style, parted on left, combed back, sideburns, low ear level.	Dark brown; hair parts left, sideburns, low ear level.
Eyes	Possibly brown. During latter part of flight, put on dark wraparound sunglasses with dark rims.	Blue eyes, wore sunglasses.
Voice	Low, spoke intelligently, possibly from Midwest section of the United States.	From Midwest

Characteristic	Heavy smoker of Raleigh filter tip cigarettes.	Heavy smoker of cigarettes; Lisa Story, Sandy, and Loretta Laurin know Walt smoked Sir Walter Raleigh cigarettes.
Wearing Apparel	Black/brown suit; white shirt; narrow black tie; black rain-type overcoat or dark top coat; dark briefcase; carried paper bag 4" x 12" x 14"; brown shoes.	Brown suit; black tie; raincoat; black penny loafers.

ABBREVIATED TIMELINE

The following timeline shows major events in Walt Peca/Reca's life interposed with the D.B. Cooper events.

Event	Date	Source
WP (Walter Peca; WR, if Walter Reca), sometime prior to 11/24/1971, rents a typewriter, types hijacking note.	November 1971	Documents
WP drives from Hartline to Spokane; takes bus to Portland; buys suit, penny loafers, tie, raincoat. Buys briefcase, alarm clock, battery, red flares, wires to construct fake bomb. Applies Super Glue to fingers.	Tuesday, November 23, '71	Documents
D.B. Cooper applies another coat of Super Glue to his fingers while in airport; buys ticket at Sea-Tac; hijacks NW 305, Portland to Seattle.	Wednesday, November 24, '71	Hijack

Event	Date	Source
WP lands in field near Cle Elum, WA, and walks to Teanaway Junction Café.	Wednesday, November 24, '71	Transcripts
Jeff Osiadacz (JO)—"Cowboy"—drives dump truck to Teanaway Junction Café, sees WP on the road.	Wednesday, November 24, '71	Transcripts
JO meets WP at Teanaway Junction Café, Cle Elum, WA.	Wednesday, November 24, '71	Transcripts
WP calls Don Brennan (Don) while WP is at Teanaway Junction Café; JO talked to Don.	Wednesday, November 24, '71	Transcripts
JO "Cowboy" telephonically gives directions to Teanaway Junction Café to man (Don).	Wednesday, November 24, '71	Transcripts
JO "Cowboy" plays in band at Grange Hall, Cle Elum.	Wednesday, November 24, '71	Transcripts
Don Brennan (Don) picks up WP and drives WP to Hartline.	Wednesday, November 24, '71	Transcripts
WP becomes W Racca, in Spokane, WA, home purchase.	July 1972	Realtor
WR obtains first passport—uses name Walter Reca.	Tuesday, March 26, '74	Passport
WR's passport shows him in Poland before Daoud shooting (which occurred on August 1, 1981, in Warsaw).	Monday, July 1, 1981	Passport
Carl Laurin (CL) begins taping WP conversations.	October 2008	

Event	Date	Source
Carl submits WR's DNA through David Damore to FBI Agent Larry Carr.	Monday, July 27, 2009	Damore Letter
Don Brennan (Don) dies.	Thursday, November 10, '11	Death Notices
CL goes to Cle Elum in search of drop area information.	June 2012	Complete Walter Peca/Reca Timeline
Wayne Willet identifies "Cowboy" as Jeff Osiadacz.	June 2012	Complete Walter Peca/Reca Timeline
WP/WR dies	Friday, February 17, '14	Death Certificate
Vern Jones interview/ videotapes Jeff Osiadacz "Cowboy"	Tuesday, July 26, 2016	Transcripts

Legend for Timeline:
WP = Walter Peca
WR = Walter Reca
CL = Carl Laurin
Don = Don Brennan
JO = Jeff Osiadacz

Chapter 10

SUMMARY AND CONCLUSIONS

Carl Laurin suspected Walt Reca was D.B. Cooper as soon as the hijacking was broadcast on the news. According to Carl, years later on a TV show about the hijacking, he and Loretta heard that D.B. Cooper had offered one of the stewardesses some money before he jumped. That, to Carl, was one of the first clues indicating that Walt was D.B. Cooper because Walt had offered and given money to the manager at the Big Boy robbery in Detroit, for which he was convicted. Walt also told Carl about this in the transcript: money given to the Big Boy manager, at 01:53:21; money offered to the stewardess on Northwest Orient Flight 305, 01:52:32.

Dirk, Vern, and I confirmed Carl's DNA account by interviewing the attorney he said he gave the DNA sample to for submission to the FBI. I photographed Carl's file at the attorney's office, and the attorney's account was consistent with Carl's. In fact, we verified as much of Carl's entire account to the extent that our resources allowed us. I feel confident in Carl's veracity.

Because of Carl's diligent work, perseverance, and evidence gathering, we (Dirk, Vern, and I) were able to assess, review, and inspect Carl's documents to help determine whether Walt Reca was D.B. Cooper. Without Carl's work, none of this would have been possible. So, let's look at the evidence, the Complete

Timeline, the Abbreviated Timeline, the released FBI evidence, and my analysis and evaluation of the evidence.[24]

The Abbreviated Timeline, above, shows the major events interposed with the D.B. Cooper hijacking event. I had to use abbreviations to make the narrative shorter and smaller to accommodate fifty-three years of history. It helps us get a quick picture of The Complete Timeline and fully appreciate all of Walt's significant life events.

By all accounts and evidence available, Walt was capable of jumping out of a 727, at night, in inclement weather with a good chance of surviving. His history showed he had the training, the skills, the will, the character, and the resoluteness to commit the hijacking.

Over several years, Walt admitted that he was D.B. Cooper to Carl verbally, on recordings, and in his Last Testament. Walt also admitted that he was D.B. Cooper to his niece Lisa Story and his sister, Sandy, confirming and validating all the details in his Last Testament. I closely reviewed and analyzed the recordings between Walt and Carl to begin my analysis by listening to Walt's responses and measuring his response times, pauses, changes in tone, inflections, tone, pitch, changes in voice patterns, and all the other variables I consider when trying to determine deception and changes in communication patterns. Walt's voice and communication patterns were consistent throughout the recordings.

Next, I analyzed the transcripts to ascertain whether Walt's communication patterns changed when Carl asked him about the D.B. Cooper case or something else. I again found Walt's responses to be consistent and without any communication pattern change in the transcripts as well. His patterns didn't change from his calibrated model. Following my extensive and intense review

---

24   See https://vault.fbi.gov/D-B-Cooper%20.

and analysis of those recordings and transcripts, my opinion is that Walt Reca was consistent with truthful statements in his admissions that he was D.B. Cooper. Again, being truthful and factual can be two different things. Walt believed he was D.B. Cooper. His statement, in my opinion, is consistent with the truth. The FBI or the crew and the passengers of Northwest Orient Flight 305 ultimately will determine whether he was factual.

After I conducted a similar review and analysis of Jeff Osiadacz's transcripts, recording, and written statement, my opinion is that Jeff Osiadacz's statements were and are consistent with the truth when he said:

1. Jeff was driving his dump truck on the road leading to the Teanaway Junction Café in Cle Elum, Washington, when he observed a man walking in the rain carrying a bundle under his arm;

2. Later, inside the Teanaway Junction Café, Jeff saw, met, and assisted that same man he had seen walking on the road;

3. Jeff knew it was the night of November 24, 1971, because he performed with a band that night at the Grange Hall (I've not been able to independently verify/corroborate this event at the Grange Hall);

4. He knew the date was November 24, 1971, because he said he learned of the D.B. Cooper hijacking the day after his performance at the Grange Hall;

5. He clearly remembers the man was wearing penny loafers (because Jeff always wanted penny loafers);

6. Based on a photograph Carl sent him, Jeff identified Walt as the man he'd seen walking in the rain along the road and as the man he'd assisted while inside the Teanaway Junction Café. (This was not a forensically sound photographic identification. Carl sent Jeff one photo.)

Here's Walt's account, as told to Carl in the transcript. (These recordings were made at least four years before Carl located Jeff, who then identified Walt in 2012):

[02:19:23] **Walt:** I give it to the guy with the tru— uh, with the dump truck— the telephone. He give him the directions.

[02:19:29] **Carl:** Oh, he gave you the directions?

[02:19:31] **Walt:** He give it to Don.

[02:19:33] **Carl:** Ohh. Oh, um—

[02:19:37] **Walt:** That's how come I remember him good, too, with his fuckin' guitar, cowboy hat, Western gear right there at, uh— *Use of the phrase "right there" in a threatening discussion.*

As part of this review, I read many FBI reports from the FBI Vault (see *https://vault.fbi.gov/D-B-Cooper%20*) detailing conversations between the airline personnel and D.B. Cooper. I found Walt's details about conversations, notes, and events to be consistent with the details in the released FBI reports. It is possible Walt read or heard some of the details about the hijacking from written accounts of the hijacking before he talked to Carl and before Carl recorded those conversations. Walt said he didn't read anything on it, just tried to forget about it. Here are excerpts from Walt on that issue, at 02:29:39:

[02:29:39] **Carl:** Right. And you never one time, as far as you can remember, seen anything on TV because you didn't have TV at Hartline or you never read anything about it in a newspaper, or— or— or a book or anything like that?

[02:29:59] **Walt:** No.

[02:30:00] **Carl:** And, you—

[02:30:11] **Walt:** —<u>right there</u>. *I* mean, *I* wouldn't drive twenty miles for a twenty-five-cent newspaper. *Use of the phrase "right there" in a nonthreatening discussion.*

[02:30:16] **Carl:** Yeah, yeah. Did— Did— Did you ever hear people talking about it? When you went to work on the dam project, did—

[02:30:25] **Walt:** No.

[02:30:26] **Carl:** You never heard anybody say, uh, "God, did you hear what happened, uh, Thanksgiving?" <u>You know</u>?

[02:30:33] **Walt:** Naw. The only thing *they* talked about, <u>right there</u>, is, uh, cows. A lot of 'em were ranchers and *they* had cows, and *they* all bought Charolais cows 'cause *they* could, uh-uh, stand the weather. The winter? *Use of the phrase "right there" in a nonthreatening discussion.*

[02:30:48] **Carl:** Uh-huh.

[02:30:48] **Walt:** But then *they* couldn't sell 'em and get a price on 'em 'cause the Charolais <u>right there</u> is a big-boned cow. *I* know more about fuckin' cows— *Use of the phrase "right there" in a nonthreatening discussion.*

[02:30:56] **Carl:** *[laughs]*

[02:30:56] **Walt:** —learned at lunchtime than the fuckin' cowboys in the old Western days.

[laughter]

[02:31:06] **Carl:** So, you never really— Is it fair to say, it's hard— This is hard to believe. Is it fair to say that you never knew what a legend that Cooper was?

[02:31:17] **Walt:** No.

[02:31:18] **Carl:** You never knew?

[02:31:21] **Walt:** No, not at all. Why— *I* mean, uh— just, uh, <u>you know</u>.

[02:31:30] **Carl:** Okay, how did you find out even that they were calling you D.B. Cooper?

[02:31:38] **Walt:** Oh, that <u>right there</u>, uh, uh, *I* don't know. ***Use of the phrase "right there" in a threatening discussion.***

[02:31:46] **Carl:** But you— But you did—

[02:31:47] **Walt:** I didn't sign on as D.B. Cooper.

[02:31:49] **Carl:** No, *I* know, but you did know, eventually— Eventually at some point of time that somebody, through some way had— had— had changed it to D.B. Cooper.

[02:32:01] **Walt:** Yeah, *it* was a long time afterwards, <u>right there</u>, when *I* just ran across an article in the paper. <u>Right there</u>, and that was, oh shit, maybe six months later or something. [Carl interjects: Yeah.] So, *I* didn't— ***Use of the phrase "right there" in a threatening discussion.***

[02:32:16] **Carl:** Did— Did you read that article?

[02:32:19] **Walt:** Did *I* read *it*?

[02:32:20] **Carl:** Yeah.

[02:32:21] **Walt:** No, *I* glanced through *it*, <u>right</u> <u>there</u>. I wanted all that shit out of my mind. ***Use of the phrase "right there" in a threatening discussion.***

[02:32:25] **Carl:** You just wanted to forget it?

[02:32:28] **Walt:** Yeah.

Let's assume Walt didn't tell the truth as to whether he was following news reports on the D.B. Cooper case. I found no evidence that the staff's or the passengers' FBI reports were released to the public before 2010. If that had been the case, Walt would have had to create the details he provided to Carl. It would be highly unlikely that those "created" details would be consistent with the crew's and the passengers' details.

Jeff's (Cowboy's) independent statement and details are not just similar but the same as the details Walt gave Carl many years earlier. Look at this excerpt from 02:16:28 between Carl and Walt (I provided more of the transcript to put everything in context):

[02:16:28] **Walt:** Yeah.

[02:16:31] **Carl:** Um—

[02:16:33] **Walt:** The—the, a neon light there at the restaurant.

[02:16:37] **Carl:** Okay.

[02:16:38] **Walt:** *It*'s dark but, <u>you know</u>, *you* can tell and it— *it*'s not a town or anything.

[02:16:42] **Carl:** Yeah.

[02:16:43] **Walt:** <u>You know</u>, *it* was just a restaurant there.

[02:16:45] **Carl:** Yeah.

[02:16:46] **Walt:** Maybe a quarter of a mile away.

[02:16:48] **Carl:** Yeah. Okay, now you're walkin' along. You're walkin' along to the restaurant.

[02:16:56] Walt: Yeah.

[02:16:57] **Carl:** And you get there, and do you remember anything or you just find a door and go in? Er—

[02:17:03] **Walt:** Yeah, *I* find the door and *I* go in. *I* ordered a cup of coffee. *My* hand's shaking real bad <u>right there</u>. *It*'s spilling <u>right there</u>, so *I* didn't want nobody to see *it*. *Use of the phrase "right there" in a threatening discussion.*

[02:17:13] **Carl:** Uh-huh.

[02:17:14] **Walt:** And *I* got some change from the waitress <u>right there</u> and *I* asked her where the telephone was and *I* called up Don. And *I* said, "*I* done *it*." He said, "*You* done what?" [Carl interjects: Yeah.] *I* had discussed *it* with *him* before. *Use of the phrase "right there" in a threatening discussion.*

[02:17:28] **Carl:** Did you have to go to the bathroom or anything?

[02:17:32] **Walt:** Oh, fuck yeah. *[laughs]* Yeah, *I* mean *I* was pissing in the woods coming out.

[02:17:42] **Carl:** Oh, yeah.

[02:17:43] **Walt:** Yeah.

[02:17:46] **Carl:** Yeah. Um, okay and there's nothing you can remember. Somebody said your—your face is beet red.

[02:17:52] **Walt:** Yeah. [Carl interjects: Um]

[02:17:53] **Carl:** Um— Do you remember any music playing in that truck stop or anything?

[02:18:00] **Walt:** No. Um, *I* was incoherent pretty near at that time.

[02:18:08] **Carl:** Yeah. Um, boy it's a wonder that when they heard about it, that they didn't say, "Hey, you know somebody seen a guy come in here that, uh," you know it was— you know, yeah, it's almost a wonder that they didn't report somethin'.

[02:18:27] **Walt:** Nobody would believe *it*, Charlie.

[02:18:31] **Carl:** Well, *I* mean.

[02:18:33] **Walt:** *I* couldn't believe *it* myself.

[02:18:36] **Carl:** Yeah, but *I* mean after it— it had happened, you know, every— everybody in the world believed that it happened after it happened.

[02:18:44] **Walt:** *It* just wasn't that noticeable.

[02:18:48] **Carl:** What made you think— just— just what made you think you were at Steven's point and, uh, Cashmere between there, *I* mean what— what gave you the idea that, that's where you were?

[02:19:02] **Walt:** *I* don't know, right there. *I* just figured that's where *I* was, but *I* guess

I wasn't. **Use of the phrase "right there" in a threatening discussion.**

[02:19:08] **Carl:** But you had to get directions from the— from somebody in the, um, in— in the restaurant in— in the, uh, the truck stop. You had to get directions to tell Don where to come and pick you up.

[02:19:23] **Walt:** *I* give *it* to the guy with the tru— uh, with the dump truck— the telephone. *He* give *him* the directions.

[02:19:29] **Carl:** Oh, he gave you the directions?

[02:19:31] **Walt:** *He* give *it* to Don.

[02:19:33] **Carl:** Ohh. Oh, um—

[02:19:37] **Walt:** That's how come *I* remember *him* good, too, with his fuckin' guitar, cowboy hat, Western gear <u>right there</u> at, uh— **Use of the phrase "right there" in a threatening discussion.**

[02:19:43] **Carl:** Oh, how— how come he was by the, um— how come he was by the telephone?

[02:19:48] **Walt:** 'Cause *I* called *him* over.

[02:19:49] **Carl:** Oh, just to tell him where you were? You just said to, "Come and get me," yeah.

[02:19:52] **Walt:** Yeah, because *I* don't know where *I* was. *He* knew where *we* were.

[02:19:56] **Carl:** Well, yeah, yeah. What's, uh— so you sat there and drank coffee for two and a half hours.

[02:20:03] **Walt:** Yeah, right about that. *It* could have been two and a half hours <u>right there</u>. ***Use of the phrase "right there" in a threatening discussion.***

[02:20:07] **Carl:** Yeah.

[02:20:08] **Walt:** *It* could have been an hour, <u>you know</u>—

[02:20:11] **Carl:** Yeah. Well, it had to be, if he lived in Everett at the time.

[02:20:15] **Walt:** No. *He* didn't live in Everett.

[02:20:17] **Carl:** Where did he live?

[02:20:19] **Walt:** Pardon, *he* lived in Seattle.

[02:20:23] **Carl:** Oh, oh, Don lived in Seattle at the time?

[02:20:26] **Walt:** Yeah.

[02:20:27] **Carl:** Oh, okay. So— but it was still a two-hour drive at least down there.

[02:20:32] **Walt:** Yeah.

I've concluded that Carl, Cowboy, and Walt have all provided truthful statements.

Let's look at a list of all the evidence that is corroborative, that leads us to believe Walt Reca was D.B. Cooper. Again, remember that the FBI rarely records its interviews with witnesses. So, its 302 reports reflect what the agents remember the witnesses saying—not always the precise words of the witnesses:

1. The tape recordings Carl provided;
2. Walt's lack of hubris on the recordings, which is consistent with Walt's truthful communication pattern;
3. The recordings, which reveal that Walt gave a free and voluntary, matter-of-fact accounting, almost mocking himself in a self-deprecating way;
4. Walt's work for known private military companies;
5. Walt's identification documents;
6. Walt's correspondence;
7. Walt's miniature spy camera;
8. Walt's Last Testament (confession);
9. Walt's forgeries;
10. Walt's aliases;
11. Cowboy's statement corroborating Walt's account;
12. Confirmation that Cowboy drove a dump truck;
13. The comparison of Walt with the FBI descriptors, including the Raleigh cigarette use;
14. Cowboy's identification of Walt as the man he saw the night of November 24, 1971, from a photo sent by Carl;
15. Walt's passport photo showing he was in Warsaw shortly before the Abu Daoud shooting (see photo);
16. Walt's vaccination records, which support his foreign travel;
17. Corroborative testimony from Lisa Story and Walt's sister, Sandy, which confirms Walt's activities and statements and his voice on the recordings;
18. D.B. Cooper's offer to gift the stewardess money before he jumped out, just as Walt had given money to the manager of the Big Boy restaurant he robbed on June 22, 1965. See [01:52:32] of the transcript. The FBI provided information about this offer by D.B. Cooper in news releases. In an FBI 302 (report form for the FBI) generated by FBI Special Agent H. E. Hinderliter [sic], File LV 164-60 (NORJAK file) on the interview of stewardess Tina Mucklow, he writes,

"Miss Mucklow recalled that she, in an attempt at being humorous, stated to the hijacker while the passengers were unloading that there was obviously a lot of money in the bag and she wondered if she could have some. The hijacker immediately agreed with her suggestion and took one package of the money, denominations unrecalled [sic] by Miss Mucklow, and handed it to her. She returned the money, stating to the hijacker that she was not permitted to accept gratuities or words to that effect. In this connection Miss Mucklow recalled that at one time during the flight the hijacker had pulled some single bills from his pocket and had attempted to tip all the girls on the crew. Again they declined in compliance with company policy."

19. Walt's statement that in July 1972, using last name Racca, he bought the home at 1204 Cleveland St., Spokane, Washington, with cash from the hijacking. The homeowner, Jim Everman, confirmed that Walter Racca purchased it for $675 cash down on a land contract.

20. The fact that no D.B. Cooper suspect fingerprints were found. Walt states he coated his fingers with Super Glue to avoid leaving fingerprints.

[00:53:38] **Carl:** Yeah. So in fact the airplane was just taxiing, it was taxiing come to think of it. And, uh, you handed her the note and, uh, uh, she— she put the note in her pocket like, <u>you know</u>, or some place and, uh, and you even [Walt interjects: smoked] Now you must have planned something because you said you put you put—

[00:54:01] **Walt:** Yeah. Super Glue.

[00:54:03] **Carl:** On your— on your fingers?

[00:54:04] **Walt:** Yeah.

[00:54:05] **Carl:** Where did you do that? In a hotel room in Portland or what?

[00:54:10] **Walt:** *I* did *it* once in Spokane before *I* left and *I* had the Super Glue with *me* and, uh, *I* did *it* at the airport, waiting. But to put another coat on.

21. The FBI 302 reports from witnesses suggesting that D.B. Cooper always wore his sunglasses, never removing them. Here is Walt in the recording:

[01:39:29] **Carl:** Yeah. Yeah. Do you ever remember taking your sunglass— glasses off well, in— in the airplane?

[01:39:37] **Walt:** *I* can't remember but *I* probably did to wipe *my* eyes, <u>*you* know</u>, *I* always do that but *I* mean, <u>*you* know</u>—

[01:39:44] **Carl:** You didn't leave—

[01:39:44] **Walt:** Not for any length of time.

22. FBI reports that state D.B. Cooper sat while the stewardesses brought everything to him. Here is Walt in the recording:

[01:38:22] **Carl:** Yeah. Now, how did you get the money? In other words, was it, was that carried back to you or did you have to go up to the front? You wouldn't have went up to the front of the airplane, you'd ordered it to been brought to you someway.

[01:38:33] **Walt:** *I* wanted everything brought to *me* where *I* was sitting.

[01:38:36] **Carl:** Okay. And— and, how— how did the parachutes get back to you? By a stewardess?

[01:38:43] **Walt:** *She* brought them back to *me*— the stewardess.

23. The FBI reports of stewardess interviews showing the stewardess didn't open the envelope D.B. Cooper gave her right away—she thought he might be *"making a pass,"* and she waited to open the envelope. D.B. Cooper called to her (Florence Schaffner) and, *"She said the man turned around and looked at her several times, and she felt that he was indicating that he wanted her to open the envelope immediately."* She then asked the man if he was "kidding" and he said, "No, Miss, this is for real." Here is Walt in the recording:

[01:43:37] **Carl:** So you did hand her— hand her the note and, uh— and— and she kind, uh— She was busy doing other things and she kind of put it in her pocket like and— and then when she, uh—

[01:43:51] **Walt:** Came back.

[01:43:52] **Carl:** Came back, she was— Yeah. After the airplane actually took off, uh, she came back to you. And— and that's when she said, "I can't believe you're actually hi— hijacking this airplane."

[01:44:05] **Walt:** And *I* said, "*I* can't believe *it* neither, but *I*'m serious."

[01:44:08] **Carl:** Yeah. Um, then do you remember what she said?

[01:44:14] **Walt:** *She* stared at *me* for a little while.

[01:44:18] **Carl:** *[laughs]* *I* would imagine— That's what *I*'da done, too.

[01:44:24] **Walt:** Yeah.

[01:44:25] **Carl:** And— and— and then did you tell her anything like, "Well, take this note up to the captain," or anything?

[01:44:32] **Walt:** Told *her* that about three times.

[01:44:35] **Carl:** You told her to take the note up to the captain?

[01:44:37] **Walt:** Yeah.

[01:44:38] **Carl:** And what did she—

[01:44:39] **Walt:** *She* was just staring at *me*.

[01:44:41] **Carl:** Okay. So, but finally, she did, though.

[01:44:45] **Walt:** Yes.

24. FBI reports stating that D.B. Cooper, after handing the stewardess the first note in the envelope, had her write his demands to take to the captain. Here is Walt in the recording:

[01:38:52] **Carl:** Yeah. Do you remember any other notes or any other information that you gave to anybody? Uh, for example, [Walt interjects: No.] when you said, "Well, when— when they bring the parachutes, don't have somebody in coveralls."

[01:39:11] **Walt:** What *I* said <u>right there</u>, everything was verbal. ***Use of the phrase "right there" in a threatening discussion.***

[01:39:18] **Carl:** Okay.

[01:39:19] **Walt:** <u>You know</u>, when *they*– writing out these notes and all that, why would *I* type something out and then go to handwriting, <u>you know,</u> in the airplane?

25. Walt identified several people by name in the recordings made in 2008, some of whom were/are alive. (I redacted some of those identifying details to protect their or their family's privacy.) When we could, we contacted those people (Jeff Osiadacz; the Spokane homeowner Jim Everman whom Walt bought his house from with proceeds of the hijacking), who confirmed Walt's accounting of events/conversations. Walt also freely provided other very specific details, such as conversations with the stewardesses, that deceptive people typically don't volunteer. In addition, Walt's free and voluntary disclosure of specific details is consistent with a truth-teller.

A prosecutor must prove the following legal elements in order to convict someone of hijacking:

- The taking, with the intent to steal, of;
- the personal property of another;
- from his or her person or in their presence;
- against his or her will;
- by violence, intimidation, or the threat of force.

Walt freely and voluntarily admitted to each and every one of these elements in the audiotapes/transcript and the

Last Testament, constituting a confession to being D.B. Cooper. A good confession contains admissions to all the elements needed to prove a criminal prosecution. Furthermore, our evidence corroborates and helps prove his confession is a good one. "Cowboy" corroborates the Cle Elum landing in Walt's confession. Walt's details are consistent with the FBI 302 reports. Even Jim Everman confirmed all the details Walt told Carl about the cash purchase of Walt's home in Spokane a few months after the hijacking.

26. And, finally, an important point for a seasoned investigator—in my more than two years of gathering evidence, interviewing witnesses, conducting analyses, and verifying statements, I never found one piece of evidence or testimony to be contradicted or refuted.

To promote objectivity, let's list the evidence we have that appears less supportive of the belief that Walt was D.B. Cooper:

1. The FBI's published flight path makes a landing in the Cle Elum area improbable. The FBI's stated flight path was reported to be up to 60 miles west of Cle Elum, Washington. If that were true, even with heavy easterly winds, a landing in the Cle Elum area was very unlikely. Yet if I were an agent, I would not want to publicize the probable drop zone for fear that hundreds of people would be in the area trampling my crime scene. Keep in mind, visibility was very poor, radar was still fairly rudimentary, and the jets dispatched to surveil Northwest Orient Flight 305 were unable to locate it. So, it's possible the FBI's publicized flight path was wrong. It's also possible the FBI, to protect the landing zone crime scene and evidence, was not eager to provide precise flight path information to the public. In an article titled "How the

Hunt for D.B. Cooper Worked," author Josh Clark wrote about information given by retired FBI agent Ralph Himmelsbach, the lead investigating agent in the early days of the hijacking. Himmelsbach interviewed the Northwest Orient Flight 305 pilot, Captain William Scott. Scott led Himmelsbach to believe the probable drop zone was "actually 40 miles east of where the manhunt had focused."[25] Forty miles east of the published landing area is much closer to Cle Elum, Washington.

Experienced pilots, as evidenced in the film documentary, tell us they would fly southeasterly out of Seattle toward Reno under the conditions on that cold, rainy, and windy night of November 24, 1971. Cooper demanded a 10,000-foot altitude with a slow speed in low visibility. Along the FBI's flight path, the pilots would have had to fly near or over Mt. Rainier (14,417 feet elevation) and Little Tahoma Peak (11,138 feet).[26] And, from the lips of a veteran commercial pilot since 1987, certified in flying the Boeing 737 and pilot for the 727 for more than 1,500 hours, Jeff Wierenga: "I wouldn't fly the FBI's [given] flight path because at some point you would have to cross the spine of the Sierra Mountain range, which is over 12,000 feet on average. The Cascade Mountain range near Cle Elum, Washington, has an average elevation below 10,000 feet";[27]

2. Walt's account does not explain the money found at Tena Bar;
3. Walt's illogical statement that he didn't know Abu Daoud survived the shooting;
4. Walt's imperfect resemblance to the composite sketch (although it is close, and composites are quite often useless and sometimes detrimental);

---

25 See https://history.howstuffworks.com/historical-events/hunt-for-d-b-cooper-worked.htm/printable.

26 *D.B. Cooper: The Real Story*, a documentary directed by Dirk Wierenga (Principia Media, 2018).

27 Jeff Wierenga provided this statement to me on June 11, 2018.

5. FBI witness reports stating that D.B. Cooper carried a paper bag (4" x 12" x 14") with him when he boarded the plane. Walt says nothing about this paper bag;

6. The FBI reports saying that D.B. Cooper bought a bourbon drink. Walt remembers he was drinking liquor, suggesting it was "Scotch and water, or somethin'." However, bourbon is liquor.

```
[01:46:06] Walter: Scotch and water or somethin'.
I don't— I don't— I'm not a liquor drinker, but
I was drinking liquor;
```

7. Carl's submission of Walt's DNA profile to the FBI. The FBI advised there was no match to the DNA they had obtained from the black tie. The best DNA evidence would have been the Raleigh cigarette butts the FBI confiscated, but, according to Agent Larry Carr, the FBI lost that evidence.

Finally, here is some very specific information divulged by Walt that would allow the FBI to determine whether, in fact, Walt was D.B. Cooper. The only persons who would know these acts occurred are D.B. Cooper, the FBI, and the people on the hijacked Northwest Orient Flight 305:

- Walt used Super Glue (he refers to it as "crazy glue") on his fingers to avoid leaving fingerprints. The FBI found no fingerprints of D.B. Cooper. The FBI might have picked up some trace evidence from the plane that would suggest the hijacker had put something on his fingers;

- Initially, in keeping with his admission that his plan wasn't well thought out, Walt intended to jump out the side door on the 727 until the stewardess pointed out the rear door. This suggests passengers boarded NW 305 from a passenger jet ramp in the front of the plane in Portland and exited the plane through the front in Seattle. The FBI, the crew, and the passengers can confirm this information—I saw nothing in the records;

- Walt dictated instructions to the stewardess, and the stewardess wrote down his demands to give to the captain.
- Walt ordered the parachutes to be obtained in Snohomish.
- On November 23, 1971, Walt drove his car to Spokane and parked his car at the bus station. He then took a bus to Portland, where he boarded Northwest Orient Flight 305.
- Walt offered a "handful" of money to the stewardess before he jumped. She refused the money.
- Walt covered the window where he was sitting to protect against snipers.
- Walt said he received a stopwatch with the parachutes;
- Walt insisted that the stewardess bring the money and the parachutes to him.
- The stewardess initially didn't believe Walt was hijacking the plane. She just stared at him until he convinced her it was real.
- The parachutes were delivered to Walt before the money and the stopwatch.
- Walt told the stewardess she was "polite and kind."
- Before he jumped, Walt told the stewardess to go into the cockpit.
- Walt addressed the stewardesses as "young lady."
- The phone records from the Teanaway Junction Café phone booth on November 24, 1971, might still be available—a task only the FBI could take on.

The scale is lopsided and strongly supports the finding that Walt Reca was, in fact, D.B. Cooper. The FBI should use the evidence in this book and Principia's film documentary to finally close the D.B. Cooper case as solved.[28]

So, was Walt Peca, a.k.a. Walt Reca, *the* D.B. Cooper? You decide.

My opinion? I determined the statements of Walt, Carl, and Cowboy to be truthful. I analyzed and evaluated the available documents and interviewed key witnesses to assess their evidentiary value, credibility, and believability. I compared our information and evidence to the FBI's.

I am convinced: Walt Peca, a.k.a. Walt Reca, is D.B. Cooper.

---

28   *D.B. Cooper: The Real Story*, a documentary directed by Dirk Wierenga (Principia Media, 2018).

WALT PECA/RECA'S TIMELINE

September 20, 1933

Walt R. Peca is born to Walter P. Peca and Jean Peca (Smith). The family lives with Walt's grandparents, who speak Russian and Polish in the home.

March 17, 1939

Joan Marie Feldhoffer, who later becomes Joan (Joni) Peca, is born.

1939

Walt's father is accidentally electrocuted while working in Farnsworth, Michigan.

1943

Ten-year-old Walt meets Willard Stahl in juvenile detention, after Walt is arrested for stealing money from pay phones. Willard becomes his best friend for life, and Walt lives for a time with Willard's family.

February 5, 1951

Walt enlists in the army at Fort Campbell, is stationed in Germany, and becomes a paratrooper.

January 6, 1954

Walt receives an honorable discharge from the U.S. Army.

1954

Walt goes to barber school under the GI Bill and, on graduation, opens a small barbershop in Royal Oak, Michigan.

March 8, 1954, through March 7, 1957

Walt is enlisted in the Army National Guard.

January 6, 1956

Carl ("Charlie Brown") Laurin is discharged from the U.S. Army.

In 1957, Carl, Art Lussier, and "Colonel" Bill Parker initially establish the Michigan Parachute Team in Saginaw, Michigan. The manager of the H.W. Browne Airport, Ward Seeley, is the only airport official who will let them modify planes (remove the door and the seats) and jump.

Walt Peca hears about the parachute group and drives up to Saginaw to investigate. He immediately joins the team. Walt receives an annulment from his first wife and starts dating Joni.

They all have weekday jobs: Carl works at the GM plant in Flint, and Art is a mailman. All have had military paratrooper training. The team members typically meet at the home of Art's parents, where they plan the weekend activities over beer and servings of beans cooked by Art's mother.

While reading the *Detroit News*, nineteen-year-old Jim McCusker notices an article that talks about some crazy guys jumping out of planes. The interview features a barber named Walt Peca. Jim looks up his phone number, calls him, and accepts an invitation to join them for a weekend jump. When Jim arrives at Walt's barbershop, he notices an extension cord running from the shop to the business next door. He quickly realizes that all of Walt's electricity is "borrowed" from the neighbor.

After Jim makes several jumps with the group, they ask him if he would like to experience flying an airplane. Jim enthusiastically agrees and sits in the pilot's seat, believing that he is getting his first lesson. The other three decide this will be a great opportunity for them all to jump together, which they have never done. They jump and leave Jim to land the plane, with only the instructions "Remember how we took off? Just do it in reverse." (Jim goes on to become an honorably decorated pilot for United Airlines, from which he eventually retires. He has allowed us to record his stories and recollections.)

The team later grows to nine members and is one of the first sport parachuting groups in the country. They perform at the Saginaw airfield on weekends and pass the hat to the crowds that inevitably arrive. Each weekend, they try to create different stunts to keep their avid fans returning.

They often challenge one another to see how close to the ground they can get in a "last to open" contest. They jump every weekend and during all seasons, including the brutal Michigan winters. Carl's most dangerous jump is when he opens at 400 feet in a blinding snowstorm.

(Today, parachutists typically jump from 13,000 feet or higher, open the canopy at 5,000 feet, and also have reserve chutes that automatically open at 2,500 feet for safety. Carl, Art, and Walt jumped from as low as 800 and as high as 3,500 feet, leaving little margin for error.)

February 10, 1958

Art's little brother Michael becomes the youngest skydiver at the age of thirteen. The conditions are not ideal that day, with the temperature 15 degrees and 30 mile-per-hour winds. Mike's landing is rough, as the chute drags him a couple hundred yards over crusty snow and ice.

March 30, 1958

Walt persuades his mother, Regina Schneidegger, in her forties, to become the first woman to jump. When she balks, Walt physically throws her out of the plane. It is her only jump.

March 31, 1958

They convince a friend, Jack Clapp, at age seventy-three, to join the group and perform his first jump. He thus becomes the oldest person on the team (and possibly in the world) to parachute.

July 4, 1958

Art agrees to parachute into Flat Rock Speedway during the races on that holiday weekend. In his homemade batwing suit, he jumps from 5,000 feet and opens the chute at 300 feet.

In July 1958, the team performs an air show for the Rotary Club in Caro, Michigan. This becomes known as the Great Caro Air Show and includes a fake failed chute, with Carl releasing a tangled reserve chute and finally pulling the ripcord about 50 feet off the ground. A drunk tries to impress some women by saying that he can do what they are doing but doesn't have a parachute. Art and Carl drag him away, put a chute on him, force him into the plane, and throw him out, using a clothesline to pull the ripcord. And finally, they announce that the town doctor will jump. Then they throw a dummy out of the plane and pretend his chute doesn't open. The dummy crashes to the ground, and they rush it into the medical tent where the doctor has been hiding. The doctor emerges, completely "revived" from this lethal fall.

Later that year, the guys agree to jump onto a horse racing track in Detroit. The betting tables are said to be operated by remnant offshoot thugs of a local mob known as the Purple Gang, who say they'll pay the team $100 for the jump. Unfortunately, the sponsors who booked this show decide not to pay the men the $100 they promised. Instead, they offer to place the $100 on a horse in the last race, which is a 20 to 1 long shot. The team members decide that since they will never get their money, they will take the chance. Walt, believing this is a great opportunity, claims to own the Cessna 170 aircraft they will jump from, which actually belongs to Ward Seeley. He uses the plane for collateral for an even larger bet. The horse finishes last, and the thugs want the plane. Walt goes into hiding.

Fall of 1958

When Walt learns that the thugs know of his whereabouts, he decides to leave town in a free rental car. (This "relocation" deal is still offered by rental car companies: they allow people to drive their cars to an office in another city for a very small fee. In the past, there was no fee.) With ten pounds of welfare cheese and some crackers, Walt heads for Fairbanks, Alaska.

December 1958

When a friend in Fairbanks refuses to parachute in a Santa suit with gifts for local orphans because of severe winds and temperatures of –40 degrees, Walt volunteers to do the jump and gets tangled up in a tree. His fingers are freezing as he tries to free himself, with the kids shouting, "Please come down, Santa."

March 1959

Carl, Art, and a friend called Porky all plan to join Walt in Alaska and fly up in Art's 1943 Stinson Reliant. Carl and Porky don't get much farther than Anchorage, then come home in May after only two months. In Fairbanks, Walt and Art earn money performing free air shows and teaching every drunk in town how to skydive.

While in Alaska, Walt meets smoke-jumper Don Brennan, who will become a good friend for life.

1960

Art and Walt head to Vegas, where they heard that the casinos are paying money to parachute jumpers. This turns out to be a lie, but they do convince a casino manager to give them free drinks and a room to perform jumps into the parking lot.

The casino manager is a good friend of the famous comedian and vaudeville actor Jimmy Durante. As a birthday present to Durante, the manager asks the guys to parachute from a plane holding a birthday cake, which results in a picture on the local paper's front page. Durante becomes friends with Walt and Art, and they communicate back and forth for years.

September 1960
Walt and Joni introduce her good friend Loretta to Carl at a party. Loretta accepts Carl's invitation to watch him jump on the weekend. The group is performing one of their "last to open" competitions, which Carl wins because his feet nearly touch the earth just as his chute opens. Loretta declares to her friends that he is crazy.

November 3, 1960
Walt and Joni get married.

September 5, 1961
Carl and Loretta are married.

September 22, 1961
Walt enlists in the U.S. Air Force Reserve as a member of the Para Rescue 305th Air Rescue Squad at Selfridge AFB. He becomes a Rescue and Survival Specialist, AFSC B92130A.

October 25, 1961, through the end of November
Walt is assigned to active duty.

November 9, 1961, through December 9, 1961
Walt takes part in Operation Long Legs II, a goodwill mission to South America with the USAF Thunderbird Team. His unit also receives a presidential citation for participating in the 1961 Berlin Air Lift. He holds the rank of Airman First Class.

(Carl reports that the military taught Walt the love of jumping, but he never enjoyed the crazy stunts the rest of the guys performed. According to Carl, Walt jumped for a reason; the rest of them jumped for fun. While sitting around drinking, on a couple of occasions Walt discussed the possibility of committing a robbery in a plane and then parachuting to safety.)

When Walt returns to Detroit, he joins the Teamsters union and is employed as a picket-line organizer. He quickly works his way up in the organization.

February 19, 1962
Walt's first child is born in Garden City, Michigan.

Sometime in 1962
Although still working for the Teamsters, Walt gets a desk job at a small airline named Zantop, where Carl and Art are pilots. Using the privileges that come with his Zantop job, Walt takes a trip to Elsinore, California, and immediately visits the local drop zone. His friends have told him that the CIA often recruits jumpers from this location. While there, he makes friends with a man named Phillip (Phil) Q. (He and Phil remain friends for many years, and Walt's address book contains numerous addresses for Phil throughout the world, including Saudi Arabia, Montreal, and Quebec, Canada.)

February 12, 1963
Planning to apply to the CIA, Walt takes a literacy test at army headquarters in Detroit, Michigan, and passes for Russian and Polish—languages he retained from his childhood.

Spring of 1963
Walt is elevated to an enforcer in the Teamsters. He is paid for his work with the Teamsters through the Sunshine Biscuit

Company, known for making animal crackers. According to Walt, he goes to the biscuit company only to pick up his checks and is paid very little money. He keeps trying to work his way up in the organization or, as he says, "Proving himself." At some point in 1963, Walt leaves his job at Zantop.

Walt completes and mails his application to the CIA.

June 21, 1963
Walt is charged with Misdemeanor Assault or Assault and Battery and found guilty.

September 18, 1963
Walt receives a letter from the CIA in Washington, D.C., informing him that "Operating Officials of the Agency have made a careful analysis of your background and experiences"; however, "we cannot at this time utilize the qualifications which you have made available to us."

Early 1964
While hanging out with a friend and drinking heavily, Walt begins to talk about robbing a bank. He tells Joni that he is going out for milk and a loaf of bread. There is no record of a robbery that night, but Walt never returns home to Joni.

October 2, 1964
Walt and Joni get a judgment of divorce.

December 20, 1964
Walt rents a plane and a pilot and parachutes down to Our Lady of Providence School in Northville, Michigan, dressed as Santa. He passes out gifts to the orphans.

June 7, 1965, at 12:11 a.m.
Walt attempts to pull off an armed robbery of a jewelry show at the Birmingham House Motel, but he makes a mistake about the date—it's the wrong week for the show.

June 22, 1965, at 4 a.m.
Still needing money, Walt commits an armed robbery of the Big Boy on E. Eight Mile Road in Detroit, with his friend James Henry LeBlanc driving the getaway car. After taking money from the safe, he tells the female manager, "You've been very nice to me, and I never had a chance to tip you." He then hands her a few $20 bills, which she accepts and stuffs down her bra. He goes outside and approaches his friend in the parked getaway car. A police officer is writing the friend a ticket for parking on the wrong side of the street, and Walt tosses his empty Tommy Gun into the bushes. The officer receives an APB that matches Walt's description, and Walt is immediately arrested. The restaurant manager visits Walt in jail shortly after the arrest and tells him she wishes they had met under different circumstances. Carl and Loretta come to see Walt in jail to offer support; however, Walt is already being bailed out by the Teamsters, who inform him that they are finished with him. Jimmy Hoffa personally fires Walt, saying that it's people like Walt who give the Teamsters a bad name.

Walt decides he doesn't want to go to prison. He tells his old friend Willard that he is leaving and asks Art to tell Joni he's sorry that things didn't work out between them. Walt jumps bail and leaves the state, moving to California to try to find Don Brennan, whom he recently met in Alaska. Walt meets up with Don in northern California. Don helps Walt get an alias by providing a Social Security number from a deceased former coworker, and Walt now becomes James O'Brennen. Don then moves on to Washington State to get more work with the Iron Workers.

Walt gets a job with the Iron Workers near Tehachapi State Prison in California. One evening in a bar, he meets ▮▮▮ (her name has been changed to protect her identity), who works at the prison as a guard. ▮▮▮ has a son at the time, and after a brief courtship, Walt moves in with her.

September 15, 1965
Walt receives an honorable discharge from the U.S. Air Force.

July 1966
Walt tells ▮▮▮ that he is moving up to Washington for better work. ▮▮▮ informs Walt that she is pregnant and is going with him.

Fall of 1966
▮▮▮ gets suspicious of Walt because his friend Don keeps calling him Walt, not the alias, James, that he is using. She calls the local police, who discover his real name. Walt is arrested and extradited back to Michigan, where he stands trial. The judge places him on probation.

▮▮▮ and her son follow Walter back to Michigan.

February 14, 1967
▮▮▮ gives birth to a boy, Walt's first child with her, in Saint Joseph Hospital in Flint. Walt begins to go by the name of Reca around this time, which he will use as his primary name for the rest of his life.

Looking to get extra money, he begins selling military automatic machine guns (Schmeisser and Sten) on the black market.

December 14, 1967
Walt is interrogated by Detective Richard Chambers from the City of Birmingham regarding the attempted robbery at the Birmingham House Motel on June 7, 1965, and denies any

involvement with the robbery. The next day, December 15, Walt phones the detective back and claims he was working at the Sunshine Biscuit Company at the time of the robbery. The detective calls the personnel manager at Sunshine, who informs him that Walt didn't begin work with them until the day *after* the robbery. No further action is taken.

July 31, 1968

Walt writes a letter to President Lyndon B. Johnson and Michigan governor George Romney, complaining about the unfair labor practices of the Iron Workers.

September 3, 1968

Walt files a complaint to the National Labor Relations Board against Iron Workers Local #25 for unfair labor practices. He also sends copies to the two senators from the State of Michigan, Philip A. Hart and Robert P. Griffin.

November 7, 1968

A judgment is issued against the union for charging excessive referral fees, which the union challenges.

Walt learns that some men he believes work for the Iron Workers union tried to kill his son by locking the child in a house trailer with the gas left on. Walt again jumps bail, and he, ███, and the kids leave Michigan and head to Baton Rouge. He gets a dog from the pound, which he names Hitler, to protect him and his family. Instead, the dog bites the mailman, and the city initiates a lawsuit against Walt. He avoids going to court by moving to Fort Lauderdale to visit Art.

In early 1969, Walt and family move into a motel near Briny Breezes, Florida.

A "hippie" band rents the motel room right under their second-story room, and the musicians play loud music into the night. Walt barges into their room and shoots up the place, putting one bullet into each of their instruments. Shortly after that, he and his family leave Florida and head to Atlanta; then he begins working his way across the country. He eventually returns to Washington State, where he finds work at the Grand Coulee Dam and continues to use the name Walt Reca.

January 1, 1971

Walt reunites with his friend Phil, who lands him a job at the Vinnell Corporation. Walt works occasionally at the Grand Coulee Dam and also performs other "odd jobs" for them.

Walt's relationship with ███ hits very rough times because his occasional work on the dam does not provide much income beyond living paycheck to paycheck. He contemplates his poor options and considers falling into the dam to get a payment from Workers Compensation, which would provide for ███ and the kids. Instead, he decides to do what he often threatened to do: rob a bank and escape using a plane.

During this time, hijackings are frequently in the news. From 1968 through 1972, there are 131 hijackings in the United States.

Walt's planning is crude, at best. His only preparation is to go into Spokane and buy a used suit, a tie, penny loafers, an overcoat, and a briefcase from a second-hand store for his disguise as a businessman. He also buys road flares, a large battery, and an alarm clock to rig up a fake bomb in the briefcase. He rents a typewriter, types out a hijacking note, and also writes one by hand. Walt then persuades ███ to spend Thanksgiving at her sister's house near Seattle, claiming that he has to work over the holiday weekend. ███ seems more than happy to have time away from Walt.

November 23, 1971

Walt drives from his house in Hartline 75 miles east to Spokane and parks his car in the bus station parking lot. He then takes a bus southwest to Portland. Walt keeps the briefcase between his legs during the bus ride to Portland.

He spends the night in a motel he stayed in previously when working in Portland. There is a businessmen's bar in the basement where the waitresses "look real nice with short skirts and nylons." He cleans the oil off his fingers with rubbing alcohol and applies quick-drying glue to his fingertips to avoid leaving fingerprints.

November 24, 1971

The day before Thanksgiving, he goes to the Portland airport and buys a twenty-dollar ticket to Seattle. In the men's room, he reapplies more glue to his fingertips before boarding the plane. He takes a seat in the rear of the plane. A chronic smoker and very nervous, he lights a Sir Walter Raleigh cigarette before takeoff, which the stewardess makes him put out. Walt typically drinks beer, but today he orders liquor. Yet even that doesn't calm him down. Shortly after takeoff, he hands the stewardess one of the notes he prepared, which says something to the effect of "Miss, I have a bomb. Come sit by me." He explains to the stewardess, Flo Schaffner, that he has a bomb in his briefcase and shows her the fake bomb he made with the lantern battery, road flares, and wires. He then dictates his demands to a second stewardess, Tina Mucklow. He requests four parachutes, two front and two back chutes; $200,000 in used twenty-dollar bills in a knapsack; the plane to be refueled; and to be flown to Mexico at 10,000 feet, at a speed of 200 mph with the flaps down to 15 degrees.

The plane lands in Seattle around 5:45 p.m., after the money and the parachutes have been secured. The money arrives in a bank bag, instead of a knapsack, which requires that Walt improvise in order to take the money with him. Walt agrees to let the passengers leave the plane and wishes them a Happy Thanksgiving.

His only concern is the possibility of a sniper, and he is careful to keep the lights to a minimum and the windows covered.

At one point, just before the plane departs, Walt offers stewardess Tina Mucklow a couple of bundles of cash, saying, "You've all been nice to me. I never had a chance to thank you." The stewardess refuses to accept the money.

The plane leaves Sea-Tac at 7:38 p.m.

The FBI obviously believes that the hijacker has a bomb on board and has to suspect that he is taking a hostage because he ordered four parachutes.

Walt opens one of two backpack chutes, which he immediately recognizes to be a good chute. He uses the cord to tie the money bag around his neck, then discards the remainder of the chute. He secures the money by wrapping the cord along the bottom of the bag, between his legs, and around his neck. He then puts on the overcoat and ties the bag again with his coat belt as well as he can. He puts the parachute on last. The chute does not have D-rings; therefore, the front chute cannot be used in the jump, even if he wanted to use it, but Walt has jumped from much lower altitudes without a reserve hundreds of times in the past. He throws the dummy chute and the briefcase with fake bomb out the back door before jumping. (That chute is never found.)

It is estimated that Walt jumps at 8:10 p.m. and lands near Cle Elum about half a mile from the Teanaway Junction Café. This is a long way from the route the FBI claims the plane took. The actual flight path is along Victor 2, which goes east out of Sea-Tac. This route quickly passes over the Cascade Mountains and arrives at a flat high plains area before crossing over the U.S. military training center. There are no large cities on this route.

The FBI claims that the plane's route followed Victor 23, which runs almost directly south. This route goes over numerous towns and cities, including Tacoma; passes over Mt. Baker and the heavily wooded area around St. Helens; and leads directly over Portland, Oregon. Professional pilots say that the first option with a bomb on board is to go over the ocean, never over a heavily populated area. With the threat of a hostage jumping, too, that option would be out. Getting the plane away from a populated area and toward a flat landing area for a jumper would be a priority. The FBI's stated route does neither. The two alternate paths merge near Portland, and both proceed to Reno.

(The FBI agent assigned to the case from Portland, Ralph P. Himmelsbach, wrote in 1986 that the drop zone where Cooper should have landed had been wrong, possibly by as much as 80 degrees: "We'd probably [spent] a hell of a lot of money and manpower searching the wrong area.")

It is estimated to be less than −10° F at 10,000 feet, with heavy cloud cover and freezing rain on the ground. Shortly before Walt lands, on the way down he sees some headlights in the darkness, along a road (Highway 970). There are two cars off to one direction and lights from what looks like a bridge. He also notices a bright light just off to the east. On landing, Walt hits a dead tree, and, while falling through the branches, he feels pain in his leg. From his experience with broken bones, he assumes that his leg is broken.

On the ground, he removes the parachute, stuffs it into the backpack, and covers it with some branches to prevent it from blowing away. He then removes his overcoat, in spite of the freezing rain and wind, and wraps it around the bank bag. He uses his belt to secure the coat to the bag. He carries this bundle over a small incline toward the road.

Walt estimates that he walks for about a half hour, limping slightly with his broken leg, toward the direction of the light he observed briefly in the final seconds of his fall. It turns out to be a café.

Inside, he takes a seat near a gentleman he refers to as "Cowboy"—a big guy wearing Western garb, with his guitar laying on the counter.

Walt goes to a pay phone in the café and calls his friend Don Brennan in Seattle, hoping that Don will have no money and will be sober. If Don has money, he will be in a bar, and if he is drunk, Walt will have to wake him from his stupor. Luckily, Don is both broke and sober. He answers the phone, and Walt says quietly, "Don, this is Walt. I did it."

"You did what?" Don asks.

"That thing I said I was going to do that night in the bar, and that there."

"I was drunk. What did you say?"

"I need a ride. Come get me, and I'll explain," Walt tells him.

Walt has no idea where he is and asks "Cowboy" to give Don driving directions to the café. Cowboy learns that Don is driving from Seattle and instructs him to drive over Blewett Pass, rather than along the other available route.

After this, Cowboy drives off in his dump truck to go to a 9 p.m. "gig" he has at the Grange Hall that night.

While waiting for Don, Walt drinks only coffee. Don arrives a couple hours later, and they begin driving to Walt's home in Hartline, Washington. Along the route, Walt shows Don the contents of his overcoat, bundles of $20 bills, and explains the hijacking. Don, a petty criminal his entire life, screams, "You did what? You know the prisons are filled with guys like us." Walt then gives Don a few of the bundles and thanks him for his help.

When they reach Walt's house and Walt gets out of the car, he reminds Don what he said about prisons and that they are now in it together. Inside the house, Walt puts the money into his old Air Force B-4 bag and slides it under his bed. He leaves the overcoat and the suit in the bedroom.

In the morning Walt calls another ironworker who lives nearby—Jerry Grady—and gets a ride to Spokane. He explains that his wife and kids are near Seattle for Thanksgiving and will be home shortly. Grady says, "You got your days mixed up, Walt. We got lots of time. We celebrate Thanksgiving today. ▮▮▮ and your kids likely won't be back until sometime tomorrow."

On hearing the news reports about the D.B. Cooper hijacking, Carl looks at Loretta and says, "What the hell did Walt just do?" That same night, Willard's father, Zephie Stahl, says the same thing: "Did you hear what Walt did?" Nobody knows that Walt is actually in Washington at the time.

On the Monday following Thanksgiving, Walt returns to work at the Grand Coulee Dam. His supervisor notices his broken leg and sends him to the doctor. For the next couple of months, Walt is assigned to a desk job in Spokane while his leg heals.

A couple of weeks after the hijacking, Walt, still limping with his leg in a cast, crosses into Canada at Sumas, Washington, and puts most of the ransom money into a safe deposit box in the Royal Bank of Canada. (Interestingly, Cooper researcher Galen Cook, a lawyer from Washington, also believes that the ransom money was deposited into a bank in Canada.)

The FBI begins to circulate the serial numbers of the hijacking money; however, the agency is at a distinct disadvantage. The ransom money consists of previously circulated $20 bills, most of them engraved and printed in 1968. The serial numbers are not sequential, and without computers, it is very difficult for banks to match the numbers. In addition, the life expectancy of a $20 bill is two to three years. When the bills are taken out of circulation, the serial numbers are not checked or recorded. Only if large purchases are made with all $20 bills will they likely be checked against the extensive list.

Early 1972

Two or three months after the hijacking, two men wearing hardhats show up at Walt's temporary place of work in Spokane and begin a conversation. They invite him to join them after work for a drink at the Brown Derby, a bar in Spokane. During that meeting, one of the men looks at Walt and asks, "Do you want to go to prison?"

Walt replies, "No."

"Then you work for us."

With that, the men immediately walk out, leaving Walt to wonder what he has just agreed to.

A few weeks later, as he prepares to go to work, the phone rings. A deep, clear voice on the phone simply says, "Walter Peca, eight o'clock tomorrow morning be at the Spokane Airport. There's a plane ticket with your name on it. Get on that plane."

He does as instructed and boards a plane to Boise, Idaho. On Walt's arrival, a man recognizes him and another passenger on sight and takes them to a restaurant. He begins asking them questions. They then go to another building near a college campus, where Walt is questioned for the next four days. None of the questions involve the hijacking or his work with the union. (Walt subsequently undergoes two years of training, which he calls "mind sculpting," until he is given his first assignment in 1974.)

March 13, 1972

Walt makes a trip back to Oakland, Michigan, where, despite twice jumping bail, he is discharged from probation.

July 1972

When Walt put the money into the safe deposit box in Canada, he kept about $1,500 out, which he planned to use as a down payment on an apartment or a house. In July 1972, he tries to rent a house at 1204 W. Cleveland Ave, Spokane, Washington, from a realtor who flips houses and sells them on land contracts to individuals. Rather than rent Walt the house, the realtor offers to sell it to him for a down payment equivalent to two months' mortgage payments, which total $685.

Walt also uses some money to buy furniture and a car. Since all of the realtor's customers pay in cash, a large deposit of $20 bills does not raise suspicion with his bank. During this time, Walt uses the last name Racca for the house purchase, which is finalized in July 1972.

(The realtor, now retired and living in Kentucky, confirms that he sold a house to Racca on a land contract. The man owned several houses around Spokane and accepted only cash for the house payments. He remembers that Racca traveled around the world.)

March 24, 1974

Even though he doesn't officially change his name to Walter Richard Reca, he gets his first passport under that name. On this passport, a convicted felon, a petty thief, and a construction worker with an eighth-grade education travels throughout the world and is admitted to some very high-security installations. His passport indicates trips to:

1974

April18: Scotland
The UK multiple times between '74 and '78

September 30, 1974

Walt and ▮▮▮ get married in Coeur d'Alene, Idaho, while both give their residence as Spokane and begin to assume the names ▮▮▮ and Walter Reca.

1975

June 18 and again on December 29: Iran
June 21: UK
Indonesia
Singapore
Saudi Arabia—Walt is reunited with Phil while in Saudi Arabia.

October 1, 1976

Walt petitions the court in Spokane, Washington, for a name change from Walter Richard Peca to Walter Richard Reca. He lists his address as Spokane, Washington.

He travels to Saudi Arabia on a three-month work permit, issued April 27, and returns again on November 23.

August 29: Amsterdam

1977

March 2 and December 24: Thailand
September 1 and October 13: Bahrain
May 5: Indonesia

1978

February 28: Saudi Arabia
June 17: Poland
June 18: Bangkok

Walt and ▮▮▮ separate for good. Although he frequently sent money to ▮▮▮ for mortgage payments, the bank has started to foreclose on their house, due to lack of payment.

New Passport Issued in 1979

1979
Algeria
July 15: France
Saudi Arabia
Houston
November16: Holland

1980
Poland
Toronto
Nigeria
Saudi Arabia

June 3, 1981
Walt receives a letter on *Detroit Free Press* stationary written in code, directing him to go to Vienna to receive his next assignment from his handler.

August 1, 1981
Poland—Walt maintains that he attempted to kill Abu Daoud on August 1 in a coffee shop in Warsaw. Daoud was the architect of the 1972 Munich massacre of eleven Jewish athletes in the Olympic Village. Walt's passport shows he was in Warsaw on July 1, 1981. Walt stated he was paid in Francs.

Sierra Leone—Several trips. According to Walt, at this time he becomes involved with smuggling diamonds out of Sierra Leone.

(Carl claims the story he wrote about the diamond smuggling was stolen from him by a book agent he hired to represent him. Carl says the movie *Blood Diamond* is very similar to his manuscript and was made into a book and a movie three years after he hired the agent. That money went to others, not to Carl.)

Holland
Saudi Arabia
France
London

1982
Sierra Leone: Multiple times
Montréal
Saudi Arabia: Several times
Poland
June 25: Scotland

Another Passport Issued in 1983
Sierra Leone
Saudi Arabia
London
Toronto
Holland

Walt also has a British passport issued in 1983 under the name Frank Drinkell.

During this time, Walt makes trips back to Michigan and reestablishes a relationship with his second wife, Joni. He begins by making a call to Joni and stating, "This is your husband, Walter." Joni responds, "I don't have a husband named Walter. You son of a bitch. You said you were going out for bread and milk years ago." Walt, the charmer, tells her, "You never said if you wanted white or wheat."

(Apparently, the line works, and they spend the final years of Joni's life together.)

April 12, 1984

Joan Peca petitions the court for a name change to Joan M. Reca.

May 21, 1985

Walt believes that it will be easy to make money by opening a pizza shop. (Carl also ran a pizza shop at one point in his life—coincidence?) Walt establishes his new business and calls it Reca's Hot 'N' Tasty Pizza in Wixom, Michigan. The building also has two apartments, which Walt rents out. Mysteriously, on May 21, 1985, the pizza shop burns to the ground, and Walt applies to the insurance company for a settlement. (Two weeks prior to the fire, Walt evicted the two tenants.)

Sergeant Michael Malloy from the Michigan State Police determines that "No accidental cause could be found" and concludes that the fire was incendiary in nature and intentionally set.

Walt claims that prior to the fire, on March 29, 1985, someone entered his apartment, stole a handgun, and set fire to the headboard on his bed. At the time, Walt filed a police report with the Westland Police Department that verified the event.

A cemetery owner testifies that he knows Walt's son, who confided that his father was going to burn down the pizza shop. Walt's son first denies this, then informs police that days before the fire, his father removed a painting that he and his wife liked and that an employee witnessed his father practice lighting a fire.

Walt and his wife, Joni, are arrested and charged with arson. Then the son suddenly recants his story and is arrested for perjury on November 5, 1985.

January 3, 1986

Assistant prosecutor Gary Tunis recommends to the prosecutor that "there be no prosecution on either the arson or perjury charges."

1986
London
Sierra Leone: Multiple times

While traveling abroad, Walt takes extensive notes about his contacts, bank accounts around the world, and safe places.

Carl's contact with Walt is nearly nonexistent from 1971 until 1985. During this time, Walt rarely gets in touch with any of his friends or family.

Other than a few small contractual work assignments, Walt essentially stops working after the pizzeria fire at the age of fifty-two. Despite no apparent income after this point, Walt frequently purchases new cars and gives his two-year-old used cars to friends who need them.

August 1990
According to a letter from David M. Nefores, CS2 in the Department of the Army, Walt alerted the U.S. Army about risks "that existed in the Middle East beyond those belonging to the Iraqi military apparatus." Nefores goes on to state, "Looking back, the information you provided was of greater concern than any of us realized at that time."

April 26, 1991
For the actions stated above, Walt is issued a commendation for "Contributing unselfishly to the support of American Soldiers, Sailors, Airmen and Marines in their joint efforts to achieve freedom from Tyranny during this historic period." Signed by Lieutenant General, USA Commanding. This is for unknown work in Operation Desert Shield/Storm.

1997
Walt follows his good friend Willard up to Oscoda, Michigan, and buys a house at 6310 Seminole Road. He also purchases many

firearms through Willard. (Being a convicted felon, Walt is not allowed to buy or own firearms). During this time, Walt lives in what Jim McCusker calls a fortress with more weapons than the local police.

1998

Walt rejoins his parachute buddies for a reunion at Art's cabin west of Pinconning, Michigan. One day Art starts singing the old Australian children's song "Waltzing Matilda." They begin to call the getaway a "Billabog," after the billabong mentioned in the song lyrics. A billabong is a lake, and due to the location of Art's cabin on a bog—a muddy marsh—the name "Billabog" seems appropriate.

> *Once a jolly swagman [traveler]*
> *Sat beside the billabong [lake]*
> *Under the shade of the Coolibah tree*
> *And he sang as he sat*
> *And waited by the billabong [lake]*
> *You'll come a waltzing Matilda*
> *With me.*

The guys adopt this as their song, and the Billabog gang decides to make the gathering an annual event each spring. At these Billabog reunions, they mostly drink, shoot guns, and retell old stories about their early parachuting days. After Carl returns home from the first Billabog, he decides to create a record of their adventures. In the past, he often jotted down his thoughts after their parachuting shenanigans, so now he begins writing his recollections of the events the guys described in their Billabog stories.

At the second Billabog in 1999, Carl gives everyone a copy of his tales, titled *The Last Barnstormers*, which Loretta had typed, copied, and bound. He has a separate chapter just for Walt—a fictional account of Walt carrying out the D.B. Cooper hijacking. Carl gives it to Walt, and Walt says that he isn't much of a reader, but Carl asks him to take it anyway.

Later in 1999 or early 2000
Carl writes a longer version of Walt carrying out the D.B. Cooper skyjacking, titled "Immaculate Deceptions." He mails it to Walt, in an effort to get Walt to start talking.

January 23, 2001
Joan (Joni) Reca dies at Tawas St. Joseph Hospital.

February 4, 2002
Walt is granted a Default Judgment of Divorce from ███ in Tawas City, Michigan.

Late April 2003
Walt tells his sister, Sandy, that he is having dreams of being in danger, due to all of the weapons in his home. Walt buries some explosives in the woods down the street from his house and hides some automatic weapons in his garage and at Willard's house.

May 9, 2003
Walt's house in Oscoda Township, Michigan, is raided by Alcohol, Tobacco, and Firearms (ATF) and the Michigan State Police. Copies of the police report show that a search warrant was issued for the "house and garages owned by Walter Richard Reca." The items to be seized are "any firearms and or heavy weapons, including but not limited to pistols, rifles, shotguns, hand grenades and explosive devices." The ATF confiscates thirty-five weapons and lots of ammunition, including:

- 38-caliber revolver
- Ruger semi-auto pistol
- 357 mag pistol
- Rugger M77 220 swift bolt action with bi pod
- 30.06 bolt action Mak-90 Sporter semi-auto rifle with 30-round clip
- Rugger M-77 Mark II
- Winchester 1300
- Marlin model 60
- Grenade launcher and grenades
- Rifle grenades
- Lots of 22-caliber rifles and pistols
- Several Tasers

Amazingly, even though Walt is a convicted felon, no charges are filed. (It's interesting that the prosecutor's office responded to our Freedom of Information Act request by saying that they had no records of the search or confiscation.)

Carl and Walt speak often by phone, sometimes three times a week, discussing various topics: their children, getting older, and so on.

May 5, 2004
"Colonel" Bill Parker dies.

Over the years, usually in a joking manner in phone conversations, Carl confronts Walt with being D.B. Cooper, but Walt denies it.

In an October 2008 phone conversation, Carl again asks Walt if he is D.B. Cooper, and Walt says he isn't. Despite this, Carl asks if he can start taping their conversations, and Walt agrees.

November 27, 2008

Finally, on Thanksgiving Day, after denying his involvement in the hijacking for more than thirty-seven years, Walt admits to Carl in a phone call, "I am Cooper."

Carl and Walt talk nearly every day and sometimes multiple times per day for the next couple of months, with the provision that the story will not be released until after Walt's death. Carl records more than three hours of these conversations on an audiotape recorder hooked to his daughter's telephone (with Walt's permission). Because Carl is unable to figure out how to record on his own home phone, calls made to and from his house are not recorded.

Over a series of conversations for the next six years, the story of Walt's life unfolds to Carl, while Carl's wife, Loretta, listens in on most of the phone calls. Walt's tales are typically accompanied by packages delivered to Carl's Florida home, containing passports and news clippings providing details of Walt's work as a contractor for the intelligence community.

Carl asks for and receives permission to write the story of Walt's life, and Walt signs a notarized permission agreement.

The Billabogs continue until **2009.**

2009

After the Michigan Parachute Team's springtime Billabog reunion, Carl stays a couple of days at Walt's house and secretly collects some DNA samples from Walt.

On returning to DeLand, Carl contacts an attorney, David Damore, and requests that he help prove that Carl's friend is Cooper. (Carl maintains that he referred to Walt only as Mr. Blank and says he told the attorney that Mr. Blank's friend picked him up after the hijacking.) Damore charges Carl a $1,000 retainer and an additional $300 for the testing. Damore sends the sample to a lab for a DNA test. Damore then sends the DNA card to the FBI agent in charge of the Cooper investigation in Seattle, Agent Larry Carr, to see if the results match the Cooper DNA. Agent Carr informs them that the match will take a couple of days.

A few days later, Walt calls Carl and yells into the phone, "Why the hell did you DNA me?" and adds, "I'm done talking to you."

Damore repeatedly inquires about the DNA results, and Carr apologizes for the delay. Finally, seventy-four days later, Agent Carr emails Damore to say that there was no match. Damore tells Carl about Agent Carr's email with the DNA results and says that Agent Carr had one unusual question. He asked whether Damore knew the name of the person who picked Cooper up after the hijacking.

After a couple of months, Walt calls Carl and begins the conversations again—but now Walt initiates the calls and phones Carl only at his house, which prevents Carl from recording him. Walt begins speaking again about the Cooper case only when he calls Carl without warning. (These conversations happen four to five times a week, up until Walt's health deteriorates shortly before his death.)

2010
Art Lussier dies. The parachute gang plans to have the next Billabog at a nearby motel because of Art's passing.

November 10, 2011
Don Brennan, the friend who picked up Walt from the Teanaway Junction Café, dies.

2012
Spurred by the numerous phone calls with Walt, Carl attempts to recreate the Cooper jump. Walt describes the landing to Carl but has no exact location, only that it was southeast of Seattle

and nowhere near Portland. Carl manages to identify the general location of the jump: Cle Elum, Washington, slightly southeast of Sea-Tac airport, not south, as the FBI reported. Carl bases his deduction on his knowledge as a professional pilot, aeronautical charts of Seattle, weather reports, and Walt's description of the route that Don drove to pick him up after the jump—they went through Blewett Pass, coming from Seattle—and the route going through Cashmere that they drove to get back to Walt's house.

June 2012

Carl and a friend decide to make the trip to Washington from Carl's home in DeLand, Florida, to see whether they can find the parachute or possibly even "Cowboy." Prior to making the trip, Carl begins calling restaurants in the area, trying to locate one that did not serve alcohol back then, yet was open late at night. A waitress at the Liberty Café tells him about the Teanaway Junction Café, which burned down years ago and was replaced with a fire station.

For the trip, they bring a metal detector, in hopes of finding some rigging from the chute. As they arrive at the general location of the jump, they see that the area is now overgrown with bushes and vegetation up to eight feet high and is on private land.

Carl then makes his way to the small town of Cle Elum, three miles distant, and begins his search for Cowboy. Remembering that Cowboy drove a dump truck, Carl goes to the nearest truck repair shop. The owner, Steve, suggests that Carl speak with Wayne Willet, who owns the local Shell station and whose father, Tom, owned it back in 1971.

Wayne is very helpful. When Carl describes Cowboy, he immediately says, "I don't know who that would be, but I know someone who would know." A couple of days later, after Carl returns to Florida, he receives a call from Wayne, explaining that he found the man. Jeff Osiadacz was the lead singer and lead guitar player for several Country-Western bands over the years and performed locally nearly every weekend. He wore cowboy attire while performing and worked as a dump truck driver for several years. He is also a former law enforcement officer.

Carl asks Wayne to give Cowboy (Jeff) his name and number and requests that he call Carl.

A few days later, Carl receives a call from Jeff. Carl asks Jeff whether he remembers meeting a man in the café in November 1971, who needed directions. Jeff responds, "Yes, I remember." Jeff recalls this meeting due to the very unusual circumstances: Walt, soaking wet and freezing, has an overcoat bundled and tied together on his lap, and Jeff takes the phone to give someone driving directions for a man who has no idea where he is. Walt calls Jeff "kid" and pays for his coffee.

Summer of 2012
Carl sends Jeff a photo of Walt, and Jeff identifies Walt as the man he met in the café.

May 2013
Carl becomes worried that something is wrong with Walt because he isn't answering the phone. Loretta encourages Carl to make the trip from Florida to Michigan to check on him. Carl finds Walt in a semi-comatose state and tries to convince him to go to the hospital, but Walt wants to wait until the next morning. Carl then cleans Walt's house, which is strewn with bits of mattress stuffing that Walt's dogs have spread throughout the house. During the night, Walt takes a turn for the worse, and Carl drags him to the car. They drive to the VA hospital, where the doctors say that Carl saved Walt's life. All during the previous day and on the day when they drove to the VA hospital, Walt and Carl discuss the Cooper case, but Carl is unable to take notes. The one comment he remembers Walt making is, "Remember that

story you wrote about me? You gave me way too much credit. I never did no planning. That's all I'm going to say right there." After Walt is safely in the hospital and stabilized, Carl returns home to Florida. It was the last time he would see Walt.

June 2013

After more than six years of conversations and with Walt's health fading rapidly, Carl and Walt discuss the idea of Walt writing out a Last Testament to provide further evidence that he is Cooper. Walt agrees and dictates this over the phone to Carl, who then has it typed up. The document is actually more of a confession of both the Cooper hijacking and the Daoud assassination attempt. On **June 20, 2013**, Carl mails the document to Walt for him to sign in front of a notary. Walt receives the document and agrees to sign it as soon as his sister, Sandy, and niece Lisa visit from Las Vegas.

August 7–12, 2013

Lisa and Sandy visit Walt, as his health gets worse. Walt confesses to Lisa that he is D.B. Cooper and hands her the confession to read. He then asks her to take him to a notary at his bank to sign the document. After reading the confession, Lisa tells Walt never to sign it because he will immediately be arrested if anyone finds out. Lisa shows the confession to her mother, and Sandy and Lisa both implore Walt not to sign the document. Walt then tells them about the hijacking, as well as the Daoud assassination attempt. He explains to Lisa that he has done far worse things that he cannot share with her because he would fear for her life. Sandy and Lisa try to convince him to go into hospice, but he's worried about his dogs.

Late August 2013

A friend drives Walt to a Canadian bank to close out one of Walt's accounts.

October 13–19, 2013
Sandy travels to Oscoda to arrange for Walt to go into hospice.

November 20–24, 2013
Lisa, her daughter Syd, and Sandy visit Walt in the nursing facility.

February 11, 2014
Sandy makes one final visit and stays a few days.

February 17, 2014
Walt dies at the age of eighty.

July 15–20, 2014
Lisa and Sandy visit Walt's house to go through his possessions, dispose of unwanted items, and ship his papers back to their home in Las Vegas. A party is held on **July 19** at a local tavern to memorialize Walt, attended by Sandy and Lisa and a few of Walt's friends, including Willard and his son Mickey (but most of Walt's friends are dead by then).

September 26, 2014
Willard dies in Oscoda, Michigan.

Mid-January, 2016
Lisa McNeilley, a freelance editor, contacts Dirk Wierenga, the director of publishing for Principia Media. Lisa informs Dirk of a manuscript that her uncle Carl Laurin is hoping to have published by a small publishing company that he can trust.

Within a week, Dirk calls Carl to discuss his manuscript. In the two-hour discussion, Carl outlines the life of his best friend, Walter Peca/Reca. Following this conversation, Dirk phones Principia Media CEO and Publisher, Vern Jones and encourages him to call Carl and listen to his story with an open mind. Vern's first response is, "You don't believe this nut job, do you?"

February 4, 2016

Vern Jones calls Carl at his home in Florida. In one and a half hours, Carl convinces him that he is indeed sane and seemingly credible. During the conversation, Carl stresses that Vern will be convinced once he sees the evidence he has accumulated over the last fifteen years.

April 1, 2016

On an unrelated trip to Florida, Vern Jones decides to visit Carl at his home. His wife, Irene, remains with their dog at the hotel after Vern explains that he will probably be back within ninety minutes. Nearly five hours later, Vern return to the hotel and tells Irene that he is completely convinced Walt was involved with the intelligence community and that alone would be an interesting story, even if he isn't D. B. Cooper.

May 8, 2016

Principia Media and Carl Laurin sign an agreement to publish Carl's manuscript.

May 23, 2016

Vern Jones and Dirk Wierenga visit Carl and Loretta's home in Florida. While reviewing the details of the evidence, Dirk notices some audiotapes tucked into a few plastic boxes in the corner. Carl informs them that they are actually conversations he taped between him and Walter in 2008–2009, discussing the hijacking and the clandestine operations that followed. These three and a half hours of taped conversations become one of the centerpieces of their investigative work.

June 2016

Realizing that many details need to be clarified, investigated, and verified, they ask Joe Koenig to join their investigative team at

Principia Media to provide advice and leadership in their search for the truth, wherever it may lead.

July 26, 2016

At this point, although they've talked on the phone, Carl has never met Jeff Osiadacz in person. (They first meet in the spring of 2018, shortly before the book launch.) Assisted by Julie Hurley and Irene, Vern visits Jeff in Cle Elum and record his recollections.

In Vern's conversation with Jeff, he explains that while driving to the café, he saw a man walking along the road hitchhiking but couldn't pick him up. The passenger seat of the dump truck had been removed, and his company prohibited employees from picking up hitchhikers. Jeff also reports that about twenty minutes later, this same guy, wet, cold, and, Jeff says, "looking look like a drowned rat," walked into the Teanaway Junction Café and sat down next to him. Jeff noticed that the man was wearing penny loafers. He remembers that detail because he always wanted penny loafers, and his parents wouldn't buy them for him. (As revealed in the **"Summer of 2012"** entry, Jeff later identified the man he saw on the road and the man he talked to in the Teanaway Junction Café as Walt Reca.)

It is shortly after this interview that Vern begins to believe Walt Reca was the real D.B. Cooper.

From this point until the book is published, two years later, the Principia team travels across the United States, following every relevant lead in their attempt to unmask D.B. Cooper.

MORE ABOUT THE AUTHOR

Born and raised in Kalamazoo, Michigan, Joe went to Kalamazoo University High on the campus at Western Michigan University and graduated in 1964. U-High closed in 1967. He was very active in sports and wasted a good deal of time and energy thinking he was good enough to play professional baseball. He then entered Engineering School at the University of Michigan in the fall of 1964. After two years of skipping classes, he transferred to Western Michigan University, thinking that by living at home, he would settle down and regain some discipline. He didn't. After two more years of wasting time, he had no alternative but to leave. On his way off the campus, he heard on the car radio a "Join your Michigan State Police" advertisement and applied. As he waited for the MSP, he gained very valuable insight into how to peacefully respond to troubled people while working for the Kalamazoo State Hospital. In May 1967, at the age of twenty-one, he joined the Michigan State Police, entering recruit school.

After surviving the intense training and regular demerits for improper bed making, he graduated in September 1967, then was assigned to the Bridgeport, Michigan, Post. There, as was the custom, he continued as a probationary trooper for the remaining twelve-month probation period. Jim Malczewski became his "Senior Trooper" and began to mold Joe into a "Trained Observer," instilling a "work hard and enjoy it" attitude and a work ethic in his "recruit." Joe served under a series of wonderful Malczewski-like mentors during his career. They are all respectfully listed in the Tribute.

In those days, the MSP transferred its troopers every two years. The thought process was to make sure troopers never got too comfortable in their work areas, reducing the risk of those troopers establishing close friendships that would inhibit their ability to enforce the law. That very ethical practice stopped years later when economics dictated a different direction, one that, at least on the surface, would be less costly. So, in 1969, Trooper Joe transferred to the Warren Post, which later became the New Baltimore Post.

While talking to students at a local school about safety, Joe noticed a beautiful teacher. That led to marrying the love of his life, Julie. While assigned to the New Baltimore Post, he identified extensive youth drug use and made community leaders aware of the problem. The community responded, which resulted in opening the New Baltimore Recreation Center. The center was funded and built by the community to help the youth find alternatives to drug use and is still in use today.

In 1974, he was promoted to detective sergeant in the Detroit Intelligence, Organized Crime Unit, located at the Detroit Armory on Eight Mile Road. During those years, he studied organized crime, both its "made" and "affiliated" mob members; the value of proper intelligence gathering; and the value of not gathering political intelligence, as a result of the "Red Squad" days. It was during these years that Joe became the MSP's lead investigator on the James R. Hoffa case and several other high-profile cases, where he learned the need to follow the money.

Because of Joe's marriage and resultant newfound maturity and discipline, he enrolled in Wayne State University's (WSU) accounting program. He carried a full load even during the

James R. Hoffa case, missing three mid-term examinations in the process. He graduated with a bachelor's degree in 1977 and later a master's degree from Eastern Michigan University, where he was a member of the Phi Kappa Phi Honor Society.

Before he was able to graduate from WSU, the college required him to pass a writing examination. He was startled to learn he had flunked it. His writing style was police style—that is, extensive use of the passive voice.

Police officers and military officers are taught early on to write using the passive voice. For example, they describe the removal of a fingerprint from a car mirror this way: "A fingerprint was obtained from the driver's side mirror by the undersigned officer." They feel (apparently) that passive voice produces a more professional report.

The active voice would dictate this: "I obtained a fingerprint from the driver's side mirror." The passive sentence contains thirteen words, while the active voice sentence contains nine. The passive voice is more complex, more wordy, and less direct. The active voice is quick, clear, and very direct. You be the judge on which is better.

Marriage put Joe on track, and he began to realize that time moved even if he didn't. He became driven to learn and build, helping create a wonderful family and earning two college degrees. In 1993, after twenty-six years, he retired from the Michigan State Police as an inspector, the assistant division commander of the Criminal Investigation Division in Southeast Michigan. (If you are interested in law enforcement, there is none better than the Michigan State Police.) In 2004, he retired again from Hartford Financial in Connecticut and relocated to Grand Rapids. In 2005, he founded his firm KMI Investigations, LLC, where he focuses on financial investigations and speaking engagements on "Getting the Truth" and the "Truth in Ethics." He's committed to lifelong learning.

"I was a voracious reader and a wordsmith. At an early age, I assiduously looked up any word I didn't know, which greatly slowed my reading rate but gave me a love for the precision and subtlety of words. Over the years, I gained an intimate and revealing understanding of the importance of words, the role words play in communication, and how people use the subtleties of words to their advantage."

His passion took him to many basic and advanced schools in interviewing and interrogation. He conducted extensive research, read and studied many books on discourse and statement analysis, and applied the learned principles to several hundred interviews. He made mistakes, but he learned a great deal and continues to fine-tune his processes. His books (*Getting the Truth and Getting the Truth: "I Am D.B. Cooper"*) are the result of his continued passion to help people understand the real message, to know truth, and to know deception.